# always up to date

The law changes, but Nolo is on top of it! We offer several ways to make sure you and your Nolo products are up to date:

**1** **Nolo's Legal Updater**
We'll send you an email whenever a new edition of this book is published! Sign up at **www.nolo.com/legalupdater**.

**2** **Updates @ Nolo.com**
**Check www.nolo.com/update** to find recent changes in the law that affect the current edition of your book.

**3** **Nolo Customer Service**
To make sure that this edition of the book is the most recent one, call us at **800-728-3555** and ask one of our friendly customer service representatives. Or find out at **www.nolo.com**.

# please note

We believe accurate, plain-English legal information should help you solve many of your own legal problems. But this text is not a substitute for personalized advice from a knowledgeable lawyer. If you want the help of a trained professional—and we'll always point out situations in which we think that's a good idea—consult an attorney licensed to practice in your state.

6th edition

# How to Win Your Personal Injury Claim

By Attorney Joseph L. Matthews

| Sixth Edition | SEPTEMBER 2006 |
| Editor | EMILY DOSKOW |
| Book Design | STEPHANIE HAROLDE |
| Proofreading | ROBERT WELLS |
| Index | MEDEA MINNICH |
| Cover Photography | TONYA PERME (www.tonyaperme.com) |
| Printing | CONSOLIDATED PRINTERS, INC. |

Matthews, J.L., 1946-
    How to win your personal injury claim / by Joseph L. Matthews -- 6th ed.
      p. cm.
    ISBN 1-4133-0519-9 (alk. paper)
    1. Personal injuries--United States--Popular works. 2. Accident insurance
    claims--United States--Popular works. 3. Liability insurance claims--United
    States--Popular works.  I. Title

    KF1257.Z9M37 2006
    343.7303'23--dc22

                                           2006048309

Quanity sales: For information on bulk purchases or corporate premium sales, please
contact the Special Sales Department. For academic sales or textbook adoptions, ask for
Academic Sales. 800-955-4775, Nolo, 950 Parker Street, Berkeley, CA 94710.

# Acknowledgments

Thanks go to several people who gave of their time and skills to help make this book happen. Annie Tillery did sometimes dizzying research with thoroughness and good cheer—and Ella Hirst took over the research detail for the 4th edition. Stephen Elias gave the manuscript a careful reading at several stages and gave numerous helpful suggestions along with unfailing encouragement. Amy DelPo and Emily Doskow have significantly improved subsequent editions of the book, combing their knowledge of the law with thoughtful and eagle-eyed editorial energies.

Another round of thanks go to Peter Lovenheim of Empire Mediation in New York and to Bill Mahoney of Aetna Insurance of California, for their consultations regarding the use of mediation in personal injury claim disputes.

Special thanks go to Richard Duane, Esq., who took time out from his busy law practice to review the manuscript and give it the benefit of his great expertise in the area of personal injury law. Both the quality and willingness of his assistance came as no surprise, since he is known to trial lawyers and clients alike as a tireless and brilliant advocate for the rights of the injured.

Last and greatest thanks are reserved for Barbara Kate Repa. Far more than merely a skilled and dedicated editor, Barbara Kate vetted this book into the world with her vast talents and compassion tuned equally to the needs of future readers and to the foibles of a wandering and sometimes wondering author. The assistance this book will provide its readers comes in large part from her untiring efforts.

# Table of Contents

## Introduction

# Appendix

## Accident Claim Worksheet

# Index

*Introduction*

# Who Can Use This Book?

You don't need any special training to handle most injury claims—just patience, perseverance, and some basic information about how the insurance claims process works. It doesn't matter if you were partly at fault for an accident as long as the accident was not entirely your fault.

You can use this book if you have been injured or your vehicle or other property has been damaged in any sort of accident that occurred when you weren't at work. And if you're injured on the job and someone other than your employer or a coworker might be partly to blame, you can use this book to seek compensation.

You should use this book if you want to receive up to 40% more in compensation for your injuries than if you hired a lawyer, and if you want to receive far more in compensation for your injuries than if you were unprepared to deal with an insurance company on your own.

The book sets out all the information you need to get a fair settlement through the insurance claims system and to:

- protect your interests after an accident
- understand what your claim is worth
- prepare a claim for compensation, and
- negotiate a settlement with an insurance company.

It also gives you strategies for what to do if an insurance company refuses to negotiate fairly.

## What Kinds of Claims Can You Handle Yourself?

There are a number of personal injury claims we believe you can safely handle yourself.

## Automobile, Cycle, or Pedestrian Accidents

Whether you make your claim against the other driver's or owner's insurance or under your own policy, and whether or not your state has some kind of "no-fault" auto insurance law, you can handle your own claims for vehicle accidents that occur:

- while you are driving or riding as a passenger, in your own car or someone else's, riding a bicycle or motorcycle, or walking
- while riding public transportation, or
- while you were at work, whether in a company vehicle or your own.

You can also get full compensation for damage to your vehicle.

## Slip or Trip and Fall Accidents

You can handle your own accident claim if you trip, slip, or fall

- on commercial property—a store, office, or other business
- at a private residence or other private property, or
- on a sidewalk, street, park, public building, or other public property.

## Home Accidents

In many cases you'll also be able to handle a claim for damages that are:

- caused by a dangerous or defective product
- caused by a dangerous or defective condition of rental premises, or
- caused by a neighbor's careless conduct.

## Miscellaneous Accidents

Finally, many other types of accidents are also simple to handle yourself, including those that are:

- caused by anyone's careless conduct
- caused by children or animals, or
- work-related accidents caused in whole or in part by someone other than your employer or a coworker.

## How to Use This Book

This book helps you understand almost any type of accident situation and most every wrinkle in the insurance claims process. You won't need all of the information here to settle your claim, but it's all here if you do need it.

The chapters are set up both to help you understand how the process works and to give you step-by-step directions for protecting your rights and receiving all the compensation you deserve.

A directory at the beginning of each chapter explains what the chapter contains and which parts of it you need to read, depending on your situation. You can go straight to the information you need while skipping whatever doesn't apply to your situation. For example, if you had a slip and fall accident, you don't need to read special rules about auto accidents; if you had a car accident and you don't have no-fault insurance, you can skip the explanation of how a no-fault claim works.

### Guide to Icons Used in This Book

 This icon lets you know when you may need the advice of a lawyer.

 This is a caution to slow down and consider potential problems you may encounter as your personal injury claim proceeds.

 A reminder.

 This icon directs you to other useful resources.

# Chapter 1

# Handling Your Personal Injury Claim

*The world's most solitary tree is located at an oasis in the Tenere Desert in central Africa. There is no other standing tree within 31 miles. In 1960, a Frenchman accidentally rammed into it with his truck.*

◆

*In 1896, there were only four automobiles registered in all of the United States. Two of them ran into each other in St. Louis.*

◆

*Walking up and down stairs is not usually considered tricky. Yet every year thousands of Americans are injured falling on stairs, often from defects in the stairs that they never noticed before the fall.*

In this crowded, hectic, and corner-cutting world, no matter how careful you are, the odds are still great you'll be injured in an accident caused—at least in part—by another person's carelessness.

And what happens after the accident can often be as exasperating as your injury. A whole lineup of profiteers lies in wait to make sizable gains from your injuries. First and foremost is the insurance industry. With their tentacles wrapped around every inch of our lives, the virtually unregulated insurance companies take 12 cents out of every dollar you earn, whether or not you are ever in an accident. Part of the insurance stranglehold comes in the exorbitant rates charged for car, home, business, and health insurance. Then, after a claim, insurers bulldoze over people who stand in the path of their profits by denying as many claims as possible and paying as little as they can get away with on the claims they are forced to honor.

The health industry joins in to increase the financial pain of an injury. Medical care is controlled by a corporate health industry creating wildly expensive medical treatment and contributing greatly to outrageous health insurance costs.

The lack of protection for lost work time also hikes up individual losses. Employers permit very limited paid time off. Americans average fewer than 11 paid nonmedical days off per year, by far the fewest of all the major industrial nations of the world. The Netherlands, for example, averages 32 days off per year; Germany, 30; and Japan, 24. And as anyone who has ever been off work for any length of time knows painfully well, the American government provides precious little backup for lost days and lost jobs.

Finally, our legal system twists rather than straightens an injured person's road to compensation. The legal system provides few alternatives for obtaining compensation outside of the lawyer-dominated claim and lawsuit system. And when lawyers are involved, they take 33% to 40% of a person's injury compensation—and run up sometimes staggering costs that come out of the injured person's pockets.

## Why You Often Can Handle Your Own Claim

Few people realize that, after an accident, it is often possible to get around some of these roadblocks to fair compensation. With basic information about how the accident claims process works, a bit of organization, and a little patience, you can handle your own injury insurance claim without a lawyer—and without the insurance company unfairly denying or reducing your compensation. In fact, you may be able to get more compensation for your injury and a faster resolution to your claim by handling it yourself instead of hiring a lawyer and paying his or her fees. And you can certainly receive more than you would if you submitted a claim yourself without knowing how insurance companies and their claims processes work.

### Settling Claims Is Cheaper for Insurers

An insurance company's willingness to settle your claim quickly has nothing to do with fairness and everything to do with the company saving money in the long run. It's simply cheaper for it to pay you than to prolong the fight.

In the first place, insurance companies must spend money to fight. The longer an adjuster works on a claim, the more money the company is spending on that claim. If lawyers get involved, the company's expenses become steeper. And if the claim actually goes to court, costs skyrocket. Therefore, once an insurance company knows it is likely to have to pay somewhere down the line—because you understand how much your claim is worth and will not drop your claim without a settlement—it makes financial sense for the company to pay sooner rather than later.

The cost of fighting claims is so great for an insurance company that it will often pay a claimant at least a small amount—what is called "nuisance value"—even if the odds favor the insured if the claim went to court. In other words, if it costs an insurance company several thousand dollars in legal costs to fight a claim in court, and there is any chance the company might lose, it is statistically much cheaper for it to pay a quarter or a tenth of that as nuisance value compensation to settle the claim early. (See "Nuisance Value" in Chapter 5.)

## The Claims Process Is Simple

Despite what the insurance industry and some lawyers would like you to think, settling an injury claim with an insurance company is usually quite simple. Most claims involve no more than a few short letters and phone calls with an insurance adjuster who has no legal training and no more information than you'll find in this book. You don't need to know technical language or complex legal rules. Your right to be compensated usually depends on nothing more than common-sense ideas of who was careful and who was careless.

## You Know Your Claim Best

You know better than anyone else—insurance adjuster or attorney—how an accident happened. You were there, they weren't. And you know best what injuries you suffered and what your physical condition and other circumstances have been since.

## The Compensation System Is Structured

The amount of fair compensation in any given case does not come out of a crystal ball that only lawyers and insurance companies know how to read. Rather, a number of simple factors—type of accident, injuries, medical costs—go into figuring how much any claim is "worth." The amount an insurance company will be willing to pay usually falls into a fairly narrow range, whether a lawyer handles your claim for you or you handle the claim yourself. An insurance adjuster who learns that you are organized and that you understand the claims process will usually settle the claim with you right away, and for virtually the same amount as if you had a lawyer.

## Save Money on Legal Fees

If you hire a lawyer to handle your claim, the lawyer will take a fee of up to 40% of your recovery—and charge you for "costs" that seem to appear out of thin air and can quickly run into hundreds of dollars. Yet, except in serious or complicated cases, a lawyer can usually gain for you, if anything, only an extra 5% to 20% above what you can obtain for yourself once you understand the process. Subtract the lawyer's fees and costs from the extra amount of the settlement, and you can actually end up losing more than a third of the money to which you are entitled.

# When You Might Need a Lawyer

Sometimes, the skills of an experienced personal injury lawyer, or at least the threat that such a lawyer presents to an insurance company, are worth the money you have to pay that lawyer to represent you. You may need a lawyer because of complex legal rules involved in your claim, because your injuries are so serious that the potential amount of your compensation might vary greatly, or because an insurance company refuses to settle the matter with you in good faith.

 **Hiring a lawyer later in the process.** If, after you have presented your claim and negotiated with an insurance company as explained in this book, you do not feel the insurer is offering a fair settlement, you can retain an attorney to finish the process for you. Or you may be able to consult an attorney on an hourly basis to see if he or she can spot a particular legal argument that might help you to move the insurance company toward a more reasonable offer. (See Chapter 11.)

## Beware of Internet "Injury" Sites

The Internet has made a tremendous amount of information readily available. But it is also a magnet for misleading and sometimes unscrupulous advertisers, including the electronic equivalent of ambulance-chasing lawyers. Some websites—often using address terms like "accident," "injury," or "hurt"— claim to offer free information about accident insurance claims. Don't be fooled! The information is mostly useless and is intended only to get you to contact the site's referral "service," which is usually just a fast-buck law firm eager to grab your case (and the 33% to 50% the firm charges) before you know what is going on.

As this book explains, in many cases you simply don't need a lawyer to get full compensation. And if you do need or want a lawyer, either to consult with or to represent you, you certainly don't want to choose one simply because the lawyer is connected to an Internet site. Most of the lawyers listed on these sites are not screened for experience or competence. And they may not even be located near you, nor be familiar with your local courts.

There is no electronic shortcut to finding and choosing among lawyers for your personal injury claim. If you decide to use a lawyer, follow the steps in Chapter 11. Those steps will show you how to locate several experienced local lawyers, and how to choose among them based on their experience and the quality of your personal contacts with them.

There are no hard and fast rules about when you do and do not need to hire a lawyer. Much of the decision has to do with how you feel things are going as you attempt to settle your claim on your own. At some point, you may feel overwhelmed—by too much work, or by some obscure legal rule the insurance company decides to throw at you. Or you may be stonewalled by an insurance adjuster who blusters that the company does not have to honor your claim at all, or who offers you only a piddling amount to settle it. In these situations, you may want to consult an attorney for advice, and perhaps have him or her take over handling the claim. These situations are discussed in detail in Chapter 11.

There are a few types of injuries and accidents that almost certainly require that you hire a lawyer. They include the following situations.

## Serious Long-Term or Permanently Disabling Injuries

Some accidents result in injuries that permanently or for a long time—more than one year—seriously affect your physical capabilities or appearance. Figuring out how much such a serious injury is "worth" can be a difficult business that may require an experienced lawyer. Even if you decide to handle the matter yourself, an injury with a long period of recovery or a permanent physical effect really requires that you consult a lawyer for an hour or two to make sure you have covered all the bases in your claim.

## Severe Injuries

The amount of your accident compensation is mostly determined by how severe your injuries were. And the severity of your injuries is measured by the amount of your medical bills and your lost income, as well as the length of time you remain in pain or disabled. Once your medical

and lost-income figures begin to rise, not only does the amount of compensation rise, but it becomes more difficult to gauge the range of fair compensation an insurance company is willing to pay. And once these figures get high and the range gets broad, it may be worth the fee you would have to pay to have a lawyer handle your claim.

In Chapter 5, we explain how to gauge how much your claim may be worth. In a less serious case, with medical costs and income loss of a few thousand dollars, it is rarely worth your money to hire a lawyer.

> **EXAMPLE:** Your medical costs and income loss are $2,500 and you fully recover from your injuries in a few months. Applying the damages formula (discussed in Chapter 5), you know that your compensation will be between $5,000 and $10,000—no lower and no higher. Therefore, you can negotiate within that range to get the highest possible amount without worrying that you might instead have received $20,000 or $30,000 if you had hired a lawyer to negotiate for you. Also, you know that even if you got $7,500 on your own and a lawyer could have obtained $10,000, the lawyer's fee and costs would have reduced your actual compensation to less than $7,500, anyway.

But when the injuries are severe and the medical costs are high—over $10,000 or so—the range of potential compensation can become very wide—from $20,000 to $100,000. Because the difference between the low end of this range and the high end is so great, it may be a good idea to take advantage of the experience of a knowledgeable personal injury lawyer to ensure that you get the highest possible amount, even taking into account that the lawyer's fee will eat up a large part of your final award.

**EXAMPLE:** Your medical bills are $15,000 and you are able to get a settlement offer of $50,000 by yourself, but a lawyer might be able to get $75,000 to $100,000 for you. Even after the lawyer takes one-third as a fee, you would be left with between $50,000 and $67,000—up to $17,000 more than you obtained on your own. And the lawyer will have done the work.

No fixed cutoff point in medical bills and lost income determines when you should consider hiring a lawyer. Some people feel more comfortable hiring a lawyer as soon as their bills reach a couple of thousand dollars, regardless of any other factors in the case. Other people would handle a similar claim on their own and avoid the lawyer's fee, even if their medical bills reached $10,000 and their potential compensation $100,000.

## Finding the Right Lawyer

Deciding that you want to consult with or hire a lawyer is one thing, and finding the right lawyer is another. Only some lawyers are experienced in personal injury claims. And if your claim were simple enough for an inexperienced lawyer to handle, you would be handling it yourself. It is important to find a lawyer who can handle your particular kind of claim, and also to find one with whom you are comfortable. (See Chapter 11.)

The only way to know whether you feel comfortable handling your own claim is to understand how compensation amounts are calculated and apply those criteria to your situation to get a rough idea of what your claim might be worth. (See Chapter 5.) Then decide—either right away or after negotiating for a while with the insurance company—whether to continue handling the case on your own, consult with a lawyer on an hourly basis, or hire a lawyer to handle your case. (See Chapter 11.)

## Medical Malpractice

If you have suffered an injury or illness due to careless, unprofessional, or incompetent treatment at the hands of a doctor, nurse, hospital, clinic, laboratory, or other medical provider, the complexities of both the medical questions and the legal rules involved almost certainly require that you hire a lawyer experienced in medical malpractice matters.

## Toxic Exposure

We sometimes become ill because of exposure to chemicals in the air, soil, or water, in products we use, or in food we eat. Even some molds that are naturally occurring can cause severe health problems. Claims based on such exposures are difficult to prove, however, and often require complex scientific data. Because the chemical and other industries have erected a huge wall to protect themselves from legal exposure while they continue to expose us to chemicals, the required evidence is very hard to come by. As a result, fighting a claim for toxic exposure requires the services of a lawyer experienced in such cases.

## When an Insurance Company Refuses to Pay

In some instances, regardless of the nature of your injury or the amount of your medical bills and lost income, you will want to hire a lawyer because an insurance company or government agency simply refuses to make any fair settlement offer at all. This is often referred to as "stonewalling," because negotiating is like talking to a stone wall. An insurance company may stonewall when it denies that its insured is at all responsible for the accident, or denies that the insured was covered for the type of accident that happened. You can also run into stonewalling when your claim is against a governmental body that claims it is immune—legally protected—from responsibility for the accident. These situations are discussed in detail in Chapter 11.

If, after repeated efforts, you are unable to obtain a fair offer, you might be forced to see whether an attorney can do better for you. In these cases, something—what the lawyer can get minus the fee charged to get it—may be better than nothing.

### Don't Be Shy— You're Entitled to Compensation

The insurance industry spends fistfuls of money each year on well-placed "news" stories to create the impression that most people who file personal injury claims are trying to cheat defenseless insurance companies. These stories often depict people grossly exaggerating their injuries or fraudulently staging fake accidents. As a result, many people are too embarrassed to file legitimate claims, or they accept far less than they are entitled to when an insurance adjuster takes a high-and-mighty tone.

The insurance industry collects vast sums of money in premiums to provide protection for every aspect of our daily lives: car, home, and business. And that money—minus the industry's huge profits—is specifically intended to compensate people injured in accidents. Injured people are not being greedy when they make insurance claims, and insurance companies are not being kind or generous when they pay them. Instead, injury compensation is exactly what we have *all* been paying for when we send in our insurance premiums, month after month, year after year. So, if you have the misfortune of being injured in an accident, don't hesitate to pursue your claim vigorously. You've paid for it.

# Chapter 2

# Whose Fault Is It? How Legal Responsibility Is Determined

The question of who caused an accident, or whose fault it was, forms the basis of any decision about who is legally responsible—or liable—for the damages that result. In other words, deciding who was at fault determines who has to pay for your injuries.

## Basic Rules of Legal Responsibility

Although lawyers and insurance companies would like people to think that legal responsibility, or liability, for an accident is a complicated question, the answer usually requires nothing more than common sense. Liability revolves around the simple fact that most accidents happen because someone was careless—or, in legal terms, "negligent." And as to this carelessness, the law applies a basic rule: If one person in an accident had been less careful than another, the less careful one must pay for at least a portion of the damages suffered by the more careful one.

## How the Law Determines Liability

A small percentage of injury accident claims are fought out in court instead of being settled beforehand. In court, an injured person must prove four basic things:

- the person who caused the accident had a legal responsibility—called a "duty of care"—to avoid harming the person who was injured
- the person who caused the accident failed to live up to that legal responsibility—committing what's called a "breach of duty"
- the accident resulted from the breach of duty—called "causation," and
- injuries and their consequences—known as "damages"—resulted from the accident.

When you negotiate your claim for insurance compensation, you probably won't be using these legal concepts to discuss your accident. The cause of your accident may well be obvious, and the only question may be how much compensation is appropriate. Even if one of these issues does arise in your case, chances are you won't hear an insurance adjuster use all these legal terms. Nor will you need to use these terms yourself. Instead, you and the insurance adjuster will almost certainly negotiate using general language about whose fault the accident was and how much your claim is worth.

However, even if you do not use or hear any of these terms, understanding the basic legal issues may give you extra confidence as you process your claim. And if one of these issues becomes a sticking point in your claim, having a complete picture of how legal liability works may help you make a clearer argument to the insurance company. After you read the section later in this chapter that applies to your specific type of accident, you may want to refer back to this section if you think one of the four points mentioned above may be difficult to prove.

## Duty of Care

A duty of care is an obligation to avoid injuring someone else or placing them in the path of danger. In most cases, every person has at least some duty of care toward others. The only questions are, to whom is a duty of care owed, and if there is a duty, how broad is it?

A common example of a duty of care involves driving a car. Everyone has a duty of care to drive in a way that is unlikely to injure pedestrians and people in other vehicles. The extent of that duty is defined by the rules of the road (usually spelled out in a state vehicle code) and by common sense, which is often described as how a "reasonable" person would act. (See "Car Accidents," below.)

In some situations, determining the duty of care is difficult because, unlike the example above, there are no laws (like a vehicle code) that spell out how a person should act. For example, a grocery store has some duty of care toward its customers' safety, but there are no specific legal guidelines on just exactly what the grocery store owner must do to satisfy that duty. The law simply requires the store to take "reasonable" steps to ensure customer safety—such as regularly checking the floors for spills and not putting heavy objects precariously on high shelves. But how frequently must the store check for spills and how high is too high? Unfortunately, there's no precise answer. If a customer has an accident involving store safety, the argument revolves around whether steps taken by the store qualified as "reasonable."

In many situations, there is no duty of care owed at all, even though there may indeed be a real injury. For example, in most states a landowner owes no duty to act reasonably toward a trespasser. If a burglar is injured on a slickly waxed floor, he'll have no case. However, a tenant or tenant's guest walking across that same lobby floor is owed a duty of care and may be able to collect if the landlord didn't take steps to warn of the danger.

## Breach of Duty

It's one thing to recognize that there is a duty of care involved in an injury situation. The next question is whether the person who owed the duty lived up to it. If not, the law calls that person's actions "negligent," or careless. Put another way, the person breached the duty of care by creating or allowing a dangerous situation above and beyond the normal level of risk we encounter while going about our daily lives. Whether the duty of care was met is the issue on which most accident cases turn.

In some cases, determining whether the duty of care has been breached isn't too difficult. For example, when a speed limit is posted, the duty of care involves observing that limit. Whether a driver was really going over that limit might be easy to show, with witness statements attesting to the car's rate of speed. If the jury believes these witnesses, they'll conclude that the driver breached that duty. Similarly, a car must stop at a red light (duty of care), but was the light red when the car entered the intersection? Again, the witnesses may be able to clearly say yes or no.

In other situations, deciding whether the duty of care was breached is more difficult, because complying with the duty isn't an "all or nothing" proposition. Think again about the example above of the speed limit. While it may be simple to show whether a driver was going over the posted speed, this isn't the end of the inquiry. As you no doubt know, drivers must always obey a "universal speed law," which directs them to drive safely under the circumstances, even if this means going slower than the posted speed. A driver's ability to show compliance with the speed limit doesn't necessarily prove the driver was obeying the universal speed law. That issue involves determining what would have been a safe speed under the circumstances. Similarly, a city must keep its roadways reasonably safe for all vehicles. But did a saucer-size hole in the pavement, which had been there for months, constitute a breach of the duty of care in that it created an unreasonable risk for bicyclists?

There often is no simple answer about whether a duty has been breached. Many of the examples in this chapter explain how to figure out what constitutes a breach of duty in particular types of accidents.

### Causation

Usually, once you have shown that someone has breached a duty toward you—for example, broken a traffic law or failed to fix a loose stairway handrail—you have established that person's legal responsibility for your injuries. But in some circumstances, the other person may claim that even if he or she was negligent (breached a duty), that negligence was not the cause—or not the sole cause—of the accident. For example, you may be able to show that another driver failed to signal before making a left turn. However, the other driver may reply that you had a stop sign and should not have entered the intersection at all until the other car had cleared it, regardless of whether it was turning. In the case of the stairs, the owner of the property may claim that your fall was not caused by the loose handrail but by your own carelessness in bounding up two stairs at a

time in an effort to get into the apartment and answer the phone.

Most arguments about causation are not all-or-nothing affairs. They are usually about how much each person's carelessness (negligence) contributed to the accident, and therefore how much each person should be responsible for the resulting injuries. (There's more about this in "How Your Carelessness Affects Your Claim," below, and in Chapter 5.)

### Damages

In legal lingo, "damages" refers to the physical and emotional injuries, property damage, and lost income someone suffers as the result of an accident. (The term "damages" is also sometimes used as shorthand for an amount of money that would be appropriate to compensate someone for injuries and related losses.)

No matter how clear it is that someone else is legally responsible for an accident, you may collect compensation only for injuries, pain and suffering from injuries, and lost income that result from the accident. This may seem obvious, but many claims for compensation are disputed because the person liable for the accident claims (through an insurance company or lawyer) that the injuries complained of were not caused by the accident. Rather, the person responsible may contend that the injuries existed before the accident, were caused by a different event such as another accident, or have been exaggerated or imagined.

### Miscellaneous Other Rules About Liability

Liability for most accidents is determined by the rules discussed above. These basic rules are sometimes supplemented by one or more of the following propositions.

- If a negligent person causes an accident while working for someone else, the employer may also be legally responsible for the accident. (See Chapter 4, "Business and Landlord Liability Coverage.")

- If an accident is caused on property that is dangerous because it is poorly built or maintained, the owner of the property is liable for being careless in maintaining the property, regardless of whether he or she actually created the dangerous condition. (See "Accidents on Dangerous or Defective Property," below.)

- If an accident is caused by a defective product, the manufacturer and seller of the product are both liable even if the injured person doesn't know which one was careless in creating or allowing the defect, or exactly how the defect happened. (See "Dangerous or Defective Products," below.)

- If the injured person was also careless, his or her compensation may be reduced by the extent such carelessness ("comparative negligence") was also responsible for the accident. (See "How Your Carelessness Affects Your Claim," below.)

## You Don't Need to "Prove" Anything

Liability insurance covers nearly every motor vehicle, home, business, and other property. (See Chapter 4.) So in virtually every accident, you will need to deal only with an insurance adjuster and not with a lawyer or judge. And making a successful insurance claim usually requires nothing more complicated than providing a clear explanation to an insurance adjuster, in plain language, of how the insured was careless and how such carelessness caused the accident. (See "Preparing a Demand Letter," in Chapter 6.)

If your explanation makes it appear likely that carelessness by the insured person or business caused the accident, the liability insurance company will pay you for your medical costs, for your lost income, and a certain amount for the pain and inconvenience you have suffered. (See Chapter 5.) Once an insurance adjuster knows that you understand how the simple rules of liability apply to your accident, the emphasis in your claim will likely shift quickly from *whether* you can receive compensation to *how much* that compensation will be.

Most liability claims are settled without anyone ever stepping into a courtroom. So, the process of negotiating with an insurance company does not require that you provide legally perfect "proof" that the insured was negligent and that the negligence caused the accident. To get compensation for your injuries, you need only make a reasonable argument that the insured was negligent, even if there is also a plausible argument the other way.

And in accidents caused by defective products, you don't need to argue at all that the insured was negligent; negligence is automatically presumed under a rule called "strict liability." (See "Dangerous or Defective Products," below.)

Making a reasonable argument that the insured was negligent shows the insurance company that if the matter later becomes a lawsuit, there is a good possibility that a court would find its insured to be legally responsible. If that were to happen, the insurance company would be on the hook for your damages, court costs, and attorney's fees. That's a lot of money, and the insurance company knows it can save quite a bit by settling with you out of court.

## Accidents Across State Lines

You may be involved in an accident while visiting another state. Or an out-of-towner may have an accident with you in your state. As this and the following chapter explain, state laws controlling accident claims may differ. For example, they may specify different time limits within which to file a claim or lawsuit, or set different standards for comparative negligence.

The basic rule is that the law of the state where the accident occurred applies. But while the location of the accident may change some of the rules to be followed, it will not affect insurance coverage. Regardless of where an accident happens, an insurance company must honor valid claims against its insured. This means, for example, that a state with mandatory no-fault vehicle insurance cannot force a no-fault settlement onto a visitor. Visitors do not have the state's insurance protection, and they are free to present a claim for full compensation just as they would in a state without no-fault insurance laws.

## Choosing Whom to Collect From

Vehicle accidents can involve the carelessness of more than one person—the drivers of two other vehicles, or a driver and a city or county that carelessly maintained a roadway. In accidents that happen at a business, both the property owner and the business tenant might be responsible. If you are injured by a defective product, both the maker and the seller are probably legally responsible.

When there is more than one other person responsible for an accident, the law provides that either one is responsible for compensating you fully for your damages. If one of them pays the entire claim, the two of them must decide between themselves as to whether the other should reimburse the one who paid, and how much. However, the law does not allow you to collect the full amount from both.

This rule about collecting from either responsible person—called "joint and several liability" or "concurrent liability"—provides you with a couple of important advantages. If one liable person is insured and the other is not, you can make your claim against the insured person for the full amount. And even if both are insured, you will have to settle your claim with only one insurance company. Initially, consider everyone you think might be responsible and notify each of them that you may be filing a claim for damages. (See "Determine Who Might Be Responsible," in Chapter 3.) Then, depending on what you discover about how the accident happened, or on which insurance company takes responsibility, you will pursue a claim against only one. (See "Preparing a Demand Letter," in Chapter 6.)

## How Your Carelessness Affects Your Claim

Even if you were careless and partly caused an accident, in most states you can still recover compensation from anyone else who was also careless and who partly caused the accident. The amount of a person's liability for an accident is determined by comparing his or her carelessness with the carelessness of the person injured. The percentages of liability determine the percentages of the resulting damages each party must pay. This rule is referred to as comparative negligence.

**EXAMPLE 1:** Bob was in a car accident in which he stopped short and was hit from behind. If the other person had been 100%

at fault, Bob's medical bills and lost income would entitle him to $1,000. However, the police accident report notes that Bob stopped short because one of a group of children next to a school looked as if he was going to dart into the street. The insurance company for the person whose car hit Bob from behind points out that Bob should have been going slowly enough in the school area to be able to stop without having to jam on his brakes.

In this case, not going slowly enough may have made Bob between 10% to 25% negligent. The person who hit him would not be liable to Bob for the full compensation of $1,000, therefore, but only for $750 to $900 (100% liability minus Bob's 25% to 10% liability = 75% to 90% liability).

**EXAMPLE 2:** Ted, who was driving the car that hit Bob, also sustained injuries. If another person had been fully responsible for his injuries, Ted's claim would have been worth $2,000. Even though Ted was 75% to 90% liable for the accident, in some states (see below), he could collect an amount from Bob's insurance equal to Bob's negligence. So, since Bob was 10% to 25% negligent, Ted can collect 10% to 25% of his $2,000 damages—between $200 and $500.

There is no formula for arriving at a precise number for a person's comparative carelessness. During claim negotiations, you and the insurance adjuster discuss the factors that make both you and the insured person at fault. Then the question of your comparative negligence will go into the negotiating hopper along with all the other factors that determine how much a claim is worth—such as the seriousness of your injury and the amount of your medical bills. (See Chapter 5.)

Comparative negligence is applied in three slightly different ways, depending on the state where the accident occurred.

## States With No Restrictions

| | |
|---|---|
| Alaska | Missouri |
| Arizona | New Mexico |
| California | New York |
| Florida | Rhode Island |
| Kentucky | South Dakota |
| Louisiana | Washington |
| Mississippi | |

In these 13 states, the general rule of comparative negligence operates without any restrictions. You are entitled to compensation for your damages in an amount based on the percentage of the other person's fault regardless of how great your own fault was.

## States With Some Restrictions

| | |
|---|---|
| Arkansas | Nevada |
| Colorado | New Hampshire |
| Connecticut | New Jersey |
| Delaware | North Dakota |
| Georgia | Ohio |
| Hawaii | Oklahoma |
| Idaho | Oregon |
| Illinois | Pennsylvania |
| Indiana | South Carolina |
| Iowa | Tennessee |
| Kansas | Texas |
| Maine | Utah |
| Massachusetts | Vermont |
| Michigan | West Virginia |
| Minnesota | Wisconsin |
| Montana | Wyoming |
| Nebraska | |

The above 33 states have a more restrictive rule, known as "modified comparative negligence." With this restricted rule, you lose your right to any compensation at all if your own carelessness made you 50% or more responsible for the accident. If you were less than 50% at fault, the rule works exactly the same as the general rule of comparative negligence (explained in the examples above). In other words, you have a right to compensation up to the percentage amount of the other person's negligence.

Keep in mind that there is no precise way of figuring the extent of your carelessness. So, in these states, the degree of your comparative negligence—including whether or not it was more than 50%—is a subject about which the insurance company has to negotiate with you.

### States With the Most Restrictions

| Alabama | North Carolina |
|---|---|
| District of Columbia | Virginia |
| Maryland | |

Four states and the District of Columbia follow a very restrictive and often unfair comparative negligence rule. In these states, you cannot recover any compensation at all if you were at all "contributorily negligent," meaning that your carelessness contributed in any way, however slight, to the accident.

In these states, it can be difficult to recover damages if the insurance company can point to anything you did that contributed to the accident. However, it is not easy for an insurance company to prove absolutely that you were partly at fault. So, even if you might have been slightly careless, you can still recover some damages from an insurance company as long as your carelessness did not obviously cause the accident.

**EXAMPLE:** Alejandro makes a sudden stop when a dog runs in front of his car. Bernice hits Alejandro from behind. There was no indication that Alejandro's driving was at all careless, but the police accident report notes than one of Alejandro's tail lights was out.

If the insurance company can show that the tail light was out before the accident, it might claim that Alejandro was partly at fault for not having his car working properly. In one of these most restrictive states, the insurance company might say that Alejandro has no right to any compensation because of his comparative, or contributory, negligence. Alejandro would respond, however, that Bernice said nothing to the police officer about Alejandro's tail light being out, so Alejandro's tail light did not contribute in any way to the accident.

Alejandro and the insurance company would then negotiate about this question, along with all the other factors in the case. Because the insurance company cannot prove that the tail light actually contributed to the accident, Alejandro would almost surely receive at least some compensation for his injuries.

### Witnesses Can Help Show Fault

If someone saw what happened in your accident and backs up some part of your version of events, you may have a strong tool in showing who was at fault. A witness could be someone else who was involved in the accident—a passenger in your car, for example—or a bystander who just happened to see what went on.

An insurance adjuster might try to convince you that what a witness says is less important if it comes from a friend or relative. But in general, that is not true as long as the friend or relative actually saw the accident; after all, most people traveling in the same car are going to be friends or relatives. If you have a complete stranger as a supporting witness, however, your case might become even stronger. (See Chapters 3 and 6.)

# Liability in Specific Types of Accidents

There are no magic formulas or special language you have to master to show why someone was at fault in any particular kind of accident. All you have to bear in mind are the general rules of liability discussed in the first section of this chapter.

You need only make a reasonable, common-sense argument about why a person or business was careless in acting or failing to act, and how that negligence caused the accident that injured you. And in accidents caused by defective products, you need not show any negligence on the part of the product's maker or seller. Instead, you need to show only that you used the product in a normal way and that the defective or dangerous part of the product caused your injuries.

The rest of this chapter discusses how these general rules are applied in specific types of accidents. Remember, though, that an insurance adjuster might claim that you, too, were negligent, or that you were using a product improperly. So, when you think about the facts of your accident, consider how the insurance company will view your actions—and begin to plan your responses.

## Car Accidents

Anyone who drives or rides in a car long enough is likely to be involved in at least a minor fender-bender. And on our crowded streets, pedestrians, too, are often involved in accidents with buses, cars, and bikes.

The rules regarding liability for vehicle accidents apply both to injury claims and to claims for damage to your vehicle.

Anyone who rides a bicycle or motorcycle knows that the roads are even more dangerous for two-wheelers than for cars. Also, special rules of the road apply only to two-wheelers. If you

had an accident riding a two-wheel vehicle, your claim is given special attention below, in "Special Issues for Bicycles and Motorcycles." But before turning to that section, familiarize yourself with the information in this section about vehicle accidents in general.

---

### Special Rules for No-Fault Policyholders

About a dozen states have some form of no-fault (also called Personal Injury Protection) auto insurance. No-fault insurance is intended to prevent people with minor auto accident injuries from filing claims for any damages other than their property damage and medical bills, like pain and suffering.

However, every no-fault plan permits claims for damages beyond medical bills in some circumstances. To see if your no-fault policy affects how you can make an auto accident injury claim, see Chapter 4.

If you are covered by a no-fault policy that allows you to file a claim for damages against the person who was at fault for your accident, proceed against that person as explained here, exactly the same as if you did not have no-fault coverage.

---

## Traffic Laws May Help Determine Fault

Figuring out who is at fault in a traffic accident is a matter of deciding who was careless. For vehicle accidents, there is a set of official written rules telling people how they are supposed to drive and providing guidelines that can help you measure liability. These rules of the road are the traffic laws that everyone must learn to pass the driver's license test. Complete rules are contained in each state's vehicle code, and they apply not only to automobiles but also to motorcycles, bicycles, and pedestrians.

Sometimes a violation of one of these traffic rules is obvious and was clearly the cause of an accident.

**EXAMPLE 1:** Bob drives through a stop sign and hits Mary's car. Going through a stop sign is an obvious violation that leads directly to a collision with someone coming through an intersection in a cross direction.

**EXAMPLE 2:** Juanita does not look carefully and moves from the left lane to the right. Another car, driven by Arlene, is already in the right lane. Arlene swerves to avoid Juanita and hits a parked car. The accident was clearly caused by Juanita's traffic violation—her unsafe lane change—and is obviously Juanita's fault, even though her car never actually hit Arlene's car.

In other situations, whether or not there was a violation will be less obvious.

**EXAMPLE 3:** Arnie merges onto a freeway. Ed does not give him room to enter, and Arnie's car strikes the side of Ed's car. A little research reveals that the rule in the state where the accident occurred is that the entering driver must give way to the driver who is already in traffic. Arnie was probably at fault.

In other situations, there may have been a traffic violation that had no part in causing the accident and therefore should not affect who is liable.

**EXAMPLE 4:** Beatrice failed to signal when she made a right turn; Chain-Fa ran through a stop sign and plowed into her. Obviously, Chain-Fa's violation led directly to the accident. If he had stopped, he would not have hit Bea. But Bea's violation probably

had nothing to do with the accident. Since Chain-Fa would have hit her whether she had gone straight or turned, signaling would not have prevented the accident.

## Accidents With Several Causes

It is sometimes difficult to say that one particular act caused an accident. This is especially true if what you claim the other driver did seems unimportant. But if you can show that the other driver made several minor driving errors or committed several minor traffic violations, then you can argue that the *combination* of those actions caused the accident.

**EXAMPLE:** Lana was driving in the right-hand lane when John changed from the left lane to the right and ran into her. In the police report, John says he had already moved into the lane before the collision and that Lana was not paying attention.

This is the kind of case where it is often difficult to show who was most at fault, and an insurance settlement for Lana might be lower because of what appears to be her comparative negligence. That is, it seems both people were at fault.

But if, through the police report or a witness, Lana can show that John was driving over the speed limit, failed to signal a lane change, changed lanes too abruptly, or committed some other driving violation, in combination with Lana's claim that he did not give her the right of way, Lana's argument for liability could be stronger.

## Where to Find Help in Showing Fault

Your argument to an insurance company that the other driver was at least partially at fault can be strengthened if you can find some official support that the other driver violated one or more rules of the road.

**Vehicle code.** One place to look for support for your argument that the other driver was at fault is in the laws that govern driving in your state, usually called the state vehicle code. A simplified version of these laws, sometimes called "The Rules of the Road," is often available at your local department of motor vehicles office. The complete vehicle code is also available at many local department of motor vehicles offices, most public libraries, and all law libraries. There is a law library at or near every courthouse and at all law schools.

In the index at the end of the last volume of the vehicle code are references to many rules of the road, one or more of which might apply to your accident. A librarian may be willing to help you with your search, so don't be afraid to ask. If you believe a rule might apply to your accident, copy not only its exact wording but also the vehicle code section number so that you can refer to it when you negotiate a settlement of your claim.

**Rule violations that always mean liability.** Many rules of the road are subject to debate with insurance companies: Did the other driver really violate the rule? Did the rule really apply in your case? Did the rule violation actually cause the accident? But there are a few situations in which the other driver is almost always found to be at fault and insurance companies don't even bother to argue about it.

**Rear-end collision.** If someone hits you from behind, it is virtually always his or her fault, regardless of the reason you stopped. A basic rule of the road requires that you be able to stop safely if a vehicle stops ahead of you. If you cannot stop, you are not driving as safely as the person in front of you.

The other surefire part of a rear-end accident claim is that the car's damage proves how the accident happened. If the other car's front end

and your car's rear end are both damaged, there's no doubt that you were struck from the rear.

In some situations, both you and the car behind you will be stopped when a third car runs into the car behind you and pushes it into the rear of your car. In that case, it is the driver of the third car who is at fault and against whose liability insurance you would file a claim.

However, even if you have been rear-ended, in a few circumstances your own carelessness may reduce your compensation under the rule of comparative negligence. (See "How Your Carelessness Affects Your Claim" in this chapter.) A common example is when one or both brake or tail lights were out, especially if the accident happened at night. Another example is when a car had mechanical problems but the driver failed to move it fully to the side of the road.

## Police Reports: Powerful Support

If the police responded to the scene of your accident, particularly if they were aware that anyone was injured, they probably made a written accident report.

Sometimes a police report will plainly state that a driver violated a specific vehicle code section and that the violation caused the accident. It may even indicate that the officer issued a citation. Other times, negligent driving is merely described or briefly mentioned somewhere in the report.

Regardless of how specific the report is, if you can find any mention in a police report of a vehicle code violation or other evidence of careless driving, it can serve as great support in showing that the other driver was at fault. Naturally, the clearer the officer's statement about fault, the easier your job will be. (See Chapter 6.)

**Left turn accident.** A vehicle making a left turn is almost always liable to a vehicle coming straight in the other direction. Exceptions to this near-automatic liability can occur if:

- the vehicle going straight was going much too fast, but that is usually difficult to prove; it would mean only that the other vehicle had some comparative liability, not that the turning vehicle could escape responsibility altogether
- the vehicle going straight went through a red light, but that is also very difficult to prove unless there were witnesses outside the two vehicles who saw the accident clearly, and
- the left-turn vehicle began its turn when it was safe but something unexpected happened that made it have to slow down or stop its turn. Nonetheless, the law says the vehicle making the left turn must wait until it can safely complete the turn before moving in front of oncoming traffic.

Also, as with a rear-end collision, the location of the damage on the vehicles sometimes makes it difficult for the other driver to argue that the accident happened in some way other than during a left turn. So, if you have had an accident in which you ran into someone who was making a left turn in front of you, almost all other considerations of fault go out the window, and the other driver is nearly always fully liable.

## Accidents Involving Cell Phones

Love them or hate them, cell phones are a fact of life. Unfortunately, they are also a fact of driving. According to the phone industry's own figures, there are more than 150 million cell phones in use, with 85% of users saying they use the phone while driving. These are disturbing numbers—and the amount of time each user is on the phone, including while driving, is rising dramatically.

Talking on the phone while driving increases the risk of an accident significantly. A number of studies have now shown beyond any doubt that a phone conversation is a major distraction. In a landmark study, University of Toronto researchers found that using a phone while driving quadruples the risk of an accident—and using a speaker or headset instead of your hands makes no difference in the risk. (See *New England Journal of Medicine*, February 13, 1997, www.nejm.org.) This is the same risk factor as driving while intoxicated. Another experiment by the University of Utah (Park City) showed that cell phone use reduces reaction time even more than a legally prohibited blood-alcohol level. The University of Toronto findings were confirmed by the Insurance Institute for Highway Safety, which published its report of cell phone use and accidents in the *British Medical Journal* in July 2005.

The explanation for the heightened risk is that there's a dramatic drop in your concentration while you are talking on the phone. When a person performs two tasks at once, the brain has a reduced ability to perform either one. The National Transportation Safety Board (NTSB) has found that a distracted driver responds up to 1.5 seconds more slowly to a road hazard than a focused driver—and that's an eternity behind the wheel.

The Harvard Center for Risk analysis reported that in 2002 cell phone use was already responsible for 6% of all U.S. auto accidents. Based on all these studies, the NTSB has issued a warning against driving and phone use. And despite massive lobbying efforts by the cell phone industry, the states of Connecticut, New Jersey, and New York and the District of Columbia all make it illegal to drive while using a hand-held phone.

If you have had a traffic accident with someone who was on the phone, you have a powerful argument that the phone use alone means the other person was at fault. You can make the other driver's phone use a central part of your demand for compensation, referring to the studies and findings described above. (For an example, see Sample Demand Letter 2 in Chapter 6.) And if the accident occurred in a state, county, or city where phone use is illegal, your argument is even stronger.

Some insurance adjusters reply to arguments that cell phone use is unsafe by citing a University of North Carolina study sponsored by the American Automobile Association. This study looked at 1995–1998 accident reports in North Carolina. It found that of drivers who admitted that some distraction contributed to their accidents, only 1.5% named cell phone use. The cell phone industry claims this shows phone use is not a significant driving danger. In fact, it does no such thing. The study includes no data about the number of cell phones in North Carolina in the mid-1990s. As a relatively poor and rural state, and in years before cell phone use hit its stride, it is likely that cell phone use in North Carolina was not that widespread. The small numbers of cell phones involved makes the study scientifically meaningless—it is like saying that the low number of alcohol-related accidents in Saudi Arabia (where alcohol is prohibited) proves that driving while intoxicated is not dangerous.

Of course, making an argument about the dangers of cell phone use depends on being able to show that the other driver really was on the phone. The police report might so indicate. Or a witness—in your vehicle, in another vehicle, or on the street—may say so. Even if you have no support, but you truly did see the other driver on the phone, you should raise the point in your demand for compensation. You may find that the other driver does not deny being on the phone, particularly if you remind the insurance adjuster that if the matter goes to court, you will

be permitted to see the other driver's cell phone records for the accident day. (See Sample Demand Letter 2 in Chapter 6.)

## Special Issues for Bicycles and Motorcycles

If you had an accident while riding a bicycle or motorcycle, you must consider all the factors that relate to drivers of four-wheeled vehicles, as discussed above. But because you were driving a two-wheeler, other things may also be important in pursuing your injury claim. These may include certain rules of the road or other legal issues that pertain only to bicycles or motorcycles. And there are certain road conditions that may present legally unacceptable hazards to drivers of two-wheelers, especially bicyclists, though they do not normally affect four-wheel vehicles. Just as important are the attitudes of insurance adjusters toward motorcycle and bicycle riders.

### Helmets and Helmet Laws

Many states have enacted laws requiring helmets on motorcycle riders. Some require helmets for all riders; others require helmets only for riders under a certain age (see "Motorcycle Helmet Laws," below). Some states have also enacted mandatory bicycle helmet laws, though only for younger riders (see "Bicycle Helmet Laws," below).

Whether you were wearing a helmet at the time of your accident may or may not be a deciding factor in your claim. It depends on your type of injury. If you suffered injuries to your head or neck, then whether you were wearing a helmet is very important.

**Helmet, no head injury.** If you were wearing a helmet and did not suffer head or neck injuries, the helmet has no legal significance—in other words, even if you had one on, your ability to collect on your claim is not helped. Even so, wearing a helmet may be worth mentioning during your claim, because it paints you as a responsible person.

**Helmet, head injury.** If you were wearing a helmet and still suffered head or neck injuries, the helmet is very important to your claim. It shows that you were not "comparatively negligent," at least as to this aspect of your claim. That is, it shows that your injuries were not made worse by your own carelessness. And it shows how much worse you might have been injured—and therefore how dangerous the other driver's conduct was—had you not been wearing a helmet.

**No helmet, no head injury.** If you suffered injuries but did not injure your head or neck, the fact that you were *not* wearing a helmet is legally meaningless, because that fact did not lead to your "damages." In other words, you would have suffered these injuries whether or not you had a helmet. This is true even if the law in your state requires you to wear a helmet.

**No helmet, no helmet law, head injury.** If you were *not* wearing a helmet and you suffered head or neck injuries, you may face difficult opposition in your claim even if the law in your state does not require you to wear a helmet. That is because helmets are known to significantly reduce or prevent head and neck injuries. So, your failure to wear a helmet can amount to a kind of "comparative negligence" on your part. (See "How Your Carelessness Affects Your Claim," above.)

Bicyclists may still be able to make a successful claim in these circumstances. The protection afforded by bicycle helmets is not as obvious or well documented as it is for motorcyclists. As a result, helmets are not required for adult bicyclists in any state. If a no-helmet bicyclist sustains head injuries, it is up to the insurance company to produce convincing evidence that a commonly available bicycle helmet would have prevented or diminished the specific injury that occurred. If an insurance adjuster makes this argument, it simply becomes another part of the negotiating process. It may weaken the bicyclist's claim, but it does not end the claim altogether. And it does not affect the bicyclist's claim for injuries to other parts of the body.

For a motorcyclist without a helmet, a claim for head or neck injuries is much more difficult to pursue. There is overwhelming documentation—which an insurance adjuster has no trouble producing—that a helmet usually significantly reduces head injuries. It then becomes the job of the claimant to persuade the insurance adjuster that the injury would have happened even with a helmet. The negotiations will revolve around the extent to which the injury would have been reduced by having worn a helmet, and therefore how much compensation for the injury should be reduced.

**No helmet, helmet law, head injury.** If either a bicyclist or a motorcyclist is required by law to wear a helmet and sustains a head injury while riding without one, it is extremely difficult to obtain any compensation for the head injury. (A claim may still be successful, however, for other injuries.) The existence of the law automatically establishes the rider's comparative negligence. To obtain any compensation, the cyclist would have to show that the injury would have occurred even if he or she had been wearing a helmet. This is a very tough task, and—if it is possible at all—almost certainly requires the services of an experienced personal injury lawyer.

## Bicycle Helmet Laws

No states require helmets for adult bicyclists. However, the following states require helmets for riders under a certain age. *Be aware, however, that local laws in many cities and towns may require a bicycle helmet even though the state has no helmet law.*

| State | Bicyclists Required to Wear Helmet |
|---|---|
| Alabama | under 16 |
| California | under 18 |
| Connecticut | under 16 |
| Delaware | under 16 |
| District of Columbia | under 16 |
| Florida | under 16 |
| Georgia | under 16 |
| Hawaii | under 16 |
| Louisiana | under 12 |
| Maine | under 16 |
| Maryland | under 16 |
| Massachusetts | under 17 |
| New Hampshire | under 16 |
| New Jersey | under 17 |
| New York | under 14 |
| North Carolina | under 16 |
| Oregon | under 16 |
| Pennsylvania | under 12 |
| Rhode Island | under 16 |
| Tennessee | under 16 |
| West Virginia | under 15 |

## General Bike Rights

All states have what are called "side-of-the-road" rules, which require bicyclists to ride on the far right side of the road, or in a bike lane, if they are not moving as fast as auto traffic. Cyclists following these rules account for the three most common types of road accidents for bicyclists:

- hitting the opening door of a parked car
- being brushed by a passing car or truck, and
- being struck by a motor vehicle turning right.

Fortunately, other laws combine with the side-of-the-road rules to help protect bicycle riders who share the streets with motor vehicles. In general, a bicycle has as much right to the roadway as a motor vehicle. Unless a specific law (as discussed below) directs otherwise, a cyclist may ride in the middle of a traffic lane and must be afforded the same rights of way as motor vehicles. You may need to remind an insurance adjuster about this more than once during the course of your claim negotiations.

The following are general descriptions of the several rules that, taken together, determine liability in roadway accidents between bicycles and motor vehicles.

**Side-of-road laws and bike lanes.** If a cyclist does not ride as fast as current motor vehicle traffic, the cyclist must ride as far to the right side of the road as possible. (On one-way streets, the cyclist may instead ride to the far left.) If a special bike lane is provided, usually on the far right of the roadway, a cyclist is required to use it.

A bicyclist may leave the side of the road or the bike lane if the cyclist keeps up with moving traffic, if the lane is too narrow to share safely with passing cars, to make a left turn, or to avoid debris or other hazards.

## Motorcycle Helmet Laws

As of 2006, only Colorado, Illinois, and Iowa have no laws requiring helmet use by any motorcycle riders. All other states have some helmet law, about half of which pertain to all riders, the other half only to riders under a certain age. ("Riders" includes both drivers and passengers, unless otherwise noted.)

| State | Motorcycle Riders Required to Wear Helmet |
|---|---|
| Alabama | all ages |
| Alaska | drivers under 18; all ages if driving on learning permit; all passengers |
| Arizona | under 18 |
| Arkansas | under 21 |
| California | all ages |
| Colorado | no helmet law |
| Connecticut | under 18 |
| Delaware | under 19 |
| District of Columbia | all ages |
| Florida | under 21; all ages if no health insurance |
| Georgia | all ages |
| Hawaii | under 18 |
| Idaho | under 18 |
| Illinois | no helmet law |
| Indiana | under 18 |
| Iowa | no helmet law |
| Kansas | under 18 |
| Kentucky | under 21; all ages if no health insurance or if driving on learning permit |
| Louisiana | all ages |
| Maine | under 15; all ages if driving on learning permit; any passenger if driver required to wear |
| Maryland | all ages |
| Massachusetts | all ages |
| Michigan | all ages |
| Minnesota | under 18; all ages if driving on learning permit |
| Mississippi | all ages |
| Missouri | all ages |

| State | Motorcycle Riders Required to Wear Helmet |
|---|---|
| Montana | under 18 |
| Nebraska | all ages |
| Nevada | all ages |
| New Hampshire | no helmet law |
| New Jersey | all ages |
| New Mexico | under 18 |
| New York | all ages |
| North Carolina | all ages |
| North Dakota | under 18; all passengers if driver under 18 |
| Ohio | under 18; all ages during 1st year of license; all passengers if driver covered |
| Oklahoma | under 18 |
| Oregon | all ages |
| Pennsylvania | under 21; all ages during 1st 2 years of license unless motorcycle safety course completed |
| Rhode Island | under 21; all drivers during 1st year of license; all passengers |
| South Carolina | under 21 |
| South Dakota | under 18 |
| Tennessee | all ages |
| Texas | under 21; all ages unless with medical insurance or completed sanctioned motorcycle safety course |
| Utah | under 18 |
| Vermont | all ages |
| Virginia | all ages |
| Washington | all ages |
| West Virginia | all ages |
| Wisconsin | under 18; all ages if driving on learning permit |
| Wyoming | under 19 |

Since a cyclist is required by law to ride close to parked cars, and a person is not permitted to open a car door unless it is safe to do so, an accident caused by the opening of a parked car door is almost always entirely the fault of the door-opener. An exception might exist if there was no motor vehicle traffic at all, thus eliminating the need for the cyclist to stay to the right. In this circumstance, the motorist who opened the car door might argue that the cyclist had an opportunity to avoid the door and thus was at least partly responsible for the accident.

**Space given by passing motor vehicles.** Given that side-of-the-road rules force cyclists to share lanes with passing traffic, a companion rule requires motor vehicles to maintain a safe space while passing. Three feet is sometimes stated as a safe distance, though it is extremely difficult to be that precise when reconstructing an accident. The problem of sufficient passing space is particularly acute with trucks and buses, and with the ever-increasing number of enormous SUVs.

Because a bicyclist has as much right to the road as does a motorist, a motor vehicle coming up behind a cyclist has a responsibility not to pass unless and until it is safe to do so. The motorist may need to slow down and wait until there is enough space, or change lanes. Except for moving to the far right of the lane, it is *not* the cyclist's duty to stop or otherwise get out of the motorist's way.

Following an accident in which you were bumped by a motorist passing in the same lane, an insurance adjuster might suggest that you were not as far to the right as you should have been. You may respond that it was the motorist's duty to wait until it was safe to pass; knocking you over was not an acceptable driving option. If the motor vehicle was any wider than an average car, you might also want to measure the width of the traffic lane, up to the line of parked vehicles, if any, where the accident occurred and

determine the width of the vehicle that struck you. Measure the width of your bicycle at the handlebars (or wider, if you were bumped on a part of your body that extends out farther than the bars). If the extra width of the motor vehicle made passing you safely at that spot difficult, you have an even stronger argument that the vehicle had no right to attempt the pass at that point.

**Right turn right-of-way.** One of the most common causes of bicycle accidents is collision with a car turning right. While making a right turn, a car passes through the path of a cyclist, whether the cyclist is traveling in a traffic lane or in a bike lane. Some of these accidents happen when a car passes a cyclist, then slows down while turning right, moving directly into the path of a bicyclist who has nowhere to turn. Or a motorist simply turns right directly into a cyclist without seeing, and often without looking for, the bike.

In either of these situations, the motorist is liable for the accident. One of the basic rules of the road is that a vehicle may not make a turn unless it is safe to do so. Because a cyclist has as much right to the road as a motor vehicle, and because side-of-the-road laws force cyclists to the right, a cyclist is entitled to continue straight through an intersection without yielding to a motorist turning right.

**Lane splitting.** Many motorcyclists, and a few bicyclists, engage in the driving maneuver known as "lane splitting." Done mostly in traffic jams, it means squeezing a bike between lanes, passing the cars in stop-and-go traffic on each side.

Lane splitting is not recognized as a legal maneuver in any state except California. In most states it is not specifically prohibited but is regularly interpreted by police and courts as unlawful. Even in California, it is legal only if done safely. And "safely" is always very much a judgment call. The mere fact that an accident happened while a rider was lane splitting is very strong evidence that on that occasion it wasn't safe to do so.

If you have been involved in an accident while lane splitting, you will have a hard job convincing an insurance adjuster that the accident was not completely your fault. Remember, in most states you need not show that the accident was *entirely* the other driver's fault; you need only show that the other driver's carelessness was a substantial cause of the accident.

Nonetheless, in a few circumstances you may be able to convince an insurance adjuster that the other driver contributed significantly to the accident and that therefore you should be at least partially, if not fully, compensated. It helps if you can show that you were riding cautiously—not speeding or weaving in and out of lanes or between cars. A police report or witness statement may help. And the extent of your experience as a cyclist may support that claim. Most important, however, is showing that the other driver did something even more dangerous than lane splitting. Most likely this would be making an abrupt lane change without signaling, or drifting from one lane into another. Again, support from a police report or witness may be crucial in convincing an insurance adjuster that the other driver's carelessness was a significant factor in the accident.

**Road surface hazards.** Because of their relative instability and the size of their tires, two-wheel vehicles are susceptible to unexpected, abrupt changes in the roadway surface. In general, the thinner the tire, the greater the risk. The most common roadway hazards are potholes, sewer grates, railroad or trolley tracks, and temporary disruptions from street construction work (street level changes, metal and wood hole covers, tar, oil, or loose gravel). Any of these hazards can cause even a careful, experienced cyclist to go down, or to lose control and veer into the path of a car.

The party most likely responsible for such an accident is the state, county, city, or other public agency that maintains the roadway. If you file a claim against a public entity, you must pay special attention to the filing requirements and time limits relating to claims against public entities. (See "Special Rules for Accidents Involving the Government" in Chapter 3.)

**Potholes.** One common reason for a pothole or similar surface break is shoddy temporary roadway repair. Very often when a street or something under it is being repaired, the construction work is done in stages. Before the work is completed, a construction crew may temporarily resurface the road with relatively weak material that will be replaced later. These temporary fixes often sink or crack almost as soon as they are done, or are done so sloppily that they leave broken or loose edges of road surface. Sometimes the repair work is merely covered over temporarily with heavy metal or wooden plates that present dangerous edges to a cyclist.

If temporary road work leaves any such hazard, whether the public entity responsible for the road is liable to an injured cyclist depends on whether there was sufficient warning of the hazard. Sufficient warning might include blocking off the repaired area of the street or placing warning signs and cones. But a warning must provide a cyclist with enough advance notice that it's possible to avoid the hazard.

The other common reason for roadway surface breaks is long-term wear and tear. In these cases, the key to whether the roadway's public agency was negligent—and therefore legally responsible for the accident—is the length of time the problem has been there. If the surface break has been there for only a few days, the public agency is generally not responsible for an accident caused by the agency failing to fix it. If the problem has been there for weeks or months, however, then the public agency's failure to fix it may present an unreasonable danger to cyclists.

Showing that the problem has been there for a while is similar to proving that a property owner is liable in a trip or slip and fall accident. (See "Accidents on Dangerous or Defective Property," below.) A witness may be able to tell you that the problem has existed—and perhaps has been known by roadway authorities—for some time. Or the condition of the road, as demonstrated by photos, may show that the break is not recent. But your ability to show that the problem has been around for some time may depend on the public agency's own records of how often the street had been inspected or repaired, and whether it had any notice of the problem before your accident. Chapter 6 explains how to obtain this kind of information.

**Sewer grates.** Sewer grates can present a serious danger to bicyclists. If sewer grate bars go in the same direction as traffic, a bicycle tire may easily become stuck between them. Cyclists have complained long and loud about this problem, and most cities and counties have responded by either changing the shape or direction of grates or partially covering them with crosshatch safety bars. However, there are still many dangerous grates on America's roadways.

If you have had such an accident, you may want to request information from the public agency about its efforts to identify and replace dangerous grates. (See Chapter 6.) But this is only a way to put some extra pressure on a city or county's insurance adjuster. The basic argument that the public agency is responsible for your sewer grate accident is simple: You have a right to cycle on a safe roadway; a direction-of-travel sewer grate presents a serious, unexpected hazard; and there are simple, inexpensive remedies for the problem, none of which the city or county undertook in the case of this particular grate.

**Rail or trolley tracks.** Trains, streetcars, and trolleys are disappearing from the American landscape. But many of their tracks remain behind. Little-used or abandoned rail tracks present hidden hazards to cyclists. They are dangerous when they run on the roadway in the direction of traffic, and even more so when they cross the roadway in a curve or at an angle. In these configurations, a cycle wheel can easily get caught in the space between rail and road, throwing the cyclist down or sideways into a motor vehicle.

Whether a public entity might be liable to a cyclist injured on a rail depends on several factors. First is the rail position. If tracks run in the direction of traffic, or cross on a curve or at an angle, they are dangerous to bicyclists. If tracks cross perpendicularly, however, they do not present a significant danger to a careful cyclist.

If the rails are dangerous, then the question shifts to what the public entity should have done about them. If the tracks are no longer in use, then the public entity could have removed or covered them. If the tracks are still in use, the public entity must at least provide sufficient warning to cyclists. Signs should warn of the tracks far enough in advance that a cyclist can safely stop or take another route. And a city, county, or state should never create a bike path or alternate route—encouraging bicyclists to travel that way—if it crosses dangerous tracks.

## Combating Negative Perceptions About Two-Wheelers

Unfortunately, the general public, including insurance adjusters, tends to consider riders of two-wheeled vehicles as second-class road citizens. This attitude arises out of negative perceptions of two-wheelers that bear little relation to reality—assumptions that all motorcyclists are wild and reckless and that all bicyclists are eccentric and careless.

If you have been in an accident riding a two-wheeler, part of your job in demonstrating who was at fault for the accident is to overcome these prejudices. To do so, there are a number of things you may be able to point out in addition to your argument about how the accident actually happened. (These are things that should be included in your letter demanding compensation from the insurance company, as explained in Chapter 6.)

Significant experience or training riding the same, or the same kind of, two-wheeler as you rode at the time of the accident is a very good indicator that you knew how to ride properly and safely. This is particularly true if combined with a clean driving record (see below). There are a number of different aspects of riding experience you might be able to cite.

- **Formal training.** If you have ever completed a bicycle or motorcycle driving or safety course, you should let the insurance adjuster know.

- **Length of time riding.** Having driven a motorcycle or bicycle (as an adult) for a long time is, in itself, an important point. So is the length of time you have spent on the particular machine (or same size and type of machine) that you were riding at the time of the accident.

- **Regularity of riding.** If you ride regularly—commuting to and from work or school, for example—you should note that fact, as well as the number of miles per day, week, or month. If you frequently ride long distances for pleasure, that, too, can be noted.

- **Type of riding.** If you were injured on a city street, the frequency with which you ride on such streets—as opposed to weekend rides in the country—is something to point out. If you were injured during commute traffic hours, your familiarity with riding during those hours can be important.

Similarly, if you were injured while riding on a highway, your significant experience in highway riding should be mentioned. Weather, too, should be noted if it might have been a factor in the accident. If it was or had been raining, you should mention your experience riding in wet weather.

- **Familiarity with specific roadway—in general.** Part of the image of two-wheelers is that riders don't know what to do in certain traffic situations and that they panic and cause their own downfalls. One way to dispel this image is to make a point of how often you ride on the particular roadway, at the same general time, that the accident happened. If you were very familiar with the roadway, its parking patterns, intersections, flow of traffic, and other potential hazards to two-wheelers, you can establish immediately that, at least by experience, you were likely to know exactly how to ride that stretch of road safely.

- **Familiarity with specific roadway—road hazard.** Experience with a particular roadway is important if you had an accident with another vehicle, as explained above. Whether familiarity is useful if you struck an unexpected hazard on the roadway depends on the type of hazard. If you frequently or regularly ride a particular street and are suddenly thrown by an unexpected hazard created by recent construction work, your familiarity with the road supports the notion that you could not have been prepared to handle this particular danger. The situation is different if your accident was caused by a sewer grate or a pothole that you contend should have been discovered and removed. In that case, if you have been riding the same stretch regularly, an insurance adjuster could argue that you should have known about the sewer grate or dangerous patch of road surface, and therefore avoided it.

- **Two-wheel driving record.** Normally, your driving record is not available to an insurance adjuster during the course of an insurance claim, and you are not required to reveal that record during claim negotiations. However, you may want to bring up your driving record if it strongly suggests that you are a cautious rider. If you have never had an accident on a two-wheeler and you have been riding for a considerable period of time, this shows that you are a careful rider. Similarly, if you have had no recent moving violations (within the past ten years) and none of the type that might be related to the cause of this accident, this also shows that you are careful and law-abiding on your bike.

- **Four-wheel driving record.** If you have had a moving violation or accident while driving a car—though not on a two-wheeler—in the past ten years, you may still make this argument, but it is somewhat weaker. If you have had any accidents or moving violations on a bike or more than one violation or accident while driving your car, forget about bringing up your driving record.

- **Protective clothing.** Particularly if you were on a motorcycle, you should point to any protective clothing you were wearing at the time of the accident. This shows that you were cautious and responsible, and that your injuries occurred despite these precautions. Even if you did not suffer a head injury, mention the fact that you were wearing a helmet, if you were. Again, this presents the picture of a responsible rider, even if it has no direct relation to the cause of the accident or to your injuries.

## Accidents on Dangerous or Defective Property

Injury accidents caused by defective or dangerous property, either inside a building or outside, are called "premises liability" accidents. Premises can be dangerous for all kinds of reasons—faulty design, shoddy construction or building materials, poor maintenance, or dangerous clutter. And dangerous premises can lead to all kinds of accidents, including slipping and falling, tripping, or having something hit or fall on you.

These accidents take place
- on commercial premises—a store, office, or other place of business
- at a residence—private home or rental property, and
- on public property—park, street, or sidewalk, government building, or public transport such as a bus or streetcar.

Regardless of how or where an accident takes place, two basic rules determine who is legally responsible.

### Owner's Duty to Keep Property Safe

The owner or occupier of property has a legal duty to anyone who enters the property—a tenant, a shopper, or a personal or business visitor—not to subject that person to an unreasonable risk of injury because of the design, construction, or condition of the property. The reason for this rule is simple: The owner and occupier have control over whether the premises are safe, while the visitor has none.

> **EXAMPLE:** An apartment building visitor trips and falls on a broken piece of linoleum in the entrance hall. The owner of the building is most likely liable for the injuries because the owner has a responsibility to maintain the floor so that broken tiles get replaced and people do not trip over them.

Other rules protect an employee who is injured on his or her employer's premises. An employee who is injured at work must make a workers' compensation claim instead of a private injury claim. (See "Workers' Compensation," in Chapter 4.) But if the employee is injured on someone's premises other than his or her employer's while at work, the employee has a right to make a claim against the owner of those premises.

### Visitor's Duty to Use Property Normally

The second basic rule of premises liability has to do with your own conduct. There is an unreasonable risk of injury if a person using the premises in a normal way has an accident caused by a dangerous or faulty design, construction, or condition of the premises, or some combination of these dangerous factors. However, a property owner or occupier is not held responsible if people get injured while acting in an unexpected, unauthorized, or dangerously careless way. You can probably already see where the arguments begin: What does using the premises in a "normal" way mean? And if there was a danger or defect, was an accident caused by that condition or by the carelessness of the person injured?

> **EXAMPLE:** People leaving a party one night are roughhousing on the stairs. One of the partygoers swings himself down the stairs on the handrail. The handrail breaks, and he is injured. Because a handrail is not a gymnastics apparatus, vaulting on one is not a normal use. The owner cannot be held responsible for the unusual and dangerously careless use of the handrail.

### Who Is Responsible for Injuries

The owner of property is often different from the occupier. For example, a store or other business may be operated by one company while the property is owned by another, or a residence may be owned by one person and rented by someone else. Both the owner and the occupier may be responsible for injuries caused by the property's dangerous condition. And because both may be legally responsible, it is up to their insurance companies to determine which one will have to respond to your accident claim. Once you file a notice of claim against both, you don't have to worry about deciding which one is more responsible. That's their problem. (See "Determine Who Might Be Responsible," in Chapter 3.)

---

## The Law Takes You as It Finds You

What happens if you have a bad knee that makes one leg a bit unsteady and it sometimes buckles if you make a sudden turn? Does that mean that the slippery floor you fell on is not legally considered dangerous because someone with two stronger legs might not have fallen?

Absolutely not.

An owner or occupant must permit no unnecessary danger to any person who might reasonably be expected to be on the property. That means little kids as well as older people, and folks with good eyesight and bad eyesight, strong knees and weak knees. The legal rule is that people must be "taken as they're found," meaning that all people, regardless of physical ability, have a right to make their way through the world without unnecessary danger—as long as they have not created that danger by being careless themselves.

Next, we explain the ways legal responsibility is sorted out depending on where your accident happened and what type of accident it was.

## Commercial Property

If you have an accident at a store, office, or other type of business, you'll need to give the company notice of the event and your injuries (see Chapter 3). The business's insurance company will either handle your claim itself or pass the matter on to the building owner's insurance company, depending on which one is responsible. The question of whether the owner or occupier is legally responsible is usually determined by where the accident occurred, as stated in the terms of the lease or other business arrangement. Again, that's not your problem—one of the insurers will let you know which one will handle the claim.

## Private Residences

The rules of legal responsibility for private residences are fairly simple.

- **Rented apartment.** If you are injured in an accident on rental property, whether you are a visitor or a tenant, responsibility for the condition of the premises is usually divided as follows:
  1. the tenant is responsible for the movable things inside an apartment, and
  2. the landlord is responsible for the immovable things inside (floors, walls, fixtures, appliances that came with the apartment) and everything outside (hallways, stairs, entrances). An exception to this rule can occur if there is something immovable inside—a floorboard, for example—that the tenant knows is dangerous but has done nothing about. In that case, the tenant

may be liable along with the landlord for injuries the dangerous condition causes.

If you are injured but are not sure who is legally responsible for the portion of the premises causing the accident, file a notice of claim against both. (See "Getting a Claim Started" in Chapter 3.)

- **Private home.** If you are injured in an accident caused by a dangerous or defective condition at a private home, the owner of the home is responsible. If the entire home is rented out, the tenant, too, might be responsible.
- **Adjoining properties.** In an accident that occurs at the edge of premises—for example, at a fence on a neighbor's property line, or on a cracked sidewalk—it may not be immediately clear whether it was one homeowner's or the other's property that caused the accident. Or it may be unclear whether the homeowner or the city was responsible for the particular part of the sidewalk that was defective. In these situations, file an initial notice of claim against both and let them sort out which one will respond to your claim.

## Slip or Trip and Fall Accidents

An extremely common kind of accident is slipping on a wet or otherwise slippery floor, stair, or ground, or tripping over something on a floor or the ground. It is a normal part of living for things to fall or drip on a floor or the ground, and some things put in the ground—a drainage grate, for example—serve a useful purpose there. Therefore, the owner or occupant of property cannot always be held responsible for immediately picking up or cleaning every slippery substance on a floor. Nor is the property owner always responsible for someone slipping or tripping on something that an ordinary person should expect to find there or should see and avoid. We all have an obligation to watch where we're going.

There is no precise way to explain when an owner or occupier of property is legally responsible for something on which you slip or trip. Each case turns on whether the owner acted carefully so that visitors were not *likely* to slip or trip—and whether the person who fell was careless in not seeing or avoiding the thing he or she fell on.

To be held legally responsible for the injuries you suffered from slipping or tripping and falling, the owner of the premises or the owner's employee:

- must have caused the spill, worn or torn spot, or other slippery or dangerous surface or item to be underfoot
- must have known the slippery or dangerous material or object was underfoot and done nothing about it, or
- should have known the slippery or dangerous material was on the floor, stair, or ground because a "reasonable" person taking care of the property would have discovered and removed or repaired it.

The third situation is the most common, but is also less clear-cut than the first two because of those pesky words "should have known." Liability in these cases is determined by common sense. The law determines whether the owner or occupier of property was careful by deciding whether the steps the owner or occupier took to keep the property safe were reasonable.

People who work at, live on, and visit property drop and spill things from time to time, and they do not always pick up after themselves. Floors become cracked, torn, or worn and slippery, and ground can become loose, broken, or unusually slippery. A person who is responsible for property must make some regular effort to check the walking safety of the premises and to do some repair and cleanup with safety in mind. On the other hand, the law does not require a premises owner to stand by round the clock to repair or clean up instantly anything that is broken, dropped, or spilled.

The law concentrates on the reasonableness of cleanup and repair efforts. Someone who makes regular and thorough efforts to keep property safe and clean is less likely to be found liable than an owner who neglects the premises. But usually accident claims arise when the matter of repair or cleanup is not very clear. As a result, you can almost always argue that the owner was not careful enough. The very fact that you tripped or slipped shows that the owner could have been more "reasonable" than he or she was. (Chapter 3 discusses how to preserve evidence of what caused a trip or slip and fall accident. Chapter 6 discusses getting information about property maintenance.)

## Did the Business Regularly Check for Safety?

In a slip or trip and fall claim, one measure of whether a business has been "reasonable" in its protection of customers is how, and how often, it checked the condition of its floors. When processing your claim, it is a good idea to request from the business's insurance company a record of the store's inspections. If the business has a very spotty inspection record, or produces no record at all, you have a strong argument that it was negligent—and therefore legally responsible—in having failed to regularly monitor the safety of the premises.

How and when to request this information from an insurance company, and what to do with the information you receive, is discussed in Chapter 6.

If you have slipped on or tripped over something and fallen, there are some initial questions you can ask to determine whether the property owner may be liable.

- If you tripped over a torn, broken, or bulging area of carpet, floor, or ground, or slipped on a wet or loose area, had the dangerous spot been there long enough so that the owner should have known about it?
- If you tripped over or slipped on an object someone had placed or left on the floor or ground, was there a legitimate reason for the object to be there?
- If there once was a good reason for the object to be there but that reason no longer exists, could the object have been removed, covered, or otherwise made safe?
- Was there a safer place the object could have been located, or could it have been placed in a safer manner, without much greater inconvenience or expense to the property owner or operator?
- Could a simple barrier have been created or warning given to prevent people from slipping or tripping?
- Did insufficient or broken lighting contribute to the accident?

**EXAMPLE 1:** On a crowded train platform, Clarence slips on a banana peel. The banana peel was dry and black—evidence that it had been dropped a long time before the accident. The train management is likely to be liable for Clarence's fall because the fact that the banana peel had been on the ground for a long time means that management was not doing a reasonable job of regularly cleaning up the platform.

**EXAMPLE 2:** On another train platform, Barbara slips on a yellow, moist banana peel. Since the banana peel had not been there

long, nothing indicates that the train management was not sweeping the platform often enough. But at this train platform there is a snack bar that sells bananas, and only one trash container, which is overflowing. The train management could be held responsible for creating the situation where banana peels need to be disposed of but providing no place for them to be thrown away. In other words, the danger of slipping on a banana peel was much greater than it needed to be because of the train management's conduct.

**EXAMPLE 3:** Martina is walking in an unfamiliar neighborhood. She sees some people unloading a truck behind a warehouse, and she goes through a gate to ask them directions. As Martina approaches, she slips on an oil spot, falls, and hurts herself. A large sign on the gate reads "Authorized Personnel Only."

The owner of the warehouse probably would not be liable for Martina's injuries. Martina was not on the premises as a shopper or regular business visitor, and the warehouse had no reason to expect that she would enter the loading area. It is not "reasonable" to require the owner to do enough cleanup to protect people who are not expected to be there. Also, anyone who enters a truck loading area should be careful where he or she steps; if Martina slipped on oil there, she probably was not careful. And the sign warned her not to enter.

Even though Martina's claim for damages would not be very strong, she might still be able to collect something for her injuries from the warehouse owner's liability insurance company. Although she was not invited into the loading area, the gate was open, and it is not totally unexpected that someone should step in there to do something normal like ask directions. The warehouse owner might be considered at least partly at fault for not having protected against danger to a person like Martina whose actions might be considered careless but weren't all that unusual.

In almost every slip or trip and fall case, your own behavior is part of the issue of who was careful and who was careless. The rules of comparative negligence (discussed above in "How Your Carelessness Affects Your Claim") help measure your own reasonableness in going where you did in the way you did just before the accident occurred. There are some questions you should ask yourself about your own conduct, because an insurance adjuster is probably going to ask them after you file your claim.

- Did you have a legitimate reason—a reason the owner should have anticipated—for being where the slippery floor or ground was? If the answer is no, you may have a much weaker claim for the property owner's liability.
- Should a careful person have noticed the slippery or dangerous spot and avoided it, or walked carefully enough not to slip or trip? This is not usually a question that can be answered simply, but if it can be—for example, slipperiness that should be obvious, such as around a swimming pool— your claim may be significantly reduced by your own comparative negligence.
- Were there any warnings that the spot might be dangerous? If so, and if the signs were easily visible, the liability of the property owner is probably lessened by your comparative negligence in not heeding the warning.
- Were you doing anything that distracted you from paying attention to where you were going, or were you running, jumping,

or fooling around in a way that made falling more likely? If so, the owner's liability is probably reduced by your comparative carelessness.

Remember that you do not have to "prove" that you were careful. But think about what you were doing, and pay careful attention to how you will describe it so that it is clear to the insurance adjuster that you were not being careless.

## Poor Lighting May Make a Bad Scene Worse

In slip or trip and fall accidents, poor lighting is often a contributing cause you should mention in your claim along with the condition of the floor, stair, or ground on which you fell. Obviously, if the light is poor, it was more difficult for you to see and avoid the dangerous spot. This is particularly true on stairs, where dim lighting, or alternating bright and dark areas, make it difficult to judge the edge of the step.

If there were lights but the bulbs were burned out, that indicates the owner was not properly maintaining the premises by regularly checking and replacing bulbs. Ask the insurance adjuster for copies of the property owner's maintenance records for the property. Those records might show how often the lighting is checked. And if there is no record of maintenance, you can argue that the lack of records indicates that the owner is not being careful enough in managing property safety. (See Chapter 6.)

## Special Concerns About Stairs

Stairs present a number of special dangers, some obvious, some hidden, that cause thousands of people to trip or slip and fall every year. With the more obvious defects—a torn or loose carpet, or a step or handrail that breaks—the liability of the property owner is usually clear. With things that have been spilled or dropped or left on stairs, the responsibility of the owner is the same as described above in any slip or trip accident.

But in addition to normal considerations of things spilled or left on stairs, there may have been additional dangers with stairs that made your fall more likely. Some defects in stairs may remain hidden even after your accident. As for these, you may have to make an effort to figure out what happened and how the stairs should have been constructed or maintained differently.

### Slippery Surfaces

A common hidden stair danger is worn-down carpet or wood that makes the "run" part of a stair—the part your foot lands on—dangerous, both going up and coming down. Even a slightly worn stair or carpet, particularly on the edge of a step, can be perilous because a person is not likely to notice slight wear and may be even more likely to slip than on obviously worn stairs.

Some stairs may have a tile or highly polished wood surface that is more slippery than stone, painted wood, or carpeted stairs. If so, the owner may have sacrificed safety for beauty and may now be liable because of that choice.

### Wet or Icy Outdoor Stairs

Many people slip and fall when rain, snow, or ice collects on outdoor stairs. The first response of an insurance adjuster is often to say that the property owner is not responsible for the weather, and that everyone must be extra careful when it has been cold, raining, or snowing. While this is partly true, it does not end the question of the owner's negligence.

Outdoor stairs must be built and maintained so that water or ice does not build up excessively on the stairs. If there was an extra buildup of rain, snow, or ice on which you slipped, the step was dangerous and the owner should be liable. Further, an outdoor step must have a surface that does not become extra slippery when wet or icy. If an outdoor step does not have an anti-slip surface, the owner has not taken reasonable safety precautions and may be liable if you slip and fall.

### Building Code Violations

Every state, and virtually every county, has a building code that must be followed by builders and owners when constructing any building, including the stairs. Your city or county building permit department, any local law library, and perhaps your local public library, will have a copy of your state and local building codes.

Check the stair requirements of the codes to see if the stairs on which you fell fail to meet any specifications. If your fall occurred on, or was made worse by, the part of the stairs that fails to meet the code, the code becomes very strong support for your argument that the stairs were dangerous.

A building code stair violation might be measured in no more than quarter inches. But even a very small violation can make a set of stairs dangerous.

You need not use technical or legal language in citing a building code violation to support your injury claim. The code simply provides you with an official declaration of the minimum of safety for a set of stairs. If the stairs you fell on did not meet the standard set by the building code, you have a very strong argument that the stairs were not reasonably safe, regardless of how, or even whether, the building code actually applies. (See Chapter 6.)

**Handrails.** Most building codes require one or more handrails on stairs of a certain width or a certain height; some building codes also have different requirements for commercial premises, multiple-unit apartments, and private homes.

Building codes also require that handrails be installed properly—that is, firmly attached—and at a certain height. Reaching for a handrail that is at the wrong height can actually cause you to fall when nothing else is wrong with the stairs.

**Improper stair height or depth.** The vertical and horizontal part of each step are called the "riser" and the "run," respectively. Building codes prescribe a maximum and minimum riser height for each step, and a maximum and minimum depth for the part on which you put your foot, the run.

If you have slipped or taken a sudden and unexplained fall on a stair, measure the stair's risers and runs, and compare the measurements with the minimums and maximums in the building code. If either the riser or the run violates the code, the stairs were defective.

The question then becomes whether the defect caused your fall. But once you have established that the stairs were defective in a basic way—the wrong height or depth—you have gone a long way toward showing that the stairs were dangerous. Unless the building owner's insurance company can show clearly that you fell because of your own carelessness, the improper stair alone will normally be enough to gain a settlement for you.

**Uneven stair height or depth.** Building codes not only set maximum and minimum stair heights and widths, they also set a maximum variance from one step to another—that is, the differences

permitted in the heights and depths of any one step from another.

The variance standard is important because when we go up or down stairs, our brains remember how far the last steps were and automatically tell our legs to move the same distance the next time. If the leg moves the same distance but the step isn't in the same place— even slightly—we may lose our balance and fall. So, even if each riser and run is within the code limits, variance from one step to another may violate another section of the code and create a dangerous set of stairs.

## Accidents Involving Children

The law assumes that children do not have the same well-formed judgment as adults do, and has fashioned special rules for compensation and liability in accidents involving children.

### Injuries to Children

Although the procedures for collecting compensation for a minor—in most states, a person under age 18—vary somewhat from state to state, in general a child has a right to compensation for pain and suffering, permanent injury, or disability in the same manner and for the same amounts as an adult. Also, a parent has a separate right to be compensated for medical bills paid on behalf of a child.

Obviously, a child cannot negotiate a claim, so a parent is permitted to negotiate on behalf of the child. In some states, the parent must get the approval of a judge before the child's claim can be finally settled. This process is usually short and straightforward, and involves nothing more than filling out a simple form and filing it with the court for approval. An insurance company you reach a settlement with can help by providing you with the proper form and giving you instructions on where to file it. It is in the insurer's interest as well as yours to see that the settlement is properly approved so that a lawyer for the child doesn't go to court months or years later and claim more money for the child. The form will also be available from the court clerk's office.

## Accidents Caused by Children

Legal liability for accidents caused by minors is based on the same notion of care and carelessness as accidents caused by adults. But the same standards of care that are expected of an adult cannot be applied to minors. Carefulness implies understanding risks, and minors—particularly young children—do not understand risks the way adults do.

The law applies different standards to different age groups when deciding whether a minor is liable for causing injuries to another person. Very young children (seven years old or under) are generally not held liable for accidental injuries they cause; they are too young to understand that they have been careless. This does not mean, however, that parents or legal guardians might not be liable for their negligence in failing to control a child. (See below.)

Once a child is old enough to know right from wrong, the child can be held responsible for *intentional* injuries he or she causes. Thus, if a child intentionally injures another child, for example, or intentionally throws a rock at a car and causes an accident, the child who commits the intentional act, and the child's parents, may be held liable.

Older children are generally held liable for negligent conduct if they did not behave carefully as measured by what other children of the same age would understand is reasonably careful. And once children become middle teenagers, they are held to pretty much the same standard as adults.

When driving a car, a minor is held to exactly the same standards as adults.

Children don't normally have much money of their own, but if a minor can be held legally responsible, there are several ways for a person injured by the minor to collect compensation. First, the actions of minors are very often covered by insurance. If a minor is driving a car, either the minor's own automobile insurance or the insurance of the car owner (parent or employer) should cover the accident.

If the accident does not involve a vehicle, a homeowner's or renter's insurance policy may cover the conduct of a minor who lives in the home, so the injured person may be able to deal directly with the parent's insurance company. (See "Property Owner and Renter Policies" in Chapter 4.)

If you are seriously injured in an accident caused by a minor and there is no insurance covering the minor's conduct, it may be worth pursuing a lawsuit against the minor. If you obtain a legal judgment from a court stating how much the minor owes, the minor will have to pay it upon coming of age—18 years old in most states—and starting to earn money. Because this process can be long and cumbersome and is usually worth pursuing only in cases of serious injury, however, it probably requires the assistance of an attorney. (See Chapter 11.)

## Injuries Caused by Animals

Pets—most commonly, dogs—cause injuries in a variety of ways: biting; clawing; jumping and knocking people down; running and barking at people and making them lose their balance; running into the street and causing vehicle accidents. A few states have laws making dog owners liable for any injuries their dogs cause away from the dog owner's property, regardless of the circumstances in which they occurred. But in most states, a dog owner is liable for injuries caused by the dog only if the owner knew or should have known that the dog was likely to cause the type of injury that occurred.

A dog owner is usually covered by homeowner's or renter's insurance for injuries caused by the dog. And a business owner is covered by business liability insurance for any injury caused by an animal kept on the premises by the owner or any employee.

In a claim for injuries caused by a dog, you and the insurance company will discuss whether the dog owner knew or should have known of a danger presented by the dog. The answer usually lies with the dog's past behavior. If the injury is a bite, and you can find any evidence that without provocation the dog had bitten, snapped, or lunged at anyone before, then you have gone a long way toward establishing a good claim. If the dog is of a "fighting breed," you may be able to recover compensation even though you cannot prove any prior incidents of actual biting or snapping at humans.

If your injury was caused by a dog jumping up and knocking you over, evidence that the dog frequently jumps up is enough, whether or not anyone has been knocked down before. If the dog is large, that too should make the owner aware of the danger, especially to small or unsteady people. And if an accident was caused by an animal running into the street, the fact that it has run out into the street before but the owner still lets the animal loose is good evidence of liability by the owner.

Accidents also occur when vehicles run into farm or ranch animals that have wandered onto a road. Generally, an owner is liable for accidents caused by an animal that strays beyond the confines of the farm or ranch property. However, if the animal is being herded along or across a road that has signs warning that animals are lawfully present, it may be the driver who is responsible for an accident. If the animal is part of a working farm or ranch, the owner's business liability insurance will deal with the accident. If the animal is not part of a business, then the property owner's home insurance should handle the claim.

## General Rules for Other Accidents

There is no limit to the kinds of accidents—some pretty strange and many beyond one's capacity to invent—that cause people injuries. The categories of human behavior that most frequently lead to injury-producing accidents—such as driving and going up and down stairs—have been discussed above, and it is impossible to list all the other possibilities here.

Regardless of the particular facts of an accident, in deciding who is legally responsible the law looks basically at one commonsense question: Did the person involved in the accident act with reasonable care, or act carelessly in a way that contributed to the happening of the accident?

In some situations, the question of whether someone is legally liable for injuries may turn on whether there is a "duty of care" to protect against injuries for someone who is not expected to be in the place where the accident happens.

> **EXAMPLE:** Sameer wanted to ask a question of the produce manager at his local supermarket. He knocked on the door of the produce back room, but no one answered. Although the door was marked "Employees Only," Sameer went in. While he was looking around for someone, he leaned against a stack of crates. The crates collapsed onto Sameer, injuring him.
>
> Sameer would not have a good liability claim because the store had no duty to protect customers who ignore Employees Only signs and wander around where they are not supposed to be.

In the basic negligence rule that everyone must take "reasonable care" to avoid injury to others, reasonable care can vary with time and place and with the relationship between people, so that the same conduct might be considered negligent in one instance but not in another.

**EXAMPLE 1:** Players are on a softball field. A foul ball accidentally strikes someone who was watching at the edge of the field. Because the players were acting reasonably in playing on a field and hitting a foul ball is a normal part of the game, they were probably not negligent. If anyone was careless, it may be the person who sat too close to the field where a ball was flying around.

**EXAMPLE 2:** One of the players in a softball game gets angry and throws his bat, accidentally hitting someone who is sitting at the edge of the field watching. Because throwing a bat in anger is not a "reasonable" part of softball, and because the person watching had a right to be there, throwing the bat is a negligent act, and the bat-thrower would be liable for the injuries caused.

**EXAMPLE 3:** People are playing softball in a parking lot and accidentally hit the ball onto the sidewalk, where it strikes someone walking by. The softball player who hit the ball would be considered negligent and held responsible. When the law balances the carefulness of people lawfully using the sidewalk against the carelessness of someone hitting a ball in an area where other people are walking, the person hitting the ball is obviously more at fault than the person walking by.

Regardless of how your accident happened, obtaining fair compensation for your injuries almost certainly involves no more than application—with simple language in a commonsense way—of the few basic principles discussed throughout this chapter:

- If you show that you were careful and the other person was careless, the careless, or negligent, person must pay for your damages.
- If a negligent person causes an accident while working for someone else, the employer is also legally responsible.
- If an accident is caused on dangerous property or by a defective product, the owner of the property or the maker or seller of the product is liable regardless of whether he or she actually created the danger or defect.
- If you were also careless, your right to be compensated is reduced to the extent your carelessness was responsible for the accident —your comparative negligence.
- You do not need to "prove" anything, only to make a reasonable argument that the other person was negligent, even if there is a plausible argument that the other person was careful.

If you apply these basic rules to your accident, you will be able to negotiate a fair settlement of your claim regardless of the specific facts or peculiar situations in your accident.

## Dangerous or Defective Products

A lot of people have heard of exploding soda bottles, and while most product defects do not make their appearance quite so dramatically, defective or dangerous consumer products are the cause of many thousands of injuries every year. "Product liability"—the legal rules concerning who is responsible for defective or dangerous products—is slightly different from ordinary injury liability law, and this set of rules sometimes makes it easier for an injured person to recover damages.

Ordinarily, to hold a person liable for your injuries, you must show that he or she was careless—that is, negligent—and that his or her carelessness led to the accident. With products sold to the general public, though, it would be extremely difficult and prohibitively expensive for one individual to have to show how and when a manufacturer was careless in making a particular product. Neither can the consumer be expected to prove whether the seller or renter of the product had a proper system for checking for manufacturer's defects, or whether the seller was the cause of the defect after receiving the product from the maker. Nor, finally, can a consumer be expected to check each product before using it to see if it is defective or dangerous, except for obviously dangerous products—a chain saw, for example, or a drain cleaner with a warning on it.

### Strict Liability Defined

The law has developed a set of special rules known as "strict liability" that allow a person injured by a defective or unexpectedly dangerous product to win compensation from the maker or seller of the product—whether or not the manufacturer or seller was actually negligent.

Here's how strict liability works. If you have been injured by a consumer product, you are entitled to compensation from the manufacturer or from the business that sold or rented the product, whether or not they sold or rented it directly to you. Strict liability operates against a nonmanufacturer who sold or rented a product only if it is in the business of regularly selling or renting those particular kinds of products. In other words, if you bought something at a flea market stall, garage sale, or thrift store that sells all kinds of things but not any one type of item on a regular basis, strict liability might not apply.

## States With a Slightly Different Rule

To win a claim for damages in Delaware, Massachusetts, Michigan, North Carolina, or Virginia, you are theoretically required to show that the manufacturer or seller was negligent in making or selling a defective or dangerous product.

However, these states have an additional rule that has the same practical effect as strict liability and makes the injury claim process move in virtually the same way.

This rule is called by the Latin name *res ipsa loquitur,* which means "the thing speaks for itself." This rule holds that if a product is sold or rented and has a dangerous defect, the defect speaks for itself that someone in the manufacturing, selling, or renting process *must* have been negligent—or else the defect would not be there.

In dealing with an insurance company for a manufacturer or seller in one of these states, just as in a strict liability state, the existence of an obvious defect is enough by itself to entitle you to receive compensation, without having to prove specifically how and where the manufacturer, seller, or renter was negligent. Of course, as with strict liability, in these states, you must still show that the defect caused the accident.

## Filing a Claim Against the Seller

It is not always easy to tell who manufactured a certain product—and some products have different parts made by different companies. But because both the product manufacturer and the store where the product was sold or rented can be held responsible, you can file an initial notice of claim against the store where the item was purchased or rented. (See "Getting a Claim Started" in Chapter 3.) Then the store will contact the manufacturer, and the two (or more) of them and their insurance companies can figure out which one will settle your claim.

## Filing a Claim Against the Manufacturer

If you know who manufactured the product but are not certain where it was purchased, file a claim directly against the manufacturer. If the product was purchased at a flea market or from a private party (such as on eBay), you cannot file a strict liability claim against the person who sold it or against the flea market proprietors—unless the seller is a business that also sells its regular products at flea markets—so in that case, too, file a claim directly against the manufacturer.

## Watch the Time

Most states have laws limiting how long after a product has been sold to the public the manufacturer or seller can be held liable under strict liability rules. The limits are usually from six to 12 years after the product has been initially sold by the manufacturer.

So, if the product in your strict liability claim is not relatively new, the insurance company for the manufacturer or seller might insist on determining exactly how old it is. They may be able to do so through a product identification number or their own product records. Another approach is for you to prove how old the product is through your own purchase records, which might include a product registration card, a receipt, a cancelled check, or a credit card bill.

If the product is several years old, the insurance company might quote your state's time limit on product liability claims and contend that they are no longer responsible under your state's product liability laws. If you want to personally check the time limit in your state, go to any local law library. With a law librarian's help, look in the general index of your state's collected laws—called codes, statutes, or general laws—under the categories "product liability," "strict liability," "manufacturer's liability," "limitations on time," or "statute of limitations."

See Chapter 8 for more on statutes of limitations.

## Rules of Strict Liability

Regardless of what steps a manufacturer or seller says it takes in making and handling a consumer product, you can make a strict liability claim—without showing any carelessness on the part of the manufacturer or seller—if all three of the following conditions exist.

1. **The product had an "unreasonably dangerous" defect that injured you as a user or consumer of the product.** The dangerous defect can come into existence either:
   - in the design of the product, making it dangerous even if it is perfectly manufactured, known as a "design defect"
   - during manufacture of the product, causing a dangerous flaw in the specific unit you wind up using, or
   - during handling or shipment after the product has been manufactured.

   **EXAMPLE 1:** Aretha bought a toaster oven, and a month after she bought it she was moving it to a different spot in the kitchen when a handle snapped off and the toaster oven fell. Not only did the oven break but so did Aretha's foot.

   Handles are supposed to help you to hold things, so a handle that breaks after only a month is obviously defective. And the defect was "unreasonably dangerous" because a handle snapping off entirely is likely to cause injury with a heavy, sharp-edged metal object like a toaster oven.

   **EXAMPLE 2:** Mack buys a refrigerator. While unloading it from his pickup truck, he grabs the fridge under one side and his wrist is badly cut by a sharp piece of metal along the bottom edge. It turns out the piece of metal was not a mistake but was a designed part of the fridge's exhaust system.

   In his claim for damages, Mack demands to know: why the piece of metal had to be close to the edge where someone was likely to be cut if they grabbed the edge; why the piece was not rounded off or otherwise protected; and why there was no warning of the danger given to the consumer. If the manufacturer has no convincing answers for all these questions, it would be held liable for Mack's injuries.

2. **The defect caused an injury while the product was being used in a way it was intended to be used.**

   **EXAMPLE 1:** Leticia is working on her house and takes a break to have a cold drink. She can't find the bottle opener, so she uses the claw end of a hammer to pry off a bottle top. The bottle breaks and badly gashes her hand.

   Because the hammer was not designed to open bottles and the bottle was not designed to be opened by a hammer, Leticia has no claim against the manufacturer of either one.

   **EXAMPLE 2:** Leticia couldn't find the bottle opener because Randy had taken it into another room to pry apart two pieces of metal. The opener has a defective crack in it which breaks, injuring Randy's arm.

   Even though the bottle opener had a defect, Randy cannot claim that the defect was unreasonably dangerous, because it did not break during a bottle opener's "normal" use. If it had broken during normal use, it probably would not have injured him.

3. **The product had not been substantially changed from the condition in which it was originally sold.** "Substantially" means in a way that affects how the product performs.

> **EXAMPLE:** Alphonso bought one of those overpriced food processors with more attachments than a centipede. Alphonso tried to use the processor to mix pizza dough. The processor jammed and a rubber washer burned out. At the hardware store Alphonso got another washer, but it didn't quite fit.
>
> When Alphonso tried to use the processor again, he noticed that the new washer made it difficult to get the blades onto the rotating stem. He finally managed to get a blade on, but when he turned on the processor, the blade flew off and cut his hand.
>
> Alphonso does not have a very good strict liability claim against the manufacturer because the food processor had been substantially changed from the condition in which it was sold—the wrong washer had been put on, making the blade fit incorrectly on the stem.

## If You Were Not the Purchaser

If you were given a gift, or bought something secondhand, your rights under strict liability laws are the same as if you had bought it yourself. Similarly, if you are injured while using a product that belongs to someone else, or by a product while someone else is using it, you have the same rights as the owner to be compensated by the manufacturer or seller—as long as all three conditions of strict liability are met.

## Awareness of the Defect

Manufacturers and sellers have a defense to claims of strict liability that may be particularly important if you have owned the product for a while. That is, you may not be able to claim strict liability if you knew about the defect but continued to use the product. If it appears—either from the condition of the product (which the manufacturer's or seller's insurance company will have a right to examine) or from your description of your use of the product—that you were aware of the defect before the accident but used the product anyway, you may have given up your right to claim injury damages.

> **EXAMPLE:** Manjusha bought an electric coffee grinder and when she got it home, she noticed that the cord at the back was loose. Instead of taking it back to the store, she reconnected it and put some electrical tape over the connection. In a couple of weeks, she turned on the grinder and got a bad electrical shock.
>
> Even though the manufacturer or seller caused the defect in the product, Manjusha's claim for damages would be weaker, because she knew the connection was defective but used the grinder anyway.

## Checking With *Consumer Reports*

For many years, one of the consumer's best friends has been the national magazine *Consumer Reports,* which regularly tests and reports on the safety and performance of many consumer products. If you have been injured by a defective or dangerous product and want to see whether others have also found the product dangerous, you can check the magazine's cumulative index. Under the type of product involved, you will be referred to all the magazine's articles in which that product has been reported on.

If you find a report that criticizes your specific brand of product as dangerous or often defective—particularly if the magazine reports accidents or injuries similar to yours—you have found strong support for your argument that the product was defective and "unreasonably dangerous." If you find such a report, make a copy of it and, when you make your written demand for settlement of your case (see Chapter 6), you may want to quote the article directly to the insurance company for the manufacturer or seller. The manufacturer's insurer will undoubtedly already know about the article, but when it knows you also know, your negotiating hand may be a bit stronger.

*Consumer Reports* can be found in any local library. You can also access it online at www .consumerreports.org.

*Chapter 3*

# Initial Steps in Settling Your Claim

## Using This Chapter

This chapter explains what you can do in the first few days and weeks after an accident to protect your right to compensation. If filing a claim against a government entity as discussed in "Special Rules for Accidents Involving the Government," you must be extremely careful to follow certain formal procedures. Otherwise, it's not necessary to do every single one of the steps suggested here in order to obtain a fair settlement. If you can't follow every suggestion, don't think that you've blown it. You haven't. On the other hand, the more of these suggestions you can follow, the more smoothly you can make the claim process flow.

The Accident Claim Worksheet in the back of the book offers you a convenient place to keep track of the numerous names, addresses, telephone numbers, dates, and other information important to your claim. Use it to stay on track.

How well you settle your accident claim can depend on how well you start it. The sooner you get organized and begin documenting the facts of the accident, the better your chances of showing an insurance company your side of the incident and receiving all the compensation to which you are entitled.

## The First 72 Hours: Protecting Your Rights

Immediately after being injured in an accident, you are probably angry, in pain, and maybe a little depressed. That is not the best frame of mind in which to get organized for an insurance claim. But taking some of the following simple steps in the first few days after your accident can help make the entire claim process easier on you—and increase your chances of receiving all the compensation to which you are entitled.

## Write Everything Down

Jot down things about the accident as soon as possible after it happens, including details of your injuries and their effect on your daily life. These notes can be very useful two or six or ten months later, when you put together all the important facts into a final demand for compensation. Having notes to remind you of all the details of what happened, and what you went through, is far easier and more accurate than relying on your memory.

Get into the habit of taking notes on anything you think might possibly affect your claim and carry your memo pad or notebook through the entire claims process. Any time you remember something you had not thought of before—while you're in the shower, just before you fall asleep, as you're biting into a pastry—write it down and put it with your other notes.

**Accidents involving the government.** If your accident might have been even partially caused by a government entity or employee—the city, county, state, or federal government, or any public agency or division (a transit department or a school district, for example)—you must file a formal claim within a short time after your accident—in some states within 30 days—to preserve the right to collect compensation. See "Special Rules for Accidents Involving the Government" for more about this.

There are several kinds of notes you should keep.

## Notes About the Accident

As soon as your head is clear enough, jot down everything you can remember about how the accident happened, beginning with what you were doing and where you were going, the people you were with, the time, and weather. Include every detail of what you saw and heard and felt—twists, blows, and shocks to your body immediately before, during, and right after the accident. Also include anything you remember hearing anyone—a person involved in the accident or a witness—say about the accident. Use the Accident Claim Worksheet in the back of this book to keep a record of these details.

## Notes About Your Injuries

In the first days following your accident, make daily notes of all pains and discomfort your injuries cause. You may suffer pain, discomfort, anxiety, loss of sleep, or other problems that are not as visible or serious as another injury but for which you should demand additional compensation. If you don't make specific note of them immediately, you may not remember exactly what to include in your demand for settlement weeks or months later. Also, taking notes will make it easier for you later to describe to an insurance company how much and what kind of pain and discomfort you were in, and for how long.

Writing down your different injuries will also help you remember to report them to a doctor or other medical provider when you receive treatment. A relatively small bump on the head or snap of the neck, for example, may not seem worth mentioning, but it might help both the doctor and the insurance company understand why a bad back pain developed two or three days, or several weeks, after the accident. Also,

by telling the doctor or other medical provider about all of your injuries, those injuries become part of your medical records, which will provide evidence later that such injuries were caused by the accident. (See "Documenting Injuries" in Chapter 6.)

### Reporting to the DMV

Many states have laws requiring that anyone who is involved in a vehicle accident causing any physical injury, or property damage over a certain amount, must report that accident in writing to the state's department of motor vehicles. Check with your insurance agent or your local department of motor vehicles to find out the time limits for filing this report; you often have only a few days. And ask whether you'll need any specific form for the report.

If you must file a report, and the report asks for a statement about how the accident occurred, give a very brief statement only—and admit no responsibility for the accident. If the official form asks what your injuries are, list every injury, not just the most serious or obvious. An insurance company could later have access to the report, and if you have admitted some fault in it or failed to mention an injury, you might have to explain that later.

## Notes About Economic or Other Losses

You may be entitled to compensation for economic loss and for family, social, educational, or other losses, as well as for pain and suffering. (See Chapter 5.) But you will need documentation. Begin making notes immediately after the accident about anything you have lost because of the accident and your injuries: work hours, job opportunities, meetings, classes, events, family or social gatherings, vacation, or anything else that would have benefited you or that you would have enjoyed but were unable to do because of the accident.

## Notes About Conversations

Make written notes of the date, time, people involved, and contents of every conversation you have about your accident or your claim. In-person or telephone conversations worth noting include those with witnesses, with an adjuster or other insurance representative, or with medical personnel.

## Confirming Letters

In the course of your claim, you may be told or promised something or given some information that you want to make sure is not later denied or changed. Immediately after the conversation, send a letter confirming what the person told you. The letter does not have to be elaborate, just a brief restatement of what was said. Make a copy for your own files before you send it. A sample confirming letter is shown below.

### Sample Confirming Letter

Paula Thompson
23 Broadway
Anytown, Anystate 00000

January 2, 20xx

Mr. Clarence Smolten
Claims Adjuster
Do Right Insurance Company
Thiscity, Thisstate 00000

Re:  Claimant: Paula Thompson
     Insured: Rocky Polletto
     Claim No. 3244949Kl00
     Date of Loss: September 9, 20xx

Dear Mr. Smolten:

This letter is to confirm our telephone discussion of January 2, 20xx in which you informed me that you would be making me an offer of settlement on behalf of the Do Right Insurance Company no later than January 15, 20xx.

Thank you for your attention to this matter.

Sincerely yours,

*Paula Thompson*

Paula Thompson

## Notify Your Own Insurance Company

Within the first 72 hours after a vehicle accident, you should notify your own insurance company of the basic facts of the incident. Most policies require people to notify the insurance company within a reasonable time after the accident in order to collect under the collision coverage to repair the car, under the medical payments coverage to pay medical bills, or under the uninsured motorist or underinsured motorist coverages. (See Chapter 4 for an explanation of each of these coverages.) You should follow this initial notice (which you will do on the phone, ordinarily) with a formal notification letter, as explained in "Write Notification Letters," below.

You should notify your insurance carrier even if your claim is against the person who caused the accident and you do not intend to file a claim under your own policy. It is not always obvious in the first few days and weeks after an accident who will be responsible—and able to pay—for your damages. To protect yourself against the unexpected need to file a claim under your own policy somewhere down the road, make sure to satisfy your policy's requirement that you give your insurance company timely notice of the accident.

## Preserve Evidence of Fault and Damages

The first few days immediately following an accident are often the most important for finding and preserving evidence of what happened—and for documenting your injuries.

### Organization Is the Key

As you move along in the claims process, you will probably gather more and more pieces of paper—notes, letters, medical records, photos. Keeping them organized can be important not only so you can find things easily, but also so you can keep track of what records and documents you have and what you still need to get.

Keep categories of documents together. For example, all your notes, witness statements, and photographs belong in one place. All correspondence with insurance companies should be clipped together in chronological order. All documents concerning medical treatment, diagnosis, and billing belong together; so do all documents concerning financial losses.

There are no special rules or tricks to organizing the file. It can be useful to separate things by category. Then keep all papers in each category in a separate file, folder, or large envelope, marked on the outside so you can easily tell one from another. Keep all of them in the same safe place.

Use the Accident Claim Worksheet at the back of the book to help get organized and keep track of the information you accumulate.

### Physical Evidence

Who was at fault for an accident is sometimes shown by a piece of "physical" evidence— something you can see or touch, as opposed to a description of what happened. Examples include a worn or broken stair that caused a fall, the dent in a car showing where it was hit, or an overhanging branch that blocked visibility on a bike path. Also, physical evidence can help prove the extent of an injury. For example, damage to the car can demonstrate how hard a collision was, and torn or bloodied clothing can show your physical injuries very dramatically.

Physical evidence that is not preserved or photographed in the first few days following an accident can get lost, modified by time or weather, destroyed, or repaired. So, any physical evidence you have—your damaged car or bike, your damaged clothing, a defective product—should be preserved exactly as it was at the accident. You can later show it to an insurance company as proof of what happened.

### Photographs

If you do not have a piece of physical evidence, or for any reason cannot preserve it, the next best option is to photograph it. Regular photos are better than Polaroids. Not only do they usually show greater detail and more accurate light conditions, but you will be able to give an insurance company prints while holding onto the negatives. Take a number of photos from different angles so that you can later pick out the ones that show most clearly whatever it is you want to highlight to the insurance company.

Take the photos as soon as possible so that they will accurately represent the condition of the evidence immediately after the accident. To establish the date the photos were taken, ask a friend both to watch you take the pictures and to write a short note stating that he or she observed you taking the pictures on that date. Get the film developed immediately and make sure the photo shop indicates the date on the back of the prints, or at least on your receipt.

## A Picture Is Worth ... A Lot

A camera can be one of your best tools in helping you get a fair settlement of your accident claim—for a number of reasons.

- Photos preserve scenes, evidence, and injuries that change over time.
- Photos often show things better than you can describe them.
- Photos sometimes reveal details you do not notice at first with the naked eye.
- Photos are dramatic. They highlight whatever they are focused on, without the distractions of surrounding sights and sounds.
- Photos are difficult to contradict. An insurance company may say you are wrong when you describe how an accident happened or how badly you were injured. It is much more difficult for the company to deny what is in a photograph.
- Photos help you focus your claim. You select which photos to show to an insurance company.
- Photos impress insurance companies. They show that you have been organized and thoughtful in preparing your claim.

You have the right to take pictures in public places, so if your accident happened in a place that is open to the public, you can go back and take photos. If the area has been closed, try to get permission from whoever is in charge—for example, if you were injured in a fall at a shopping mall, ask the mall manager or security people if you can go past the barriers. If the manager or security people deny your request, make a note of that, and be sure to note the date, the name of the person who denied your request, and the reasons given for not allowing you to take photographs. Then write to the insurance adjuster for the mall, explain what happened, and demand permission to get in and take the pictures you need. Tell the adjuster that it is "bad faith" to refuse permission to examine and photograph the scene of the accident. Chapter 8 explains what bad faith is in the section called "What to Do When You Can't Get a Settlement."

## Car Damage Proves Injuries

You may be one of the many people who have been in a car accident (often, a rear-ender) and suffered injuries that are very painful but not medically obvious. These kinds of injuries—to the spine or joints, or to muscles—can cause great discomfort and life disruption but do not show up dramatically on X-rays or other imaging devices. As a result, your doctors may be unable or unwilling to state an opinion about the exact nature and extent of your injuries. And insurance companies can make it difficult for you to collect full compensation because you have no medical evidence that clearly shows the injuries.

Strong physical evidence of damage to your car can help support your claim for compensation. Showing that your car suffered damage supports the argument that you, too, were harmed. Receipts and work orders for car repair can serve as supporting evidence. But these often include only brief descriptions of the damage. If you supplement them with clear photos, your argument to the insurance company will be considerably stronger. So, before repairs are made, photograph any damage to your car—even if slight—from several angles. An impact that only dents a fender can still cause someone in the car a painful injury. It helps to show that dent.

## Returning to the Scene

If an accident occurred somewhere other than in your home, return to the scene as soon as possible to locate any evidence and photograph any conditions you believe may have caused or contributed to the accident. You may be amazed to find something that you were not aware of when the accident occurred but that may help explain what happened: a worn or torn spot on which you fell, a traffic light that isn't working. While looking around, you may also find someone who saw what happened or who knows of other accidents that happened in the same spot. (See "Witnesses," below.)

Take photographs of the accident scene from a number of different angles—particularly your view of things right before the accident—to keep a good picture of the scene in your mind. Photograph the scene at the same time of day as your accident occurred. For vehicle accidents, photograph the scene on the same day of the week to show the appropriate amount of traffic.

## Witnesses

A witness to an accident can be immensely valuable to you in making your case to an insurance company. Witnesses may be able to describe details that confirm what you believe happened, backing up your story. And they may provide information you were not aware of but that shows how the other person was at fault. Even a witness who did not actually see the accident may have seen you soon after you were injured and can confirm that you appeared to be hurt. Or a witness may have heard a statement made by another person involved in the accident indicating that someone other than you was at fault.

However, time is of the essence. If witnesses are not contacted and their information confirmed fairly soon after the accident, what they have to say may be lost. People's memories fade quickly, and soon their recollections may become so fuzzy that they are no longer useful. Also, a witness might no longer be around if you wait too long.

**Dealing with witness-strangers.** People whom you don't know but who saw your accident may be helpful to your claim. They may be able to tell you something useful, such as the fact that a dangerous condition has caused previous accidents on the same spot, in addition to verifying your version of what happened.

Look for such witnesses by returning to the scene and talking with people who live or work within sight of the accident spot. With traffic accidents, another place to look for witnesses is in the police report. If the police responded to the scene of your accident, they probably will have made a police report, also called an accident report or collision report. The report may list the names, addresses, and phone numbers of witnesses. (See "Documenting Liability," in Chapter 6.)

If you find people who witnessed your accident, and what they saw indicates that someone else was at fault, act promptly.

- Write down witnesses' names, addresses, and home and work phone numbers, or as much of that information as they are willing to give. If they will give an address but not a phone, or a work phone but not home, don't push. You need them to be on your side, so don't scare them away or irritate them.
- Talk with witnesses about what they saw and ask exactly where they were when they saw it.
- If witnesses seem cooperative, ask whether it would be all right if you type up what they told you and send it to them to check

for accuracy. Explain that you may need a written statement to back up your facts when you make your claim to the insurance company. If the witnesses consent, write down what they told you as soon as possible—on the spot, if they are willing to be that patient. Then send a typed copy to them, politely asking them to review it, sign it, and send it back to you in a return envelope you provide.

- If witnesses seem uncomfortable about getting involved even though they support your version of what happened, jot down quickly what they have told you and ask them on the spot to read it to make sure it's accurate. Ask them to sign the description to show that it's accurate. Be sure to get an address or telephone number so that you can later prove to an insurance company that this statement was from a real person. Once you have the handwritten statement, you can also contact the witness to get him or her to sign a typed version if the handwritten statement is difficult to read.

**Witnesses you know.** Many witnesses to accidents are people we know. If a friend, relative, or acquaintance witnessed your accident, or your pain and suffering following the accident, your job is essentially the same as with a stranger, only easier. You don't have to go looking for the witnesses, and you usually don't have to worry that they will disappear quickly. But go over the facts of the accident with them while their memory is fresh—and make notes of what they tell you so that, if necessary, you can later type up a statement and have them sign it.

Sometimes an insurance adjuster will independently track down witnesses—from information in a police accident report or otherwise—and will get in touch with them. Because it may be important for you to contact the witnesses first, to learn what they saw or heard and to prevent the insurance adjuster from putting false or distorted recollections into their heads, speak with your witnesses as soon as possible and discuss the possibility that an insurance adjuster might call. Witnesses do not have to discuss the accident with the insurance company if they do not want to. And they certainly have a right to limit the extent of their involvement to the statement that they have already given you. But be careful. Although you can tell witnesses that they have the *right* not to talk to the insurance company, do not tell them not to talk. That would be interfering with the other side's right to obtain information and could jeopardize your claim. The decision about whether or not to talk to the insurance company should be left up to each witness so that the witness can remain as independent, and therefore as believable, as possible.

## Documenting Your Injuries

The best ways to preserve evidence of your injuries are by reporting all of them promptly to a doctor or other medical provider, and by photographing any visible marks, cuts, bruises, or swelling, including any casts, splints, bandages, or other devices that you are using on your own or based on a doctor's prescription. Without an early medical record of all your injuries, and photos if possible, it will be more difficult later to convince an insurance company that you were injured in the ways and to the degree you claim. Visible injuries heal and will not look as serious later. And failing to seek immediate treatment can lead an insurance company to believe that your injuries were not so serious, or even that you invented or exaggerated them after the accident.

**Get immediate medical attention.** Where to go for treatment is first and foremost a medical decision. But the kind of treatment you get, and the type of medical provider from whom you receive it, can affect how much your claim is worth. (See Chapter 5.)

You may think it sounds obvious to tell you to get prompt medical care, and to let the medical people know about *all* your injuries, pains, and discomforts. But too often, people try to do without medical care, or report to a doctor only what seems to be their worst injury. They may end up with no medical records of their injuries, or with records of one injury but not of another that seemed to be minor but proved to be very painful and persistent.

Of course, the high cost of medical care often makes people reluctant to begin treatment unless absolutely necessary. But in the case of an accident in which someone else was at fault, that person or business, through its insurance, will be obligated to repay you for all reasonable medical expenses as well as the pain and suffering caused by your injuries. (See Chapter 5.) And getting medical treatment is the best way to support your claim that you have gone through pain and suffering. So, even if you have to pay for medical treatment now, you will benefit from the prompt attention and also from the documentation of what those injuries really are. Be sure to save all bills, receipts, letters, and other documents relating to your medical treatment. Use the Accident Claim Worksheet in the back of this book to help organize your medical records.

## Med-Pay vs. Medicare

If you are injured in a car accident, and you are over 65 and have both Medicare coverage and medical payments coverage under your own auto insurance policy (called "med-pay"), you're usually better off using your med-pay coverage to pay for your medical bills from the start. Both med-pay coverage and Medicare pay without regard to whose fault the injury was, but Medicare requires that you reimburse it out of later settlements with a third party, while not all med-pay provisions have that same requirement. So, the first thing to do is check the terms of your insurance policy. If there is no requirement of reimbursement out of a third-party claim settlement, then using the med-pay coverage is better than using Medicare, which will ask for reimbursement. Chapter 4 has more about med-pay and Medicare.

## Getting a Claim Started

Starting the claim process is simple. You don't have to know who was at fault in the accident; you only have to think about who *might* have been at fault. And in the beginning, you don't have to give the people involved, or their insurance companies, any detailed information about the accident or your injuries. All you have to do is notify them that there was an accident at a certain time and place, that you were injured, and that you *intend* to file a claim. Even filing a formal claim against the government is simple, as long as you do so within the legal time limit. (See "Time Limits for Filing a Claim," below.)

It is best to start your claim early, preferably within the first few days, and certainly within the first couple of weeks, after the accident. The sooner you get started, the sooner you may be able to settle your claim. If you wait too long to notify those responsible (or their insurance companies), you may have to explain why you waited.

Rather than get into that hassle, notify those responsible as soon as possible that you intend to file a claim for your injuries. After you give this initial notice, you can move at your own pace in processing and negotiating your claim with the insurance company or government agency that winds up taking responsibility.

Filing a notice of an injury accident with people or agencies does not obligate you to file a claim against them later. But if you do file a claim later, they will not be able to say that the claim has unfairly surprised them.

## Determine Who Might Be Responsible

Before you can notify anyone of your intention to file a claim, you have to decide whom to notify. At this point you don't have to try to decide who is actually responsible; instead, you should notify all those who *might* be responsible. Be creative and think of everyone possible; you can always narrow the list later.

In general, who is responsible for an accident depends on the type of accident in which you were involved.

### If You're in a Vehicle Accident

If you were in an accident in a car or on a motorcycle or bicycle, any of the following might be responsible:

- the drivers of all vehicles involved—including the vehicle in which you were riding if you were a passenger—whether or not they actually hit you or your car
- the owners of all vehicles if the owners are different from the drivers
- the employer of a driver of any vehicle if the employee might have been on company business at the time of the accident (if it is a government employer, see below)
- the parent of a minor who was driving, or who owned a vehicle involved in the accident, or of a minor who otherwise contributed to the accident
- anyone not in a vehicle who contributed to the accident, such as someone jaywalking or a property owner who allowed something to obstruct or interfere with the roadway
- your own vehicle's insurance company, if you need to make a claim under your own uninsured motorist, medical payments, collision or no-fault coverage (see Chapter 4 for an explanation of these insurance coverages).

### If You Slip or Trip and Fall, or Are Struck by an Object

If you trip on stairs or a sidewalk, or fall down or get hit by something, look to any of the following:

- the person who caused you to fall or caused an object to strike you
- the owner of the property on which you fell or from which the object came
- the renter of the property on which you fell or from which the object came
- the owner of the business at which you fell or from which the object came
- the parent of a minor who caused you to fall or who caused you to be struck with an object

- the employer of a person who, apparently during work time, caused you to fall or to be struck with an object, regardless of where the accident occurred.

### If You Are Injured by a Dangerous or Defective Product

If you're injured by a product and strict liability applies, any of these entities might be responsible:

- the business where you, or someone else, purchased or rented the product
- the business where you were supplied with the product to use on the business's premises
- the manufacturer of the product.

## Write Notification Letters

Once you have determined every person or entity that might be responsible for your accident, your next step is to notify each of them that the accident happened and that you were injured. This may mean you send more than one letter— for example, one letter each to the business and to the person who owned the property where you fell. If it was a vehicle accident, also notify your own insurance company if you believe you might file a claim under your own medical payments, collision, or uninsured motorist coverage. (See Chapter 4 for an explanation of these coverages.) If you have no-fault (Personal Injury Protection) automobile coverage, you must file a notice with your own insurance company immediately.

## Using Email in Negotiations

Email is a convenient way to communicate, and many of us use it as a matter of course in our daily contact with others. And it certainly has its place in your communications with insurance adjusters—but that place is limited. We recommend using email only for minor, logistical matters, such as arranging an inspection time for your vehicle or informing the adjuster that your demand letter is on its way. Don't use email for a letter of notification or a demand letter. If you send an email to confirm an agreement that you and the adjuster have made, follow it up with a regular letter. And in general, try to conduct your negotiations on the telephone—the in-person contact is much more effective in getting your point across than email, which is easier to ignore and doesn't give the adjuster a real sense of who you are.

Write a letter of notification even if the others involved have assured you they will notify their insurance companies. If you know the other party's insurance company, you may also send a copy of your notification letter to that company's claims department (including the other party's policy number, if you know it). Your notification should be a simple typed letter giving only basic information and asking for a written response. It should not discuss fault, responsibility, or the extent of your injuries; you will discuss those things later on. The initial notification letter should do the following:

- Provide your name and address. You do not have to include your phone number if you do not want to. Once you begin dealing with an insurance adjuster, though, you will probably want to be able to communicate over the phone as well as by letter. You are free to put whatever restrictions you want on such calls—for example, only at home but not at work, or vice versa; only in the evening but not during the day, or vice versa.

- Include the date, approximate time of day, and general location of the accident. The details of the location, if they become important, can be discussed later. In this letter, you need only to give a description identifying the accident you are talking about, for example: "at the intersection of Main and Howard Streets," or "at your store in the Broadway Shopping Center."

- If your letter is to an individual or business rather than to an insurance company, ask those involved to refer the matter at once to the appropriate insurance carrier—and request that they inform you by return letter which insurance carrier it is.

- If your letter is directly to an insurance company, ask that it confirm by return letter whom it represents and whether it is aware of anyone else who might be responsible for the accident.

- If you are writing to your own automobile insurance company after a vehicle accident, include not only information about the accident but also the basic information you have about the other driver and vehicle—name, address, telephone number, license number, and insurance policy.

**⚠ Double check before mailing.** Include the date on every letter—and make a copy for your own files before sending it.

## Sample Notification Letters

Here are examples of letters giving first notification that you have been in an accident.

### Sample Letter to an Individual With Whom Maria Jones Had an Auto Accident

Maria Jones
123 Pine Street
San Dimas, TX 00000

February 12, 20xx

Henry Parks
45 Webster Avenue
Hollowtown, TX 00000

Dear Mr. Parks:

You and I were involved in an automobile accident on February 9, 20xx at the intersection of 4th Street and Appian Way in San Dimas, Texas, in which I was injured and my car was damaged. Please provide me with the name and address of your insurance carrier and forward this letter to it regarding coverage of the accident.

Very truly yours,
*Maria Jones*
Maria Jones

### Sample Letter to Maria's Own Automobile Insurance Company If She Had an Insurance Policy Without No-Fault Coverage

(See Chapter 4 for more information about your own insurance coverage.)

Maria Jones
123 Pine Street
San Dimas, TX 00000

February 12, 20xx

Claims Department
Safety Plus Insurance Company
888 Pesky Boulevard
Dallas, TX 00000

Re: Insured, Maria Jones
    Policy No. 9HQ-678-B
    Date of Accident: February 9, 20xx

To Whom It Concerns:

I was involved in an automobile accident in which I received personal injuries and damage to my vehicle on February 9, 20xx at the intersection of 4th Street and Appian Way in San Dimas, Texas.

The other person involved in the accident was Henry Parks, 45 Webster Avenue, Hollowtown, Texas 12346. He was driving a red 1989 Chevrolet pickup with Texas license plate number B899 324.

At this time, I intend to proceed against Mr. Parks rather than file a claim under my own medical payments or collision coverages. However, I reserve the right to file a claim under either or both of those coverages.

Very truly yours,
*Maria Jones*
Maria Jones

## Sample Letter to Maria's Own Automobile Insurance Company If She Carried a No-Fault Policy

(See Chapter 4 for more information about your own insurance coverage.)

---

Maria Jones
123 Pine Street
San Dimas, TX 00000

February 12, 20xx

Claims Department
Safety Plus Insurance Company
888 Pesky Boulevard
Dallas, TX 00000

Re: Insured: Maria Jones
     Policy No. 9HQ-678-B
     Date of Accident: February 9, 20xx

To Whom It Concerns:

I was involved in an automobile accident in which I received personal injuries and damage to my vehicle on February 9, 20xx at the intersection of 4th Street and Appian Way in San Dimas, Texas. The other person involved in the accident was Henry Parks, 45 Webster Avenue, Hollowtown, Texas 12346. He was driving a red 1989 Chevrolet pickup truck with Texas license plate number B899 324.

At this time the extent of my injuries is not clear, and I reserve my rights under my policy to proceed under my Personal Injury Protection coverage as well as to proceed against the others responsible for the accident.

Please confirm in writing that you have received this notice. Thank you for your attention to this matter.

Very truly yours,
*Maria Jones*
Maria Jones

---

## Sample Letter to a Business Where Robin Smith Had a Slip and Fall

---

Robin Smith
6922 Main Way
Sintex, NH 00000

February 12, 20xx

Snack-n-Chat Restaurant
666 Alamo Circle
Grinel, NH 00000

To Whom It Concerns:

At approximately 8:00 p.m. on February 9, 20xx I was a customer in your restaurant when I slipped just outside the entrance to the restaurant and fell, injuring myself.

Please refer this matter to your insurance carrier. Please also inform me by letter at the above address of the name and address of your insurance carrier.

Thank you for your prompt attention.

Sincerely,
*Robin Smith*
Robin Smith

## Sample Letter to an Insurance Company That Insures the Premises Where Robin Smith Had a Slip and Fall

Robin Smith
6922 Main Way
Sintex, NH 00000
(111) 443-4433

February 20, 20xx

Claims Department
All Risk Insurance Company
6000 Breakneck Boulevard
Houston, TX 12355

Re: Your Insured: Snack-n-Chat Restaurant
Claimant: Robin Smith
Date of Accident: February 9, 20xx

To Whom It Concerns:

Please be advised that I received injuries in an accident on February 9, 20xx on the premises of your insured, the Snack-n-Chat Restaurant. Please confirm in writing to the above address that your company has issued liability coverage to the Snack-n-Chat Restaurant.

Please also advise whether Snack-n-Chat Restaurant contends that anyone other than the Snack-n-Chat Restaurant may be in whole or in part legally responsible for accidents on or near the premises.

As requested, please respond in writing. If necessary, I may be reached by telephone at the above number between the hours of 7:30–8:30 a.m. or 6:30–9:00 p.m. Monday through Friday.

Thank you for your prompt attention to this matter.

Yours truly,
*Robin Smith*
Robin Smith

## Sample Letter to the Parents of a Child Who Caused Walter Pasheha to Fall in an Accident

Walter Pasheha
37 9th Avenue North
South Fork, IN 00000

February 12, 20xx

Norbert and Rosetta Stone
3757 East Bowden Lane
South Fork, IN 00000

Dear Mr. and Mrs. Stone:

On February 9, 20xx I was injured in a fall in front of your residence caused by wooden blocks left on the sidewalk by your child or children. Please refer this matter to the insurance carrier of your homeowner's liability insurance policy and have the insurance carrier contact me directly at the above address.

Thank you for your cooperation.

Very truly yours,
*Walter Pasheha*
Walter Pasheha

**Make sure the letters get there.** There is no need to send your initial notification letter by certified or registered mail. But if you receive no response from the other party or its insurance company within two weeks of sending your notification letter, you should repeat the process, this time requesting a return receipt from the post office.

# First Contact With Another Person's Insurance Company

By the time you get home from an accident, your phone may already be ringing—and the caller may well be an insurance adjuster or another representative of the other person involved. Or perhaps you will hear from someone as soon as your notification letter has been received.

Very often, insurance adjusters will try to get you to say or write an immediate statement about what happened, or about your injuries or lack of injuries, so that they can pin you down before you know what really happened or how badly you are injured. Or they will make a quick offer of a small amount of money, in the hope that you will jump at it instead of developing a full claim for compensation. Do not rush to give detailed information or to take any money.

The guidelines below will help you decide what to say and do during your first postaccident contacts with the other person or an insurance adjuster or representative.

## Phone Conversations

Your first conversations after an injury may be difficult. You may be agitated and in pain. But common sense and a few guiding principles will help keep you from saying anything that will adversely affect your claim.

**Remain calm and polite.** Although you may well be angry about the accident and your injuries, taking out your anger on the insurance adjuster does not help you get compensated. Insurance adjusters are used to dealing with angry claimants, but they are human and do not respond kindly to abuse. You may not know exactly how or when an insurance adjuster's good will may pay off—in promptly handling your claim, or in believing you about something it is difficult for you to prove. Meanwhile, it is a good idea not to lose

your temper with or heap abuse on the agent during your negotiation process.

**Identify the person you speak with.** Before you discuss anything, get the name, address, and telephone number of the person you are speaking with, the insurance company he or she is with, and the person or business the company represents.

**Give only limited personal information.** You need only tell the insurance adjuster your full name, address, and telephone number. You can also tell what type of work you do and where you are employed. But at this point you need not explain or discuss anything else about your work, your schedule, or your income. You do not have to give detailed family or other personal information.

**Give no details of the accident.** Insurance adjusters or other representatives may try to get you to "give a statement" about how the accident happened. Or they may simply engage you in conversation during which they will subtly try to get you to tell them about the accident. Politely refuse to discuss any of the facts except the most basic: where, when, the type of accident, and the vehicles involved if it was a traffic accident. Say that your investigation of the accident is still continuing and that you will discuss the facts further "at the appropriate time." Later, you will be making a written demand for compensation in which you will describe the accident in detail.

If you are asked about witnesses and you know of some, respond that there "may be" witnesses and that you will let the insurance company know "at the appropriate time." Do not commit yourself to identifying witnesses or to providing witness statements. Also, if they ask you about witnesses, ask them if they know of any.

If adjusters or representatives ask about potential responsible parties other than you and their insured, give any basic identifying information you may have and a general description of how these other parties were involved, but do not discuss the accident in detail. Also, ask whether the adjuster is aware of anyone else who might be responsible for the accident.

**Give no details of your injuries.** Naturally enough, an insurance adjuster is going to want to know about your injuries. Do not give a detailed description yet. You might leave something out, or discover an injury later, or your injury may turn out to be worse than you originally thought.

Later, when you know the true extent of your injuries and treatment, your written demand for compensation will include a complete medical description of your injuries. Until then, give only a very general description of injuries ("I've hurt my knee and back" or "My wrist is broken and I have neck and back pain") and tell the adjuster you do not yet know how severe your injuries are. Also, tell the adjuster that you will be seeking or continuing medical treatment. You do not have to say which doctors or other medical providers you are seeing, and you should not yet give the adjuster their names or addresses.

**Take notes.** As soon as your conversation is over, write down all the information you received over the phone, as well as whatever information you gave to, or requests you made of, the person with whom you spoke. Get in the habit of taking notes on all conversations with anyone from the insurance company. Be sure to include in your notes the date and time of each conversation.

**Resist the push to settle immediately.** Insurance adjusters sometimes offer a settlement during the first one or two phone calls. Quick settlements like that save the insurance company work. More important, they get you to settle for a small amount before you know fully what your injuries are and how much your claim is really worth. Don't take the bait. Agreeing may seem like a simple way to get compensation without having to go through the claims process, and a quick settlement is often tempting, but it will almost certainly cost you money, perhaps quite a bit.

**⚠ Safeguard your records.** Do not agree up front to give another person's insurance company access to your medical, employment, or any other personal records. Later in the claims process, you will be presenting the adjuster with the appropriate records. And do not agree to be examined by a doctor who is affiliated with or recommended by the insurance company. You have a right to see only the doctors or other medical people you want—and the insurance company has no right to have you examined unless your claim actually becomes a formal lawsuit and goes to court.

**Set limits on conversations.** In your first contact with an insurance adjuster, make it clear that you will not be discussing much on the phone. Not only should you give very limited information in this first phone call, as discussed above, but you should also set clear limits on any further phone contact.

Let the adjuster know that until you have finished investigating the accident and have completed medical treatment, you do not want to discuss any further either how the accident happened, what your injuries are, or what a settlement amount should be. Ask that the adjuster communicate with you in writing until you present your written demand for compensation and actual settlement negotiations begin.

In some situations, however, it may not be practical to stop all phone conversations. For example, if you have been in an auto accident, you may need to discuss repairs to your car. If you do need to speak to the adjuster again in person, set whatever limits you want on the place and times—home or work, morning, evening, weekends—for telephone contact.

There are good reasons to limit your phone conversations with insurance adjusters. Some will call frequently in an attempt to get you to settle quickly, and they can become a real nuisance. It's good to nip this in the bud.

More important, until you have had a full opportunity to investigate and think about the accident, and to determine the extent of your injuries, you will not have accurate information to give. And if you give incomplete or inaccurate information on the phone, the insurance company may try to make you stick to it later on. Some insurance adjusters are good at getting you to say things that could be considered an admission of some fault on your part, or that limit the seriousness of your injuries. It is therefore much better to have no discussions at all until you have made your compensation demand in writing and you are fully prepared to discuss a settlement.

**Refuse to give recorded statements.** Many claims adjusters immediately push you to give a tape-recorded statement, or casually ask if they may record your phone conversation, claiming it will protect you later. Do not agree to have any conversation recorded. You have no legal obligation to be recorded, and it is against the law for an adjuster to record you without your permission.

The reason you should refuse is that most people tense up when they know they are being recorded, and forget to say important things or describe things clumsily or incompletely. A verbal statement or conversation is almost never as precise and thorough as the written correspondence you will later send the insurance company. Also, recordings take on far more importance than they deserve as evidence of what happened. It can be nearly impossible later to correct or expand on what you have said in a recording. This is even more of a problem because adjusters usually request the recorded statements at an early stage of the process, when you may not yet have a clear picture of the extent of your injuries.

Politely but firmly decline an adjuster's request to record your statements. Tell him or her that you are not comfortable with recording, and that when your information is complete, you will provide it in writing.

## Written Communications

**Do not sign anything.** Among the first things you may receive in the mail from an insurance company handling an accident claim are various forms an adjuster may describe to you as "just routine" or "normal procedure." However, these forms may give the insurance company direct access to your medical, personal, or work records—or even be a disguised release from any liability for the accident. No matter what an adjuster says about any forms, do not sign anything sent to you by another person's insurance company.

At this stage, you are not required to give the insurance company permission to get any records or information about you. Later in the claims process, you will send certain medical and income loss information, but in your own time and on your own terms. If you are pressured to sign any forms, politely refuse and emphasize that you will relay all necessary information at the appropriate time. If the adjuster continues to pressure you, you may need to take other steps to get the adjuster to back off. (See Chapter 8.)

Often an insurance company's first contact with you will be a simple letter informing you that it represents so-and-so regarding an accident on such-and-such date, and that you should get in touch concerning any claim you may have. But insurance companies also sometimes ask for information from you—about the accident, your injuries, your doctors, or your work. Until you are ready to make a formal demand for settlement, you are not obligated to give any more information than the things described above in the explanation about your first notification letter. Insurance companies are supposed to do their own accident investigation, and you are not required to do their work for them.

## First Contact With Your Own Insurance Company

Initial contact with your own insurance company is slightly different. Your relationship with your own insurance company is established by your policy, which is a contract between you and your insurer. You may be obligated by the rules of the policy to provide your company with more information than you would to someone else's insurance company.

Some of the common differences are discussed here.

### Notification Through Your Agent

If you give notice of the accident to your insurance agent rather than to the company's claims office, ask the agent for a letter stating the date you provided the information and confirming that the information has been passed along to the company's claims department. You should receive a confirming letter from the claims department. If you do not, contact that department directly with the information.

If you actually file a claim for compensation under a provision of your own policy, your insurance company will have the following rights:

- direct access to your medical and work records (see "Release of Medical and Work Records," below)
- to payment from you if you collect from any responsible third party; this is called "subrogation" (see "Right of Subrogation," below)
- to cooperation from you (see "Cooperation," below), and
- to inspect your vehicle (see "Right to Inspect Your Vehicle," below).

### Release of Medical and Work Records

Virtually all insurance policies give the insurance company the right to examine the policyholder's medical and work records directly. So, your own insurer is likely to send you a form entitled Authorization for Release of Records, or something similar. If your own company sends you such a form, you must sign it if you want your company to process your claim. On the other hand, many companies do not actually bother to obtain and go through your records; it's too much extra work for them. Instead, your company may simply wait for you to send them your medical records and income loss information, along with your settlement demand.

**⚠ Read any release of information carefully.** Although you are obligated to allow your insurance company access to certain records, it's a good idea to review with care any release that the adjuster sends you. Some release documents ask for authority to obtain every type of record imaginable, including credit records and medical records dating back to time immemorial. For most accidents, only more recent records are relevant, and information like your credit history is almost never relevant to your injuries. If you believe a release is too broad, cross out the portions that you do not agree with, and initial the document next to the changes. Then sign and return it along with a letter explaining to the insurance company why the information to which you declined to give access is not relevant.

### Right of Subrogation

Your own insurance company may send you a form entitled Right of Subrogation. This form says that if your insurance company pays you any compensation under your own policy, the company then has the right to recover that money from whoever was responsible for the accident.

Once your insurance company pays you, it stands in your shoes with regard to the damage for which it compensated you. For example, if you have your own company pay for the repair of your vehicle (under your collision coverage) instead of waiting to settle a property damage claim against another driver, your company may recover that amount from the other driver's insurance company. Once your own company pays you, you may not personally pursue a claim for the same property damage against the other party, except to the extent that you were not compensated for any deductible under your own policy. (See Chapter 7.)

Sometimes the subrogation form will ask for your signature, but more often it will just be a notice. If you are asked to sign, go ahead and do so—it's the insurer's legal right in any event.

### Cooperation

Most policies say that in order to be entitled to collect on a claim under your own policy, you must cooperate with the insurance company in its investigation of the accident. That means that, if asked, you must give it the names of witnesses, the medical providers you are seeing, and a statement about how the accident happened.

However, you need only to cooperate in a reasonable way. For example, the insurance company is entitled to a statement about how the accident happened, but you don't have to write an essay or undergo an interrogation nor do you have to give a tape-recorded statement. You don't have to repeat information you have already given. And you don't have to go places or do things on the company's schedule. Be reasonable, but make sure the insurance company is reasonable in return.

### Right to Inspect Your Vehicle

If you intend to file a claim under the collision or vehicle damage coverage of your own auto policy, you must allow your insurance company to inspect the damage before you have it repaired. (See "Processing Your Claim," in Chapter 7.)

## Special Rules for Accidents Involving the Government

As mentioned several times, there are special rules to follow if your accident might have been *even partially* caused by a government entity or its employee—the city, county, state, or federal government or any public agency or division. This would include, for example, an accident with a municipal bus or a car driven by a local, state, or federal employee during work time; an injury suffered because of the dangerous condition of a building or other property owned or operated by a government agency; or an accident caused by an employee of a government agency during the course of his or her work.

In general, governments get to set their own rules for who can sue them, for what, and how. To pursue a claim against a government entity, you must carefully follow your state's specific rules for such claims. In particular, you must file a formal written claim against the government entity responsible for your injury within a relatively short time after your accident—usually 30 to 180 days. If you fail to file a claim within the time limit, or fail to include required information, you may forever lose your right to collect compensation.

## Filing a Claim

If you believe that a government entity was in any way at fault for your injuries, file a claim against it. So, for example, if you are in a three-vehicle accident involving you, another car, and a city bus, file a claim against the city even if you believe the other car was primarily at fault. It may turn out that the other driver was uninsured. Or the bus was more at fault than you first realized, and the driver of the other car will be only partially responsible. In either case, you would have to look to the city for compensation—and if you have not filed a formal claim in time, you will not be allowed to seek damages against it.

## Time Limits for Filing a Claim

Each state has its own time limits within which you have to file a formal claim against a government entity. Some limits are as short as 30 days after the accident, although most are six months. If you have been in an accident that may involve government liability, check your state's time limit so that you are sure to file your claim on time. (See below for a state-by-state listing of all time limits.)

No matter what time limit you are up against, do not wait until the last minute to file your claim. You might have forgotten to include something, or you might have picked the wrong government entity—and you may have trouble correcting the error before the time runs out.

## Contents of the Claim

The claims that state laws require you to file are usually simple lists of basic information in plain language. Some cities, counties, and states have specific claim forms that you can pick up at the office of your local city or county attorney, but most require only a plain signed piece of paper with the information clearly written or typed.

Although there may be slight variations in the information each state requires, all claims should include the following:

**Name and address of claimant.** "Claimant" means the person injured. If you are filing a claim on behalf of a minor, list the minor's name and the name of the parent or guardian, as follows: "Claimant Robert Logan, a minor, by Andrea Logan, parent."

**Address to which notices are to be sent.** Your home address, unless you want official notices from the government agency to be sent to your work address (or some other address) instead.

**Date, place, and circumstances of the accident.** Do not go into any detail here. Just generally describe what happened, such as: "On January 13, 20xx, I was driving north along 4th Street approaching the intersection of Broadway when a municipal bus pulled into my lane and struck my car."

**Nature of your injury and other loss.** Do not go into detail. Describe your injuries very generally— "neck and back injuries," "wrist injury." Mention lost income, without stating how much, and any other losses you incurred—for example, damage to car, clothes, or other property.

If a form asks you to list your medical expenses, list what you have incurred so far, but also state: "Medical treatment is continuing." This will protect you in case you have to receive more treatment after you have filed your claim.

**Public employees who caused the injury.** If you know the name of the driver of the bus or car, put it down. If you don't know who directly caused the accident, do not bother trying to figure out which government employee was legally responsible for the accident. Simply say: "Not known."

**Amount of compensation claimed.** Pick a figure considerably higher than you think your case is worth. (See Chapter 5.) So, for example, if you think your case is worth $3,500 to $5,000, make a claim for $25,000. A high number is useful because you may have to file your claim before you have completely recovered from your injuries and therefore before you know how much your claim will be worth. Also, the figure in the claim is just an "opening bid." Once you actually start negotiating for a settlement, you will narrow the figure down. (See Chapter 6 and Chapter 8.)

**The date and your signature.** Make sure to date and sign the claim.

## Sample Claim Against the Government

The sample claim below is for an accident Martin Johnson had when he tripped in a hole in the public parking lot of the county medical building where he was going for a medical appointment. He sprained his left wrist and right knee in the fall, and also jammed his back. His medical bills, at the time of filing the claim, were $680. He missed two weeks of work for which his pay was $1,450.

## Sample Claim Against the Government

CLAIM OF MARTIN JOHNSON
AGAINST WABASH COUNTY

The claimant's name is Martin Johnson, 323 Cannonball Lane, Wabash, Missouri 00000.

All notices regarding this claim should be sent to 323 Cannonball Lane, Wabash, MO 00000.

This claim arises from injuries I suffered on January 13, 20xx when I tripped in a hole in the county parking lot next to the county medical building on East Pine Street, Wabash, Wabash County, Missouri. I was in the parking lot after having parked my car there on my way to an appointment in the county medical building.

As a result of the fall, I suffered injuries to my left wrist, my right knee, and my back and neck. I missed two weeks of work as a result of my injuries.

I do not know the name of any public employee who may have caused this accident.

I claim compensation in the amount of $20,000.

Dated: February 10, 20xx

*Martin Johnson*
Martin Johnson

## Where to File a Claim

The clerk's office of the government agency or entity you believe was responsible for your accident is the first place to contact about filing your claim. For example, if you have a claim to file against the county, check with the county clerk's office. It might accept claims directly, or direct you to another agency, such as the county attorney or controller's office. If your claim is against the state, call the state board of claims, board of control, or state attorney general's office to find out where to file. After you talk to someone, send them a confirming letter repeating what they told you about where and how to file. Keep a copy for your records

If you are not sure whether your claim is against the city, the county, or some state agency, file a separate claim against each of them. In most states, it does not cost anything to file a claim against the government, and filing in each place will protect you against failing to file against the correct entity before the time limit runs out. If it turns out later that one or another government entity was not responsible, you can simply ignore or drop your claim against it.

**Double check the date.** When you take or send your claim for filing, make an extra copy and ask the clerk to mark on your copy the date on which the office received it. If you mail in your claim, include at least one extra copy and a return envelope with a request that they send you back a copy stamped with the date it was filed. If you have not received a dated copy near the end of the time limit, go to the office in person to file your claim, making sure your copy is marked "received" or "filed," and that it includes the date.

## What Happens After You File a Claim

While there may be some variety in the way different claims against the government are handled, there are some common procedures you can expect to be followed.

### Contact by Government Claims Adjuster

Soon after you file your claim, you may be contacted by a claims adjuster. This person might work directly for the government entity involved in the accident or for the city, county, or state

attorney's office, or might be a private claims adjuster for the government entity's insurance company. In any case, deal with this person as you would an insurance adjuster representing a private business or individual. That is, until you are ready to make a formal demand for settlement and begin actual negotiations, give only the basic information discussed earlier in this chapter. (See "First Contact With Another Person's Insurance Company," above.) Your formal demand for settlement and the negotiation process will come later and will operate the same as with a private insurance company. (See Chapters 6 and 8.)

### Notice of Insufficiency

The first thing that may happen after you file your claim is that you receive a letter from the government telling you that your claim is insufficient because it failed to include some required information such as a date or location. Getting a notice of insufficiency does not mean that your claim has been denied. It simply means that, before your state's time limit is up, you must provide the government entity with the missing information, in writing.

### Negotiating a Settlement

In some states, government entities will negotiate with you about a settlement only after your formal claim has been denied in writing (see "If Your Claim Is Denied," below) or after the time period has elapsed within which the government has a right to grant or deny your claim (see "If Your Claim Is Neither Granted Nor Denied," below). In other states, the written claim and its denial are usually nothing more than a formality, and the government entity will begin to negotiate with you as soon as you file your claim. Regardless of when it begins, the negotiating process is exactly the same as with the insurance company for a private business or individual. (See Chapters 6 and 8.)

### If Your Claim Is Denied

The formal claim process is intended to give the government a chance to investigate your claim before you are allowed to take the government to court. But the process is usually just a formality, and almost all formal claims are denied. Official denial of your claim does *not* mean the government will refuse to compensate you for your injuries. A denial merely ends the formal claim process and legally permits you to file a lawsuit against the government, if necessary. Once the formal claim is denied, the government entity will negotiate with you about settling your claim just as if it were a private business.

In most states, the government has only a limited time after you file your formal claim—30 to 180 days—in which to grant or deny it. Within that time, you should receive a written notice from the government officially denying your claim. The significance of the formal written denial is that it permits you to file a lawsuit against the government agency if you do not agree to settle the case. And in some states, the government entity will not begin to negotiate with you until the formal claim is officially denied.

### If Your Claim Is Neither Granted Nor Denied

Often, a government entity receives your formal claim and you never hear anything more about it. Instead of officially granting or denying the formal claim, the government simply ignores it. In this situation, the claim will be considered denied after the government's time period for granting or denying it has run out. You are then legally permitted to pursue your claim against the government, by lawsuit if necessary, just as if you had received an official written denial. Note,

however, that the government's silent denial of your formal claim also starts the clock running on the time within which you can legally file a lawsuit, just as if it had denied your claim in writing.

 **Check the time.** In many states, the official written denial of your claim permits you to file a lawsuit against the government entity, but also begins the running of a time period within which you must file a lawsuit. Check "Summaries of Time Limits for Filing Against the Government," below, for the time period in your state within which you can file a lawsuit after your claim is denied.

### If You Miss the Filing Deadline

For some time after an accident, you may not realize that a government entity was to blame. And by the time you do realize it, the time period within which to file a formal claim may have passed. If so, it does not necessarily end your chances of collecting compensation from the government, although it does make the task much harder. Most states permit you to file a late claim if you can show good reason for the delay.

What is legally required to establish a good reason, however, can vary greatly from state to state. In some states, it means that you were not aware the government entity was responsible. In others, you must show that you actually investigated who was responsible but you received incorrect information or otherwise made an excusable error.

No matter what your reason, if you missed the deadline, file your claim anyway, along with an explanation of why it is late. The government entity may still grant you permission to file the claim. If it does not, in most states you can then go to court to ask permission to file a late claim. For that process, though, it is best that you seek the assistance of a personal injury lawyer. (See Chapter 11.)

## Summaries of Time Limits for Filing Against the Government

This section lists, for each state and for the federal government, the time within which you must file a formal claim against a government entity that you believe is at least partly responsible for an accident.

In addition to these time limits for filing a formal claim, some states also have special time limits for filing a lawsuit against a government entity. The lawsuit time limit for filing against a government entity may differ from that state's time limit for filing a lawsuit against a private party. The latter deadlines are listed at the end of Chapter 8.

In parentheses following each state's time limit is the state statute establishing this time limit. The time-limit rules are contained in the official laws of the state, called statutes. Statutes are identified by individual number, and in some states by an article or title number as well. In this listing, common legal abbreviations are used. For a guide to the abbreviations, see the discussion of no-fault laws in Chapter 4.

### United States

Two years to file formal claim against any agency of the federal government; suit within six months from date denial was made. (28 U.S.C. § 2401(b).)

### Alabama

Six months to file formal claim against a municipality. (Ala. Code § 11-47-23.)

One year to file formal claim against county. (Ala. Code § 11-12-8.)

### Alaska

Two years to file formal claim. (Alaska Stat. § 09.10.070.)

### Arizona

One hundred eighty days to file formal claim; lawsuit within one year. (Ariz. Rev. Stat. Ann. § 12-821 and § 12-821.01.)

 **Double check the laws.** Because laws change frequently, always double check the time limit listed here. There are at least two ways to double check. The first is to call your city or county attorney's office and ask. Although the government officials may be the ones defending against your claim once you file it, they are under a legal obligation to give you correct filing information. As with all communications concerning your accident, record the name and position of the person who gives you the information.

Another way to double check the time limit is to go to your local city, county, or law school law library and ask the librarian to help you find the current law. This listing gives the title and number of the law for each state, so it will be easy for the law librarian to help you find the information you need.

### Arkansas

The law in Arkansas permits claims against government entities only in limited circumstances, when the government entity involved may have liability insurance. (Ark. Stat. Ann. § 21-9-301.) If a personal injury claim is permitted, a claimant has five years from the date of the accident in which to file it. (Ark. Stat. Ann. §§ 19-10-209 and 16-56-115.)

If you file a claim against a government entity and are informed that the government has immunity (meaning that no claim is permitted, no matter who was at fault), consult an experienced personal injury attorney to discuss possible ways of getting around the immunity laws.

### California

Six months to file formal claim. (Cal. Gov't Code § 911.2.) Government entity must accept or reject claim within 45 days after receipt, or else it is deemed denied. (Cal. Gov't Code § 912.4.)

After denial or the date the claim is deemed denied, you have six months to file a lawsuit against the government entity. (Cal. Gov't Code §§ 913 and 945.6.)

### Colorado

One hundred eighty days to file formal claim. (Colo. Rev. Stat. § 24-10-109.)

Lawsuit must be filed against a government entity within two years after the accident. (Colo. Rev. Stat. § 13-80-102.)

A special rule requires that a lawsuit against a law enforcement or firefighting agency must be filed within one year after the accident. (Colo. Rev. Stat. § 13-80-103.)

### Connecticut

Written notice of intention to commence lawsuit against a municipality or public agency must be filed within six months; lawsuit must be filed within two years. (Conn. Gen. Stat. Ann. § 7-101(a)-(d).)

Claims against the state are filed with state claims commissioner within one year after accident. (Conn. Gen. Stat. Ann. §§ 4-147 and 4-148.)

If accident was caused by the condition of state property, you also must give notice within a "reasonable time" to the agency in control of that property. (Conn. Gen. Stat. Ann. § 4-146.)

Lawsuit against the state must be filed within one year of denial of claim (called "authorization" of lawsuit) by claims commissioner. (Conn. Gen. Stat. Ann. § 4-160.)

### Delaware

One year to file formal claim by written notice. (Del. Code Ann. title 10, § 4013(c), and title 10, § 8124.)

### District of Columbia

Six months to file formal claim. (D.C. Code Ann. § 12-309.)

### Florida

Three years to file formal claim both to the Department of Insurance and to the specific entity or agency responsible for the accident. (Fla. Stat. Ann. § 768.28)

Four years to file lawsuit. (Fla. Stat. § 11.065.)

### Georgia

Two years to file formal claim against the state. (Ga. Code Ann. § 28-5-86.)

Six months to present claim against local government. (Ga. Code Ann. § 36-33-5.)

### Hawaii

Two years to file an action. (Hawaii Rev. Stat. §§ 661-5 and 662-4.)

### Idaho

One hundred eighty days to file formal claim. (Idaho Code § 6-905 and § 6-906.)

Two years to file lawsuit. (Idaho Code § 6-911.)

### Illinois

One year to file formal claim against state government; two years to file lawsuit against state government in Court of Claims. (Ill. Ann. Stat. Ch. 705, §§ 505/8(d), 505/22(h), and 505/22-1.)

One year to file a lawsuit (no claim time limit) against a local government entity. (Ill. Ann. Stat. Ch. 705, §§ 10/8-101.)

### Indiana

Two hundred seventy days to file formal claim against the state. (Ind. Code Ann. § 34-13-3-6.)

One hundred eighty days to file formal claim against other government entities. (Ind. Code Ann. § 34-13-3-8.)

### Iowa

Two years to file formal claim against the state. (Iowa Code Ann. § 669.13.)

### Kansas

No formal claim against government entity is required; lawsuit within same time limit as if against private party. (Kan. Stat. Ann. § 75-6103.)

### Kentucky

One year to file formal claim against state. (Ky. Rev. Stat. § 44.110.)

### Louisiana

No formal claim required. In general, the same rules apply regarding time to file a lawsuit as if against a private party, but some special limits apply regarding service of a lawsuit. (La. Rev. Stat. Ann. §§ 13:5101-13:5111.)

### Maine

One hundred eighty days to file formal claim. (Me. Rev. Stat. Ann. vol. 14, § 8107.)

Two years to file lawsuit. (Me. Rev. Stat. Ann. vol. 14, § 8110.)

### Maryland

One year to file formal claim against the state; three years to file lawsuit. (Md. Ann. Code, State Gov't., § 12-106.)

One hundred eighty days to file formal claim against local government entities. (Md. Ann. Code, Courts & Judicial Proceedings, § 5-304.)

### Massachusetts

Two years to file formal claim; three years to file lawsuit. (Mass. Gen. Laws Ann. Ch. 258, § 4.)

### Michigan

Six months to file formal claim against the state. (Mich. Comp. Laws § 600.6431.)

Two years to file lawsuit. (Mich. Comp. Laws § 691.1411.)

Special rule: 120 days to file formal claim regarding defective highway or public building. (Mich. Comp. Laws §§ 691.1404 and 691.1406.)

### Minnesota

One hundred eighty days to file formal claim against the state. (Minn. Stat. Ann. § 3.736(5).)

One hundred eighty days to file formal claim against local government. (Minn. Stat. Ann. § 466.05.)

### Mississippi

Formal claim against state or local government must be filed at least 90 days before filing a lawsuit. Lawsuit must be filed within one year of the accident, but no lawsuit may be filed while the claim is pending ("pending" means the claim is filed but not yet approved or denied). While a claim is pending, the one-year limit on lawsuit is extended (statute of limitations is "tolled") up to 95 extra days for claims against the state, 120 days for claims against a local government entity.

If claim is denied, the claimant has only 90 days from the date denial is received to file a lawsuit. If claim is never formally approved or denied, the claimant must file a lawsuit within 90 days from the end of the "tolling period" (the 95 or 120 days following the filing of the claim). (Miss. Code Ann. § 11-46-11.)

### Missouri

Ninety days to file formal claim against city government. (Mo. Ann. Stat. §§ 77.600, 79.480, and 82.210.)

Otherwise, no formal claim needed against state, county, or city.

### Montana

Must file a claim within the same period that is given to file lawsuit against private person. Government entity has 120 days after claim is filed to grant or deny it. During the 120 days, time is suspended toward the statute of limitations. (Mont. Code Ann. § 2-9-301.)

### Nebraska

One year to file formal claim against city or county; two years to file lawsuit against city or county. (Neb. Rev. Stat. §§ 13-919, 13-920.)

Two years to file formal claim against state. (Neb. Rev. Stat. § 81-8227.)

No lawsuit may be filed until claim denied or until six months has passed with no decision on claim. (Neb. Rev. Stat. § 81-8213.)

Two years to file lawsuit against state (Neb. Rev. Stat. § 25-218), but this two-year statute of limitations period is suspended while claim is pending, up to six months. (Neb. Rev. Stat. § 81-8227.)

### Nevada

Two years to file formal claim. (Nev. Rev. Stat. Ann. § 41.036.)

### New Hampshire

Sixty days to file formal claim against all government entities other than the state; three years to file lawsuit. (N.H. Rev. Stat. Ann. § 507-B:7.)

One hundred eighty days to file formal claim against the state; three years to file lawsuit against the state. (N.H. Rev. Stat. Ann. § 541-B:14.)

### New Jersey

Ninety days to file formal claim; may file lawsuit six months after claim is filed and must file within two years after date of accident. (N.J. Stat. Ann. § 59:8-8.)

### New Mexico

Ninety days to file formal claim. (N.M. Stat. Ann. § 41-4-16.)

Two years to file lawsuit. (N.M. Stat. Ann. § 41-4-15.)

### New York

Ninety days to file formal claim against city; one year to file lawsuit. (N.Y. Gen. Mun. Laws § 50-e.)

Ninety days to file formal claim against county; one year to file lawsuit. (N.Y. County Law § 52.)

Ninety days to file claim against the state (or notice of intent to file claim if, within the 90 days, the claimant is unable to arrive at a final claim figure, such as if medical treatment is incomplete). (N.Y. Court of Claims Act § 10.)

### North Carolina

Three years to file formal claim against the state. (N.C. Gen. Stat. § 143-299.)

### North Dakota

One hundred eighty days to file formal claim (N.D. Cent. Code § 32-12.2-04); three years to file lawsuit against state (N.D. Cent. Code § 28-01-22.1) or against other government entity. (N.D. Cent. Code § 32-12.1-10.)

### Ohio

Two years to file lawsuit in the Court of Claims. (Ohio Rev. Code Ann. § 2743.16(A).)

### Oklahoma

One year to file formal claim. Lawsuit must be filed within 180 days after denial of claim. (Okla. Stat. Ann. tit. 51, §§ 156(B) and 157.) Claim is deemed denied if government takes no action within 90 days.

### Oregon

One hundred eighty days to file formal claim. (Ore. Rev. Stat. § 30.275.)

### Pennsylvania

Six months to file notice of intent to sue. (42 Pa. Con. Stat. Ann. § 5522.)

### Rhode Island

Three years to file lawsuit. (R.I. Gen. Laws § 9-1-25.)

### South Carolina

No requirement to file formal claim, but if claim is filed, must wait to file lawsuit until claim is denied or 180 days passes with no decision on claim. Two years to file lawsuit if no formal claim is filed; three years to file lawsuit if claim is filed. (S.C. Code Ann. §§ 15-78-90 and 15-78-110.)

### South Dakota

One hundred eighty days to file formal claim. (S.D. Codif. Laws Ann. § 3-21-2.)

### Tennessee

One year to file claim against state with State Board of Claims. (Tenn. Code Ann. § 9-8-108.)

Claim is mandatory against city or county. No time limit to file claim, except that no suit can be filed until 60 days after claim has been filed; claimant has one year in which to file suit. (Tenn. Code Ann. §§ 29-20-304 and 29-20-305.)

### Texas

Six months to file formal claim. (Tex. Civ. Prac. & Rem. Code § 101.101.)

### Utah

One year to file claim. (Utah Code Ann. §§ 63-30-12, 63-30-13, and 63-30-14.)

One year from denial of claim to file lawsuit; if no formal denial, then claimant has one year plus 90 days from date claim was filed in which to file lawsuit. (Utah Code Ann. § 63-30-15.)

### Vermont

No notice requirement other than lawsuit must be filed within statute of limitations.

### Virginia

Six months to file formal claim against city or town. (Va. Code Ann. § 8.01-222.)

One year to file formal claim against state or transportation district. (Va. Code Ann. § 8.01-195.6.)

### Washington

Formal claim against state must be filed within statute of limitations; no suit until 60 days after claim filed. (Wash. Rev. Code Ann. §§ 4.92.100 and 4.92.110.)

Formal claim against town, city, or county must be filed within statute of limitations; no suit until 60 days after claim is filed. (Wash. Rev. Code Ann. § 4.96.020.)

### West Virginia

No formal claim time requirement; two years to file suit. (W.Va. Code § 29-12A-6(a).)

### Wisconsin

One hundred twenty days to file formal claim against local government entity (Wis. Stat. Ann. § 893.80) or against state. (Wis. Stat. Ann. § 893.82.)

### Wyoming

Two years to file formal claim; suit must be filed within one year after claim filed. (Wyo. Stat. Ann. §§ 1-39-113 and 1-39-114.)

■

*Chapter 4*

# Understanding Insurance Coverage

## Using This Chapter

This chapter helps you understand what each type of insurance will cover and the consequences for you: when it will pay, how much it will pay, and how it affects payments received under other coverage.

**You can skip this entire chapter if:**
- your accident didn't involve a vehicle
- it is already clear who was responsible for your nonvehicle accident, and
- you have contacted that person's liability insurance company.

In such a case, that insurance company will likely be the only one with which you need be concerned.

**Read this chapter if:**
- you have any doubt about whether certain insurance will cover your accident, or
- you have questions about which of several insurance coverages is best for you to pursue.

Proceed directly to the section that covers the type of accident in which you've been involved.

Read "Motor Vehicle Insurance" for motor vehicle accidents, and check "No-Fault Laws: State Summaries" to see whether your state has no-fault insurance that will affect your claim.

"Nonvehicle Liability Insurance" covers business liability, homeowner, renter, and personal liability insurance for nonvehicle accidents.

"Your Own Health Coverage and Accident Claims" explains when to use and when not to use your own health coverage, instead of auto insurance coverage, to pay for your accident injuries.

There is at least one good thing about insurance companies' having their hooks in everyone's lives. If you have an accident, there's a good chance there will be an insurance company around from which you can collect compensation for your injuries. And finding the insurance coverage is usually a simple matter. With most accidents, it will be obvious who was at fault, or liable—and that person or business usually will have some kind of liability insurance. You merely have to contact that insurer and submit your claim as described in this book.

But there are some situations when you might not be certain which insurance policy covers your accident. Or there may be some confusion because more than one insurance coverage— yours as well as the other party's—is available to you, under different terms and for different amounts.

## Motor Vehicle Insurance

The first and usually the only place a person injured in a vehicle accident turns for compensation is to the other driver's liability insurance company. Almost all states require that every registered vehicle or licensed driver have some vehicle liability insurance. And even where it is not required by law, most drivers have some liability coverage.

Considering the cost of today's medical care, the minimum amount of coverage legally required in some states is quite low—$5,000 or $10,000 total per accident victim, $10,000 to $20,000 total for all injured people per accident. But in most states, the required minimum is higher, and many people carry coverage well above the legal requirement. As a result, except in the case of uninsured or underinsured drivers or very serious accidents, the person at fault is likely to have sufficient liability insurance to pay for all your damages.

## Summary of Motor Vehicle Insurance Coverages and Terms

The following are brief descriptions of the types of coverage that auto insurance companies offer. The specific workings of each coverage are explained throughout this section; property damage is discussed in Chapter 7. Coverage varies slightly among insurance companies, so check your own policy to determine the exact rules of coverage and claims. Also, all coverage is limited to the dollar amounts specified in a particular policy.

**Liability.** Policies often refer to this type of coverage as third-party liability or bodily injury and property damage liability. If you are at all legally responsible—that is, liable—for an accident, liability coverage compensates other people for their injuries and damage to their property. When you have been injured in an accident that is not entirely your fault, you can file a claim under this type of coverage with the other driver's or car owner's insurance company.

**Personal Injury Protection (PIP).** In states with no-fault insurance laws, your own insurance policy provides this coverage to pay for your medical bills.

**Uninsured Motorist.** This coverage provides compensation from your own insurance company if you or the occupants of your vehicle are injured in an accident with someone who was at least partly at fault but who did not carry liability insurance. Some uninsured motorist coverage also includes property damage.

**Underinsured Motorist.** If you are injured in an accident with someone who has liability insurance in an amount too small to cover the full amount of your damages, your own underinsured motorist coverage, if you have it, may make up the difference.

**Medical Payments.** This coverage in your own insurance policy may pay a limited portion of your medical bills, or those of any occupant of your car, regardless of who was at fault in an accident. Medical payments coverage in some insurance policies requires that you reimburse your insurance company if you later collect from the other driver.

**Collision.** Your insurance company pays for damage to your own vehicle—minus your deductible—regardless of fault.

If the other driver or owner has no insurance, or has insufficient coverage to pay you fully for your injuries, you may be able to get additional compensation through the uninsured or under-insured motorist coverages of your own policy. (See "Your Own Vehicle's Coverage," below.) Your own policy may also provide medical payments coverage for immediate payment of some medical bills. However, medical payments coverage should be used with caution. If the medical payments provision of your policy requires you to reimburse your company if you receive a third-party settlement, you may save

money by using your general health insurance or other health coverage instead. (See "Your Own Health Coverage and Accident Claims," below.)

## The Other Driver's Liability Insurance

Most of the time, the question of coverage will not even come up. The driver of the other car in your accident will be covered by liability insurance and that's all you'll need to know. But disputes over liability coverage do develop. Most of them revolve around whether the driver or vehicle in the accident fits into any of the specific categories included or excluded from a liability policy. Below is a quick guide to common inclusions and exclusions.

## What Drivers Are Covered?

**Named insured.** The named insured is the person or people named in the policy. Liability policies cover named insureds no matter what car they are driving.

**Spouse.** Even if a husband or wife of the named insured is not named on a policy, auto liability insurance almost always covers him or her as well, while driving any car. If a husband and wife no longer live together, however, the policy will not cover accidents caused by a spouse not named on the policy unless that spouse was driving the covered vehicle with the permission of the named spouse. (See "What Vehicles Are Covered?" below.)

**Other relative.** Any licensed driver living in the household with the named insured who is related to the insured by blood, marriage, or adoption, usually including a legal ward or foster child, is covered regardless of what car he or she is driving.

**Anyone driving the insured vehicle.** Any person who is using, with permission, a vehicle specifically named in the policy is covered. So, someone who steals the car is not covered because he or she was not using it with permission. The permission question also comes up if, for example, a teenager lets another teen drive a car without the parent owner's permission. In that case, an insurer might argue that the parent's policy does not cover the unrelated teenager who was driving.

### Understand Overlapping Medical Coverages for Auto Accidents

If you have been in a motor vehicle accident, two sources may be immediately available to pay your medical bills long before you settle your claim against the other driver: the medical payments coverage of your own auto insurance policy, and your own health insurance, including Medicare and Medicaid. It is a good idea to understand how these insurance policies interact before reaching out for any of the coverages.

Either type of coverage might require you to repay any amounts it pays if you also collect damages from another person's liability insurance. Whether health insurance or medical payments coverage of an auto policy requires you to repay depends entirely on the terms of the policy or contract. Before using either type of coverage, read your policies to see if repayment is required. If one does and the other doesn't, you may save hundreds and even thousands of dollars by using the nonrepayment coverage. For a full explanation of this matter, read "Your Own Health Coverage and Accident Claims," below.

Some auto policies also exclude coverage for an employee using an employer's personal car for business. In that case, though, a person injured in an accident could file a claim for compensation under the business's liability insurance.

## What Vehicles Are Covered?

**Named vehicles.** Any vehicle named in the liability coverage declaration is covered. An accident in a vehicle not named in the declaration is covered only if a named insured (see above) was driving.

**Added vehicles.** Any car, utility vehicle (see below), or other vehicle with which the named insured replaces the original named vehicle, and any additional vehicle the named insured owns during the policy period, is also covered. Some policies, however, cover replacement or additional vehicles only if the insured person notifies the company of the new or different vehicle within 30 days after it is acquired.

**Temporary vehicles.** Coverage extends to any car not owned by the named insured, or by another resident of the household, used as a temporary replacement—including rental cars— for any insured vehicle that is out of use because it needs repair or service, or has been destroyed.

**Utility vehicles.** Most policies cover an insured person driving a few types of vehicles somewhat larger than a normal passenger car, but only up to a limit. This usually means coverage is limited to a sport utility vehicle, pickup, flatbed, delivery, or panel truck to a certain rated load capacity stated in the policy. Larger vehicles might be covered if they are specifically listed in the owner's individual policy. The same holds true for a motorcycle: To be covered, it must be specifically named in the policy. Most policies, however, do not cover utility vehicles while used for business.

### States With No-Fault Auto Insurance Coverage

The following states have some form of no-fault automobile insurance law. If you live in one of these states, read "No Fault Automobile Insurance," below, to see how no-fault rules affect which insurance will pay your claim.

| | |
|---|---|
| District of Columbia | Minnesota |
| Florida | New Jersey |
| Hawaii | New York |
| Kansas | North Dakota |
| Kentucky | Pennsylvania |
| Massachusetts | Utah |
| Michigan | |

Even if you have no-fault auto insurance coverage, in many circumstances you can also file a claim against the other person's liability insurance company. No-fault plans always permit such additional claims when the nature or extent of your injuries moves beyond the limits of the no-fault policy.

## What Damages Are Covered?

Generally speaking, liability insurance covers the following costs: medical costs for diagnosis and treatment of injuries, property damage, loss of use of damaged property, expenses incurred, and lost income. In addition, an injured person is entitled to a certain amount of "general damages," also referred to as pain and suffering. (See Chapter 5.)

## Liability Coverage by More Than One Policy

More than one person's liability policy may cover your damages. When that happens, one insurance policy will provide what is called "primary" coverage, while the other will provide "secondary" or "excess" coverage. The primary coverage will pay your damages, and the secondary policy will kick in only if the limits of the primary policy aren't enough to cover all your damages. In those cases, the secondary coverage will pay to the extent necessary to make up the difference between the limits of the primary policy and your total damages.

> **EXAMPLE:** You are injured in a car accident and you are entitled to $20,000 in damages. The driver of the other car, however, has only $15,000 worth of liability insurance coverage. You could collect the $15,000 under the driver's primary insurance coverage. If there was any secondary coverage under the policy of another person partly responsible for the accident, you would collect the remaining $5,000 of your total damages from the insurance company issuing that secondary coverage.

You will not have to worry about figuring out which policy is primary and which is secondary. When more than one person is at fault in an accident, file a notice of claim with the insurance companies for everyone who was at fault. (See Chapter 3.) The insurance companies will then notify you which one will be primary and which one secondary. The primary insurance company is the one with which you will negotiate your claim initially.

The availability and sources of double coverage depend on facts such as who owns the vehicles involved in your accident and how much insurance they have.

## When You Are a Passenger

If you are a passenger in a vehicle involved in an accident, you may file an injury claim under both (1) the liability insurance coverage of the driver or owner of the car you were in and (2) the coverage of the driver or owner of any other vehicle involved. You cannot collect from both drivers or owners any more than your total claim is worth, but if one driver or owner does not have insurance to cover your total damages, you can make up the rest against another. And you can collect against the other driver or owner even if that person was not greatly at fault, because as a passenger you weren't at all at fault.

> **EXAMPLE:** You are a passenger in car X, which has an accident with car Y in which car Y seemed to be most at fault, but car X was also partly to blame. Your total damages are $20,000, but the driver of car Y has only $15,000 worth of insurance coverage. After you collect that $15,000 from car Y driver's insurance, you can collect the remaining $5,000 from car X's insurance.

If either driver was using a car belonging to someone else, you may also look for compensation from the insurance company of the car's owner.

You may not, however, file a liability claim against the driver of the car you are riding in if the driver is a relative with whom you live. In that case, you are considered an "insured person" under liability insurance—and an insured person cannot file a liability claim against his or her own liability coverage.

In the immediate aftermath of your accident, you may also file a claim under the medical payments coverage of your driver's or owner's auto policy. Medical payments coverage is not based on liability and therefore does not require any discussion with insurance companies about who was at fault. But medical payments coverage does not include compensation for pain and suffering, lost income, or anything other than actual medical bills—and those only up to the limits of the coverage. If you do collect under medical payments coverage and then later also receive liability compensation from that same insurance company, the amount you collected under medical payments will be deducted from your liability settlement. And sometimes, you're better off using your health insurance instead. There's more about this below.

**EXAMPLE:** You are injured in an auto accident and have $2,500 in medical bills in the first two weeks. You can immediately collect that amount under the medical payments provision of the insurance policy of the driver of the car you were riding in.

It turns out that the driver of the other car was uninsured, and so you file a liability claim against the driver of the car you were riding in. You settle that claim for a total of $10,000. The settlement amount you actually receive from the insurance company, however, will be only $7,500—your $10,000 settlement minus the $2,500 medical payments you received earlier from the same company.

## When the Other Driver Is Not the Owner

If you have a car accident and the other driver doesn't own the vehicle he or she was driving, the liability insurance of both the driver and the owner may be available to compensate you for your injuries. If either the driver or the owner is uninsured, the liability policy of the one who is insured will compensate you. If both are uninsured, you will have to turn to your own uninsured motorist coverage.

## Employer's Liability for Employees

If the driver of a car or other vehicle is using the vehicle on the job, then the driver's employer is liable for any injuries caused in accidents for which the employee was at fault. This is true whether the employer is a private individual, a business, or a public agency. This rule of employer liability applies whether you were the driver of another vehicle, a pedestrian, a passenger in the employee's personal car being used on the job, or a passenger in the employer's car being driven by the employee. (See "Business and Landlord Liability Coverage," below.)

Whether someone is on the job while driving is not always a simple question. In general, any time someone is performing any duties related to work, he or she can be considered on the job even though he or she may also be doing personal business and driving a personal car. For example, running errands in a personal car during lunch is not considered work-related, but if the employee is also picking up or dropping off something for work, the lunchtime driving becomes "on-the-job" time. Likewise, commuting to and from work generally is not considered on-the-job driving, even in a company car. But if the driver has to make work-related stops on the way, or has to drive to and from a job site other than the usual place of business, the driving might legally be considered on-the-job driving.

The question of whether someone was on the job when he or she had an accident is not usually something you will need to sort out. Most drivers have personal automobile liability insurance, so if you believe the driver might have been on the job, send a notice of the accident to both the employer's business insurance company and to the driver's personal insurance company. Then the two insurers will have to sort out which one will provide the primary coverage.

Only if the driver is personally uninsured, or has insurance coverage so low that it does not provide full compensation for your injuries, will you have to concern yourself with the question of whether the employee was on the job when the accident happened. If there is no simple answer, then the issue becomes another factor thrown into the general hopper of negotiations—along with whose fault the accident was and how much your injuries are worth.

Sometimes, the issue of whether an employee was on the job can become both very significant and very complicated. If the only available insurance is through the employer and the insurer is arguing that the employee wasn't working, you may need to hire a lawyer to sort things out. See Chapter 11 for more about hiring a lawyer.

### Parents' Liability for Minors

Usually, a minor teenager who is driving a car or motorcycle will be covered by either his or her own insurance or a parent's insurance policy. If the minor is not named on a parent's insurance policy, or if the car the minor is driving is owned by a parent, the parent is liable, which means that you can collect from the parent's insurance company.

If the minor is the registered owner of the car or motorcycle but has no insurance, most states make the parent responsible for damages—usually limited to between $5,000 and $25,000—caused in an accident when the minor is at fault. So, if you are involved in an accident with a minor who has little or no insurance coverage, you may be able to file a claim against a parent and collect from one or both policies up to the limit of your damages.

### When You Are Driving Someone Else's Car

If you were driving someone else's car when you were in an accident caused by a third party, you may make a claim for all your damages against that other driver. But you may also make a claim for immediate payment of your medical bills only, up to the coverage limit, under the medical payments coverage of the owner of the car you were driving. For damages to the car, the owner of the car must file a claim against the other driver.

Occasionally, the condition of the vehicle you are driving contributes to an accident. Brakes may fail, lights can go out, tires might be bald. If someone lends you a car, the owner is legally responsible to the extent the car's unsafe condition contributes to an accident. Therefore, if a borrowed vehicle's unsafe condition contributed to your accident, file a claim for damages not only against the driver of the other vehicle but also against the owner of the vehicle you were driving. If it is determined that the unsafe condition of the vehicle you were driving was the sole cause of the accident, a claim against the owner would be your only source of compensation.

If you are driving someone else's car and have an accident with an uninsured driver, the uninsured motorist coverage of the owner of the car you were driving is usually the primary coverage, and your own uninsured motorist coverage is secondary. Notify both your own insurance company and the company that insures the car you were driving, but expect to negotiate a settlement only with the company insuring the car you were driving. (See "Your Own Vehicle's Coverage," below.)

## When Several Others Are Responsible

It is not uncommon for more than one other person to contribute to a car accident. It may have been the drivers of two other vehicles, or another vehicle plus a hazard in the roadway. Whatever the combination, if more than one person contributed to the accident, file a claim under the liability insurance of both.

You cannot collect more than the full amount of your damages from all of them together, but you can collect up to the entire amount of your damages from any one of them, depending upon their percentage of fault and your comparative fault. If the coverage of one person at fault is not sufficient to cover all your damages, you can collect the remainder of what your claim is worth from the other person who was at fault.

> **EXAMPLE:** You are involved in a three-car collision with cars driven by Anice and Jim. You file a claim against both of them. Anice was most at fault, so her insurance company pays you up to the limits of her liability coverage of $15,000. But your total damage claim was worth $20,000. You can collect the remaining $5,000 value of your damages from Jim's insurance company.

It is not your responsibility to figure out which one of the other drivers should pay you first or most as primary coverage. When you notify the insurance companies for both of the people responsible for the accident, the companies will decide between themselves which will be the primary coverage and which will serve as secondary coverage. Then you can negotiate a settlement with the insurance company that identifies itself as the primary coverage, and settle with the secondary company only if the primary coverage is not enough.

## Your Own Vehicle's Coverage

Usually, the liability insurance of the person who was at fault for an accident pays for all of your damages. But you might also need to file a claim under your own policy—in addition to or instead of a claim against another person—if:

- You have an accident in which both driver and owner are uninsured, or an accident with a hit-and-run driver. You will have to file a claim under your own uninsured motorist coverage. (See "Uninsured Motorist Coverage," below.)
- You have an accident in which the insurance coverage of the person at fault is not enough to fully cover your damages—a situation that sometimes arises when several other people are injured. You will have to file a claim under your own underinsurance coverage, if you have it. (See "Underinsured Motorist Coverage," below.)
- You want an immediate payment to cover your medical expenses. Your own medical payments coverage may provide immediate coverage, but you must decide beforehand whether it is better to use your health insurance instead. (See "Medical Payments Coverage" and "Your Own Health Coverage and Accident Claims," below.)

## Uninsured Motorist Coverage

Unfortunately, there are numerous cars and drivers on the road today without liability insurance—in large part because of the inflated cost of that insurance. If you have an accident with an uninsured vehicle or driver, the place to turn for compensation for your injuries is the uninsured motorist (UM) coverage of your own vehicle insurance policy. That coverage might even pay for the damage to your vehicle—though you must check your policy to see whether, and under what terms, your UM coverage pays for property damage. If property damage is not included in your UM coverage, you can look for property damage compensation under the collision coverage of your policy. (See Chapter 7 for an explanation of property damage claims.) If your uninsured motorist coverage does not include property damage and you do not carry collision coverage, you will have to pay out of your own pocket for damage to your vehicle.

Most UM coverage will pay up to your policy's UM limits for injuries caused to:

- you while driving or riding in the vehicle named in your policy, while driving or riding in any vehicle you do not own, or while a pedestrian
- a relative who lives with you and is injured while driving or riding in the vehicle named in your policy
- anyone else riding in or driving your insured vehicle with your permission, or
- anyone riding in a vehicle you are driving but do not own.

UM coverage places limits on when you may collect compensation and on how much you may receive:

- Some UM coverage includes accidents with unidentified hit-and-run drivers. Such coverage doesn't apply unless you or your vehicle were actually hit by the other car; being forced off the road by a driver who disappears is not sufficient. If your UM coverage includes hit-and-runs, your policy probably requires you to notify the police within 24 hours of the accident.
- Other UM coverage includes hit-and-runs only when you are able to identify the driver or the vehicle.
- If you are injured while on the job, your UM payments will be reduced by any workers' compensation or other disability payments you receive.

- If you receive payments for medical bills from your own insurance company under medical payments coverage, the amount you are entitled to recover under UM coverage will be reduced by the amount of those medical payments. (See "Medical Payments Coverage," below.)
- If you or a relative are injured by an uninsured motorist while you are in another person's car, the UM coverage of that other car's owner is the primary coverage, and your own UM coverage is secondary. You can collect from your own UM coverage only the amount of your damages that is not covered by that car owner's UM policy.

If you file a claim under your UM coverage, an insurance adjuster from your insurance company will handle your claim just as if it were a regular liability claim. You will negotiate with the adjuster about the other person's liability, the extent of your own comparative negligence, and the extent of your injuries and other damages. (Liability is discussed in Chapter 2; how much your claim is worth in Chapter 5; how to prepare your claim in Chapter 6; and how to negotiate a settlement in Chapter 8.)

## Underinsured Motorist Coverage

Some drivers carry enough insurance to meet the state's minimum liability insurance coverage requirement but not enough to cover all your damages for a particular accident. Because the other driver has some insurance, your uninsured motorist coverage does not apply. However, if you have what is called "underinsurance coverage" in your own vehicle policy, you may be able to collect compensation beyond what the other driver's insurance will pay.

Once you have settled a claim with the other driver's insurance company, negotiate with your own insurance company about how much more than this amount your case is worth. Up to the extent of your underinsurance policy limits, you can collect this extra amount from your own company. However, any medical payments coverage you have collected from your own insurance company will be deducted from the amount you collect from it in underinsurance coverage.

> **EXAMPLE:** To pay medical bills right after an accident, you collect $2,000 from your own insurance company under the medical payments coverage of your automobile policy. Several months later, you settle your accident claim against the other driver for $15,000, which was the limit of the other driver's liability coverage.
>
> Your own underinsurance coverage has $50,000 policy limits. You convince your own insurance company that your claim is worth a total of $25,000. Under your underinsurance coverage, you can collect an additional $8,000—the $25,000 total value of your claim minus the $15,000 you collected from the other person's liability insurance, and minus the $2,000 medical payments.

To collect under your underinsured motorist coverage, you must first show your insurance company that the other driver was underinsured. Obtain from the other driver's insurance company a letter that includes the policy limits for that person's liability coverage, and a statement that you have settled your claim with that company for an amount equal to the policy limits.

You probably will not even have to make a special request for such a letter. When you negotiate your case with the other driver's insurance company, the documents you exchange in finally settling the claim may already include the information you need.

## Medical Payments Coverage

Most vehicle insurance coverage will pay up to certain limits for medical bills arising out of an accident—*regardless of who was at fault.*

The following people are usually covered by medical payments provisions:

- you or any relative who lives with you, when driving or riding in your insured vehicle or in anyone else's
- anyone else who is driving with your permission or riding in your insured vehicle, and
- anyone riding in someone else's vehicle while you or a covered relative is driving.

Medical payments provisions usually do not cover accidents occurring:

- on a motorcycle or other two-wheeled vehicle, unless that vehicle is specifically listed in the policy
- while anyone was a passenger in a car owned or used by you or a relative if that car was not listed in your insurance policy
- in a vehicle other than a regular passenger car if used in business
- during the course of the injured person's employment, if those injuries are also covered by workers' compensation laws, or
- while you were driving another person's car, unless you have already claimed and collected the maximum of that car owner's medical payments coverage.

Under the terms of medical payments coverage in some policies, the insurance company has a right to recover the amount it paid you in medical payments if you also collect damages from a third source—such as the liability insurance company for the other driver. If your policy has such a reimbursement clause and you eventually receive a settlement from another source, you will have to repay out of your settlement the amounts you received under your medical payments coverage.

**EXAMPLE:** Shortly after an accident, you collect $1,000 in medical payments coverage from your own insurance company to pay for immediate hospital bills. Several months later, you collect $7,500 in damages from the driver of the other car involved in the accident. Because the medical payments coverage in your policy requires reimbursement, you are now required to repay your own insurance company the $1,000 medical payments it made to you, reducing the amount you have in pocket to $6,500.

If you have health insurance that does not require repayment, you can avoid this whole issue simply by using your health insurance to pay your medical bills rather than your medical payments coverage.

### Collision Coverage for Property Damage

If your own policy includes coverage for property damage—also known as collision coverage—and you are in an accident in which someone else was at least partly at fault, you can claim compensation for damage to your vehicle either from your own insurance company or from the other driver's insurance company. (See Chapter 7 for a discussion of when it is best to file under one policy or another, and how best to file and process your claim.)

### Claims Against You

When there has been an accident in which you were a driver, there may be damage claims against you even though you were only slightly at fault. Regardless of how much or little the other person's damages are, your claim and the other person's claim have no effect on one another. You pursue your damage claim against those you believe were at fault—and the amount you receive is reduced by the degree to which you were comparatively negligent, regardless of how much or how little negligence the other driver accepts responsibility for in his or her claim against your insurance company. (See Chapter 2.)

Any person involved in the accident who believes you were partly responsible for his or her injuries or other damages may file a claim against you through your liability insurance company. Regardless of the degree of your fault, your liability insurance company must defend you in any claim or lawsuit—and must provide a lawyer to represent you in court if necessary. And it must settle and pay any claim against you up to the limits of your liability coverage. The success or failure of anyone else's claim against you has no bearing on your claim against others.

### No-Fault Automobile Insurance

The following states have some form of no-fault automobile insurance law—often referred to in policies as Personal Injury Protection (PIP):

| | |
|---|---|
| District of Columbia | Minnesota |
| Florida | New Jersey |
| Hawaii | New York |
| Kansas | North Dakota |
| Kentucky | Pennsylvania |
| Massachusetts | Utah |
| Michigan | |

No-fault auto insurance is a little like cod liver oil. Everyone's heard of it, most everyone's been convinced it must be good for you, a lot of people have been forced to take some, but nobody seems to know whether it does any good. One group, however, has clearly benefited from no-fault: the insurance industry. Although lower insurance rates was one of the basic promises on which no-fault was sold to legislators, it has failed to deliver lower costs to the consumer. About half the states that originally adopted no-fault laws have since repealed them.

In general, no-fault coverage eliminates injury liability claims and lawsuits in smaller accidents in exchange for direct payment by the injured person's insurance company of medical bills and lost wages—up to certain dollar amounts—regardless of who was at fault for the accident. No-fault often does not apply at all to vehicle damage; those claims are still handled by filing a liability claim against the one who is responsible for the accident, or by looking to your own collision insurance.

After you file your PIP claim, you may also be able to file a liability claim against the person at fault. The circumstances under which you can file a liability claim vary from state to state and are explained in the following sections.

Prompt payment of medical bills and lost wages without any arguments about who caused the accident is the simple part of no-fault. But most no-fault insurance provides extremely limited coverage to the injured person:

- It pays benefits for medical bills and lost income only. It provides no compensation for pain, suffering, emotional distress, inconvenience, or lost opportunities.
- It does not pay for medical bills and lost income higher than the PIP benefit limits of each person's policy. PIP benefits often fail to reimburse fully for medical bills and lost income.

## Do You Have No-Fault? You Can Tell Just by Looking

Whether you have no-fault coverage and the amount of PIP benefits you carry—that is, the amount of medical bills and lost income your own insurance company will pay regardless of fault in the accident—depends on your individual insurance policy. To determine whether you have PIP coverage and what your PIP benefits are, read your policy carefully. If your policy includes PIP protection, file your first claim for injury compensation—medical costs and lost income only, up to the dollar limit of your coverage—with your own insurance company, following the procedures set out in the PIP section of your policy.

### Liability Claims Are Also Allowed

To make up for what PIP benefits do not cover, all no-fault laws also permit an injured driver to file a liability claim, and a lawsuit if necessary, against another driver who was at fault in an accident. The liability claim permits an injured driver to obtain compensation for medical and income losses above what the PIP benefits have paid, as well as for pain and suffering and other general damages, the same as a liability claim in a state without a no-fault law.

Whether and when you can file a liability claim for further damages against the person at fault in your accident depends on the specifics of the no-fault law in your state. (See "No-Fault Laws: State Summaries," below.)

No-fault states have different types of thresholds that an injured person must reach before being permitted to file a claim for full compensation against those at fault for an accident. Some states have a monetary threshold only, some states have a serious injury threshold only, and some states have both. States with both requirements permit a liability claim if an injured person meets either one.

## States With Monetary Thresholds

The no-fault laws in the states listed below allow a liability claim and lawsuit against the person at fault whenever the injured person has medical expenses over a certain limit. The threshold limit is listed next to each state. Once you have reached that medical expense threshold, you are free to file a regular liability claim against those who are at fault for your accident. All of these states also permit a liability claim or lawsuit if a certain "injury threshold" is met instead of the medical expense threshold. (See "States With Serious Injury Thresholds," below.)

| | |
|---|---|
| District of Columbia | your policy's PIP benefit amount |
| Hawaii | your policy's PIP benefit amount |
| Kansas | $2,000 |
| Kentucky | $1,000 |
| Massachusetts | $2,000 |
| Minnesota | $4,000 |
| North Dakota | $2,500 |
| Utah | $3,000 |

Medical expenses that count toward reaching this threshold include not only the obvious things most medical insurance covers—costs of an ambulance, hospital, clinic, doctor, nursing, and laboratory—but also other professional health services, including dental work to repair or replace injured teeth, physical therapy, and chiropractic care. To find out what is counted toward the threshold limit in your state, look at the definition of medical expense in your own no-fault (PIP) insurance policy.

The monetary threshold can be reached only by counting covered medical expenses that are "necessary." Occasionally, the insurance company for the person at fault might argue that you have not reached the threshold because a particular medical treatment or service you received was either not really related to the accident or not necessary to treat your injuries. The insurance company could claim that after subtracting or reducing that supposedly unnecessary medical expense, your medical expense total does not reach the no-fault threshold and, therefore, you are not permitted to file a liability claim.

> **EXAMPLE:** Your state has a medical expenses threshold of $1,000. You have medical expenses of $1,250, including $650 for physical therapy.
>
> The insurance adjuster for the person at fault in your accident claims that there was no evidence that most of the physical therapy did any good. The adjuster claims that half the physical therapy expenses were unnecessary, reducing the necessary physical therapy expenses by $325. When that $325 is subtracted from your total medical expenses, the total shrinks to $925, less than your state's threshold and therefore not enough to allow you to file a liability claim in addition to your PIP benefits.

How to avoid this problem and how to deal with an insurance adjuster who tries this tactic are discussed in "Documenting Injuries" in Chapter 6, and in Chapter 8.

## Collecting Benefits: Once Is All You Get

Under some PIP policies, if you file a liability claim and recover damages after you also collected PIP benefits, your own PIP insurance company has a right to be reimbursed by you for the amount it paid you. Under these policies, no-fault coverage works just like an auto policy's medical payments coverage—except that it also pays for some amount of income loss. (See "Your Own Vehicle's Coverage," above.) In other words, the amount of liability compensation you get is reduced by whatever your PIP coverage already paid you.

Under other no-fault policies, your PIP insurance company does not have a right to reimbursement from you, but it does have a right of "subrogation"—which means it can recover your PIP benefits directly from the liable person's insurance company. Under those subrogation policies, you can't collect damages from the other person's insurance that duplicate any amounts your PIP coverage paid you.

Carefully read the terms of your own PIP benefits coverage to see whether your PIP insurance carrier has a right of reimbursement or subrogation.

**Keep track of medical expenses.** As you receive treatment for your injuries, keep track of how close you are to reaching your state's no-fault threshold level. There are times when we all have difficulty choosing whether to undergo one more examination or one more treatment toward the end of a course of a treatment for a particular injury. If you are close to reaching the threshold level for being allowed to file a liability claim for damages but are not certain you will reach it, the need to go over the threshold might be another thing to consider when deciding whether to undergo that final treatment or to have that final examination.

And the fact that you could choose not to undergo a particular examination or treatment does not mean that the treatment is medically unnecessary. A treatment or examination is medically necessary if it serves a reasonable diagnostic or therapeutic purpose.

### States With Serious Injury Thresholds

The states listed below permit an injured person to file a liability claim against those at fault in an accident if the insured had a "serious" injury, regardless of how much was spent on medical treatment. Injuries that qualify as serious are defined by each state's law, as indicated. If you meet your state's injury threshold, follow all the other information and directions in this book on filing and settling a liability claim.

**District of Columbia:** Substantial permanent scarring or disfigurement, substantial permanent impairment, or substantially total impairment lasting 180 days.

**Florida:** Permanent injury or significant and permanent scarring or disfigurement.

**Hawaii:** Significant permanent loss of use of a body part or function, or permanent and serious disfigurement resulting in mental or emotional distress.

**Kansas:** Permanent disfigurement, fracture of weightbearing bone or compound, comminuted, compressed, or displaced fracture of any bone, permanent injury, or permanent loss of a body function.

**Kentucky:** Permanent disfigurement, fracture of weightbearing bone or compound, comminuted, compressed, or displaced fracture of any bone, permanent injury, or permanent loss of a body function.

**Massachusetts:** Permanent and serious disfigurement, fractured bone, substantial loss of hearing or sight.

**Michigan:** Serious impairment of a body function or permanent and serious disfigurement.

**Minnesota:** Sixty days disability, permanent injury, or permanent disfigurement.

**New Jersey:** "Serious impact" on the life of the injured person.

**New York:** Significant disfigurement, bone fracture, permanent limitation of use of body organ or member, significant limitation of body function or system, or substantially full disability for 90 days.

**North Dakota:** Serious and permanent disfigurement or disability of more than 60 days.

**Pennsylvania:** Serious injury.

**Utah:** Bone fracture, permanent disability, or permanent disfigurement.

The categories of injuries legally considered "serious" by the various state no-fault laws are explained below.

**Bone fracture:** The probable fracture of any bone, as shown by X-rays and a doctor's statement, that was the result of the accident—that is, was not an old fracture. Some PIP laws require that the fracture be of a "weightbearing bone"—large bones of arm or leg, or a vertebra. Some also define serious injury as the compound, "comminuted" (meaning crushed or splintered), displaced, or compressed fracture of any bone. And other state laws merely mention "fracture," which would include chipped or cracked bones or vertebrae as well as full breaks.

**Permanent injury:** In some states, a "permanent" injury (if the term "disabling" is not included) can permit a liability claim even if the injury is not a severe one. For example, a broken bone that will remain crooked can be a permanent injury even though it is a small bone like a finger or toe and its crookedness does not affect the use of hand or foot. Similarly, a joint that suffers ligament, cartilage, or other damage may be permanently injured if the joint is not as strong or as flexible after healing as it was before the injury. Neck and back injuries are common in automobile accidents, and any injury to the spine that cannot be corrected without surgery might be considered a permanent injury, even though it may not prevent you from working or performing other normal daily life functions.

Laws using the word "significant" to describe a threshold permanent injury require that the injury be more serious than in states that do not use that term.

**Disabling injury:** Some state no-fault laws speak in terms of "disabling" injuries rather than "permanent" ones. In these states, your medical records must show that you have suffered some loss, though not necessarily total loss, of the function of a part of your body. For example, if you cannot straighten your arm all the way out because of an elbow injury, or you can no longer bend and pick up heavy things because of a back injury, your injury may be disabling even though you still have most of the use of your arm or back.

In some states the loss of function has to be "significant," while in others it does not. Under some rules, the injury has to be "permanent" as well as disabling, while other rules require only that the disability last more than 60 days.

## The Threshold Is a Subject for Negotiation

Because of the sometimes vague definitions of the threshold injury categories under PIP laws—and the subjective nature of many medical evaluations—it may not be clear whether your injuries qualify under your state's no-fault threshold. But you don't have to have a surefire qualified injury to pursue a liability claim. The issue of whether your injury qualifies is something to negotiate with the insurance company.

File your liability claim against the person at fault and include the no-fault threshold question among the other issues you will be negotiating with the insurance company. (For explanation of how to prepare and negotiate a claim for serious, permanent, or disabling injury, see Chapters 6 and Chapter 8.)

In general, an injury is "disabling" if, despite medical treatment and the passage of time, you suffer a loss of function that interferes in some way with your ability to perform normal functions of daily life, including your particular kind of work. Differences of opinion between you and an insurance company about whether an injury is disabling, or whether the disability is significant or permanent, become part of the normal negotiation process that takes place when you file a claim.

**Permanent disfigurement:** Disfigurement refers to what can be seen. Scarring is the most obvious example. A scar of any sort on the face is disfiguring if it can be seen by normal observation. Scarring on other parts of the body is considered disfiguring if large or severe enough. Other examples of disfigurement might be a broken nose that heals crookedly, the loss

of the tip of a finger or toe, or any other change in the shape or coloration of the body that is visible to others. If scarring is visible only when you wear shorts or a bathing suit, for example, it may be worth less in damages than a facial scar, but that doesn't necessarily mean it is not "disfiguring."

## Nonvehicle Liability Insurance

Although everyone is aware that insurance covers most automobile accidents, it's also true that coverage pays compensation to those injured in most other kinds of accidents as well. From business insurance to property owners' coverage, if you have been injured almost anywhere, it is likely there is some insurance to cover your damages.

### Business and Landlord Liability Coverage

Virtually every commercial property owner and business carries liability insurance covering injuries for which the business or property owner could be held legally liable—usually in amounts high enough to compensate for almost any injury. A broad range of people and accidents are usually covered by this type of insurance, including:

- any customer or business visitor accidentally injured because of a dangerous physical condition of the business premises
- any customer or business visitor accidentally injured by an employee of the business
- any person other than a coworker accidentally injured by an employee of a business if the employee was engaging—on or off the business premises—in work-related conduct at the time of the accident

- any person injured by the dangerous or defective condition of a product made, sold, or rented by a business, and
- any person accidentally injured by the dangerous or defective condition of rental property.

If you have been injured on business property, file your claim against the business owner. If the owner of the business claims the accident was the legal responsibility of the property owner from whom the business owner leases or rents, it is up to the insurance companies for the business owner and the property owner to decide between themselves which one will compensate you for your damages. You do not have to get involved in that decision. File your notice of claim with the business owner, and if the property owner's insurance company determines that it will cover your damages instead, it will notify you.

## Workers' Compensation

Every state has workers' compensation laws to compensate people who are injured on the job. In general, any time you have been injured while working for an employer, whether at your place of work or while doing business away from your normal job site, workers' compensation will cover your medical bills and lost wages.

In work-related accidents, a workers' compensation claim is the only claim you are allowed to file against your employer. In other words, if you are injured at work, you cannot file a liability claim against your employer even though a customer or visitor injured in the same way could file such a claim.

However, if anyone other than your employer or a coworker was even partly responsible for the accident, you are free to file your own liability insurance claim against that person or business. In the "regular" liability claim, you can collect

damages beyond the payment of medical bills and lost wages.

And if for any reason your accident is not covered by workers' compensation insurance, you are free to file a liability claim against your employer just as you would against anyone else responsible for your injuries. The following are situations in which workers' compensation will not cover an accident:

- if you were working as an independent contractor and not as an employee
- if an intentional act by your employer or coworker (for example, assault or willful violation of health and safety laws) caused your injury, or
- if your employer failed to maintain workers' compensation coverage.

**EXAMPLE:** While driving your car on company business, you are rear-ended by another car. You have $650 worth of medical bills and lose three days of work. You can file a workers' compensation claim for the $650 medical bills and for your lost wages. You can also file a regular liability insurance claim against the other driver in the accident. In that liability claim, you can seek compensation for your pain and suffering caused by the accident.

If you file both a workers' compensation claim and a private liability insurance claim for the same accident, the workers' compensation system automatically has a lien against any compensation you recover from the liable person or business. A lien means that if you recover any damages from the liable person or business, you have a legal obligation to repay to workers' compensation any money it paid you for medical bills or lost wages. Notice of this lien is usually included in any papers you receive from workers' compensation, but the law says the lien exists whether or not you receive any such notice.

## Property Owner and Renter Policies

Any time you have an accident caused by a defective or dangerous condition in someone's home, on someone's property, or in the common areas of an apartment or condominium building—such as hallways, stairs, or parking areas—the property owner or renter, or both, is probably liable to you for your injuries. And in most such cases, the property owner and sometimes the renter will have liability insurance to cover your injuries.

Landlords of residential income property (residences that they own but that others live in) have business liability insurance similar to the liability insurance carried by other businesses.

Homeowner's and business liability policies also frequently cover injuries caused by the insured party even if the accident occurs away from the business or home, except for most vehicle accidents. This all-inclusive coverage is known as "personal liability," "all perils," or "comprehensive family liability" coverage and similar names. It can cover your injuries in many situations in which you might think there would be no insurance coverage at all.

Here are some examples of accident situations in which personal liability coverage might apply.

**EXAMPLE 1:** Jack goes to the park and hits a softball that injures Candy, who is sunbathing in the picnic area nearby. If Jack had personal liability coverage as part of a business, homeowner's, or renter's policy, Candy could file a claim even though the accident took place away from Jack's business or home. The definition of "covered liability" in the personal liability coverage includes "all amounts the insured shall become legally obligated to pay" because of "any occurrence." Since neither the activity of softball nor the location of the park is

specifically excluded in the terms of the policy, the accident would be covered.

**EXAMPLE 2:** Eleven-year-old Johnny and his ten-year-old cousin Madonna, visiting from out of state, are up in a tree throwing rotten fruit at passing cars. A tomato splats on Roger's windshield, causing him to swerve his car and crash into Vera's Jeep parked in her driveway. Roger's injuries are probably covered by Johnny's parents' homeowner's policy. Johnny is covered because he is a "relative" living with the named insured—one or both of his parents.

And if it was Madonna who threw the tomato, the insurance would still cover the accident because she was a minor "in the care of" the insured when the accident happened, even though she does not live with Johnny's parents. Even though the kids were not at home when they caused the accident, the personal liability coverage of the homeowner's policy covers injuries caused by "any occurrence," without being limited to accidents on the property.

Although an automobile accident is involved, it would be covered by the homeowner's policy. Homeowner's policies exclude vehicle accidents if they are caused by an insured driving a vehicle. But here, because those the policy covered were not driving, the fact that the accident involved a car does not matter.

Vera can file a claim under Johnny's parents' coverage rather than against Roger, because the kids caused the "occurrence" that resulted in damage to her Jeep, and because personal liability coverage includes property damage.

Personal liability insurance may also cover injuries caused by:

- animals (the animal's owner would be liable and therefore covered by a personal liability policy), and
- a condition of the insured's property that causes an accident off the property (such as an overgrown bush that blocks a driver's view of an intersection, contributing to a car accident, or a tree root that has grown under the sidewalk causing it to buckle and someone to fall over it).

In fact, any kind of conduct that causes an accident and does not involve the insured driving a vehicle, may be covered by the personal liability coverage in a business, homeowner's, or renter's insurance policy. So, if there is any reason why someone (other than the driver of another car) is legally liable to you for an injury accident, it is worth pursuing a claim if that person has personal liability coverage.

## Personal Liability Coverage: What's Included, What Isn't

The following are common coverages and exclusions in business, homeowner's, or renter's personal liability insurance:

**People Insured**
- the named insured (the person named in the policy)
- any relative living with the named insured, and
- any minor living with or in the care of the named insured.

**Covered Liability**
Coverage is for any amount, up to the coverage limits, that the insured becomes legally obligated to pay as damages because of bodily injury or property damage caused by any occurrence, subject to exclusions contained in the policy.

**Exclusions**
Usually excluded—*not* covered—are accidents caused while the insured is operating a vehicle or watercraft; accidents on premises other than the named premises, that are owned, rented, or controlled by the insured; or accidents that occur in the course of any business operated by the insured other than a business named in the policy. Some policies also exclude intentional acts, such as assaults, that lead to accidental injuries.

## Your Own Health Coverage and Accident Claims

Normally, when you are ill or injured, you look to your own health coverage—through health insurance or a health maintenance organization (HMO), Medicare, or Medicaid—to take care of your medical bills. When you have been injured in an accident, however, you may also eventually receive compensation from another person's insurance company, or from your own vehicle insurance company if you had an accident with an uninsured motorist.

If you do receive compensation for your injuries but your medical bills have already been paid through your health coverage, you may be obligated to repay some or all of the amount to the health plan. Whether and how much you have to repay varies with the type of plan, and is determined by the terms of your policy or membership agreement with the health plan and by how the plan enforces those terms. Many health plans pay no attention to whether accident insurance compensates you for the same injuries that the health plan covers, and you get to keep your whole settlement. Other health plans, however, specify that you must reimburse them out of any accident insurance award you receive.

Following an auto accident, you may have the option to pay medical bills through either your health plan or through the medical payments provision of your auto insurance policy. As discussed earlier, determine immediately whether your health plan or your vehicle insurance medical payments coverage requires you to reimburse it fully if you collect later from another source. If one requires reimbursement and the other does not, you are usually better off using the one you don't have to repay.

## Health Coverage With an Insurance Company

Whether you must reimburse your private health insurance company depends on the terms of your health insurance policy. Read your policy to see if there is a section entitled "Right to Reimbursement." If so, and if the policy states that a right to reimbursement applies to third-party claims, then the insurance company has a right to ask you to repay it any amounts that it paid related to your injuries from the accident.

Even if a health insurance company has a right under the policy to seek reimbursement from you, whether it actually does so depends on whether it knows you have filed an accident claim. When you file your health insurance claim, it may ask whether the injuries were the result of an accident. It may also ask whether or not you have filed a claim for damages against the liable party. But if your claim form does not pose such questions, the insurance company may have no idea that you have filed and settled a claim for damages. Even if the company does file a request for reimbursement, you don't necessarily have to repay the full amount it claims. (How liens work and how to negotiate a smaller reimbursement are discussed in "Liens on Your Settlement Money" in Chapter 9.)

## Health Coverage With an HMO

Health maintenance organizations (HMOs) are group health plans that not only provide coverage for illness and injury but actually provide or arrange for the treatment. Most HMO membership agreements require you to reimburse them for medical expenses they have expended for accident injuries if you also receive compensation from the person at fault for the accident. When processing your claim for compensation (see Chapter 6) you will have to request copies of your medical records and billing from the HMO, which will probably alert the HMO that you are also filing a liability insurance claim.

When you're a member of an HMO, you will not have actually received a traditional bill for your treatment. When the HMO sends you copies of what it decides the cost of your treatment would have been, it will probably also send you a notice of the right to be reimbursed, called a lien. As with a health insurer's right to reimbursement, you may not have to repay the full amount the HMO claims. (See Chapter 9 for tips on negotiating a smaller reimbursement.)

### Employer's Self-Insured Health Plan

If you work for a large company or organization, it may provide you with its own self-insured health care plan instead of health insurance through an outside company. If so, the employer has a legal right to require you to reimburse it out of your damage award for any medical expenses the health plan pays you. Whether your company's plan actually contains this right to reimbursement depends on its specific terms. Check with your union or with your human resources office to see if your plan has a reimbursement clause. If it does, you should still try to negotiate for a smaller reimbursement. (See Chapter 9.)

### Workers' Compensation

If you receive workers' compensation benefits for a job-related accidental injury and also receive a damage award from a person other than your employer, the workers' compensation system has a right to be reimbursed by you for any amounts it paid for medical care. When it comes to seeking reimbursements, the workers' com-

pensation system operates slowly. Even if it has been many months since you collected both your workers' compensation claim and your liability damages, don't spend all your liability damages too quickly. A workers' compensation representative might still come knocking on your door one day asking for repayment of the money.

### Medicare and Medicaid

Medicare and Medicaid (called Medi-Cal in California) are federal government programs that provide some medical coverage for people who are older than 65 (Medicare) and for people with low incomes (Medicaid). Both Medicare and Medicaid have a legal right to reimbursement from you if you collect a damages award from a person liable for your injuries.

Because Medicare and Medicaid are huge and sometimes inefficient bureaucracies, they do not always realize that you have filed a claim for damages against a third party. Consequently, they do not always notify you right away that you must repay them out of your compensation. However, there is no legal time limit for Medicare or Medicaid to seek reimbursement. Even if you've settled your claim and Medicare or Medicaid hasn't requested reimbursement for accident-related medical bills, don't feel comfortable spending all your compensation money. Set aside an amount equal to what Medicare or Medicaid actually paid, and hold onto it for at least a year. That way, you will be prepared if the government suddenly asks to be reimbursed.

## No-Fault Laws: State Summaries

Below are descriptions of state no-fault laws. Also listed are miscellaneous other rules you should know.

## Terms Used in These Listings

**Statute.** No-fault rules are contained in the official laws of the state, called statutes. Statutes are identified by individual number, and in some states by an article or title number—referring to the actual volume in which the law can be found—as well. For example, the Hawaii no-fault law is found in the Hawaii Revised Statutes, title 24, section 431:10C-306.

**Legal abbreviations.** In this listing, common legal abbreviations are used when referring to the statutes. They include:

**Stat.**     statutes

**§**     section, referring to the specific numbered statute

**et seq.**     Latin for "and following." It appears after the number of a statute and means that the sections that immediately follow also apply to the same subject.

**Rev.**     revised, signifying that these are the updated statutes

**Gen.**     general

**Ann.**     annotated, meaning the volumes also include lists of cases that interpret the laws

**Art.**     article: The laws denoted this way have been divided into large separately numbered chunks, each chunk called an article, and within each article are numbered sections.

**PIP.** Personal Injury Protection, the official name for no-fault coverage. The PIP insurance carrier is your own insurance company with which you have no-fault coverage.

**Monetary threshold.** In some no-fault states, you are permitted to file a liability claim in addition to your PIP claim if your medical expenses have reached a certain level, called the monetary threshold. (See "No-Fault Automobile

Insurance," above.)

**Injury threshold.** In some no-fault states you are permitted to file a liability claim in addition to your PIP claim if your injuries are of a certain level of seriousness, usually defined by either the type of injury or its permanent effects. (See "No-Fault Automobile Insurance," above.)

**Right to reimbursement.** In some states, if you collect both PIP benefits and liability compensation from the party at fault, your PIP insurance carrier has a right to have you repay it for the PIP benefits.

**Make sure the law is current.** Laws change frequently. If you become involved in a dispute with an insurance company over the application of your state's no-fault rules, it's best to double check the exact language in its latest version. You can find the no-fault laws at your local law library, or you can access them online at www.nolo.com/statutes/index.cfm.

### District of Columbia

*Statute:* D.C. Code Ann. § 35-2101 et seq.

*Monetary threshold:* medical expenses or lost work income greater than PIP benefits actually available

*Injury threshold:* substantial permanent scarring or disfigurement, substantial permanent impairment that significantly affects the ability to perform professional activities or usual daily activities, or substantially total disability for 180 days

*Right to reimbursement*

### Florida

*Statute:* Fla. Stat. Ann. § 627.730 et seq.

*Injury threshold:* permanent injury, or significant and permanent scarring or disfigurement, or significant and permanent loss of important bodily function

*Right to reimbursement*

### Hawaii

*Statute:* Haw. Rev. Stat., Title 24, § 431:10C-306.

*Monetary threshold:* medical expenses or damages in excess of $5,000 in benefits provided by no-fault policy

*Injury threshold:* significant permanent loss of use of part or function of body, or permanent and serious disfigurement resulting in mental or emotional distress

### Kansas

*Statute:* Kans. Stat. Ann., ch. 40, art. 31, § 40-3101 et seq.

*Monetary threshold:* $2,000 in medical expenses

*Injury threshold:* permanent disfigurement, any fracture of weightbearing bone or compound, comminuted, compressed, or displaced fracture of any bone, permanent injury, or permanent loss of a body function

### Kentucky

*Statute:* Ky. Rev. Stat. Ann., Title XXV, § 304.39-010 et seq.

*Monetary threshold:* $1,000 in medical expenses

*Injury threshold:* permanent disfigurement, any fracture of weightbearing bone or compound, comminuted, compressed or displaced fracture of any bone, permanent injury or permanent loss of a body function

### Massachusetts

*Statute:* Mass. Gen. Laws Ann., ch. 23, § 6D.

*Monetary threshold:* $2,000 in reasonable medical expenses

*Injury threshold:* permanent and serious disfig-urement, fractured bone, or substantial loss of hearing or sight

### Michigan

*Statute:* Mich. Comp. Laws § 500.3101 et seq.

*Injury threshold:* serious impairment of a body function or permanent and serious disfigurement

Note: Michigan's threshold for a liability claim is the toughest in the country, but Michigan's PIP benefits are the highest, with no limit on medical expenses paid and the highest and longest income loss benefits.

*Right to reimbursement*

### Minnesota

*Statute:* Minn. Stat. § 65B.41 et seq.

*Monetary threshold:* $4,000 in medical expenses

*Injury threshold:* 60 days of disability, permanent injury, or permanent disfigurement

Note: Claim against liable party allowed only for amounts not paid by PIP coverage

### New Jersey

*Statute:* N.J. Stat. Ann. § 39:6A-1 et seq.

*Injury threshold:* "serious impact" on the life of the injured person

### New York

*Statute:* N.Y. Ins. Laws § 5101 et seq.

*Injury threshold:* "serious," which includes significant disfigurement, bone fracture, permanent limitation of use of body organ or member, significant limitation of use of body function or system, or substantially full disability for 90 days

### North Dakota

*Statute:* N.D. Cent. Code § 26.1-41 et seq.

*Monetary threshold:* medical expenses over $2,500

*Injury threshold:* "serious," which includes serious and permanent disfigurement, or disability of more than 60 days

## Pennsylvania

*Statute:* 75 Pa. Cons. Stat. § 1701 et seq.

*Injury threshold:* "serious injury"

Note: Cannot recover medical expenses or income loss from liable party that were already paid under PIP benefits

## Utah

*Statute:* Utah Code Ann. § 31A-22-306 et seq.

*Monetary threshold:* medical expenses over $3,000

*Injury threshold:* permanent disability or impairment, permanent disfigurement, or dismemberment. ■

Chapter 5

# How Much Is Your Claim
# for Injuries Worth?

You may have heard that insurance companies use a secret mathematical formula to figure out how much compensation should be paid to someone for accident injuries. The formula part is true, but it certainly isn't secret. And the formula doesn't actually determine how much compensation someone receives. It is just a device insurance adjusters use to begin the process of figuring out how much a claim is worth. A final determination about compensation is not made until several other facts are considered.

This chapter explains how insurance adjusters use the compensation formula and how they combine it with other facts to arrive at a figure they are willing to pay for a personal injury claim. Once you understand how the compensation formula works, you will be able to negotiate confidently for a final settlement figure within the same range an attorney would have gotten for you. And you will have saved the cost of paying the attorney.

In general, a person liable for an accident—and therefore his or her liability insurance company—must pay an injured person for:

- medical care and related expenses
- missed work time or other lost income
- pain and other physical suffering
- permanent physical disability or disfigurement
- loss of family, social, and educational experiences, and
- emotional damages resulting from any of the above.

While it is usually simple to add up the money spent and money lost, there is no precise way to put a dollar figure on pain and suffering, and on missed experiences and lost opportunities. That's where the damages formula comes in.

## The Damages Formula

At the beginning of negotiations on a claim, an insurance adjuster will add up the total medical expenses related to the injury. These expenses are referred to as "the medical special damages" or simply "specials." As a way to begin figuring out how much to compensate the injured person for pain and suffering, permanent disability, and emotional damages—together called "general damages"—the insurance adjuster will multiply the amount of special damages by about one-and-a-half to three times when the injuries are relatively minor, and up to five (and sometimes more) times when the injuries are particularly painful, serious, or long-lasting. After that amount is arrived at, the adjuster will then add on any income you have lost as a result of your injuries.

That total—medical specials multiplied by 1.5 to 5 (and occasionally higher), then added to lost income—becomes the number from which negotiations begin.

> **EXAMPLE:** Mary was injured in an auto accident. Her medical specials—the cost of her medical treatment—amounted to $600. There were no permanent effects from her injuries. Applying the damages formula to her claim, an insurance adjuster would begin with a figure of between $900 and $3,000 (1.5 to 5 x $600). This is added to Mary's lost income of $400 to get the figure from which negotiations will begin as compensation for Mary's injuries.
>
> Once this figure is arrived at, the adjuster would then factor in all the other variables discussed in this chapter to determine how much total compensation the insurance company was willing to pay Mary for her injuries.

## Insurance Adjusters Don't Reveal Their Formula

During negotiations on an insurance claim, adjusters usually will not tell you what formula they use to arrive at how much they believe a claim is worth, or even that they are using any formula at all. They are following a basic rule of negotiations: Do not let the other side know how or what you are thinking. Since the insurance adjusters won't let you know what formula they are using, it's probably a good idea not to let them know your thinking, either. Instead, you will simply negotiate total settlement amounts.

## The Deciding Factor: Which End Is Up?

There are two important points to remember about a damages formula. One is that the figure arrived at by multiplying special damages is only the starting point for reaching a settlement amount. After this starting point is reached, other facts about the accident and your injuries come into play. The second point is that because the starting formula could be anywhere between one-and-a-half to five times specials (and sometimes even more), it can produce considerably different numbers depending on which end of this multiplier spectrum is applied to your claim.

Several things determine which end of the damages formula to apply to the special damages in your claim.

- The more painful the type of injury you suffered, the higher the end of the formula you use.
- The more invasive and longer-lasting your medical treatment, the higher the formula.
- The more obvious the medical evidence of your injury, the higher the formula.
- The longer the recovery period from your injuries, the higher the formula.
- The more serious and visible any permanent effect of your injury, the higher the formula.

The rest of this chapter explains how these considerations raise or lower the numbers you plug into a damages formula, as well as the things that can increase or decrease your compensation once the formula has been arrived at. At the end of the chapter are a number of examples of accident injury situations with descriptions of the accidents, injuries, treatments, and expenses, plus explanations of how damages in those cases would be calculated.

## How Injuries Affect Compensation

As mentioned above, the amount you have spent on medical bills while having your injuries diagnosed and treated is referred to by insurance adjusters as medical special damages, medical specials, or simply specials. Medical specials are part of the damages formula used to figure out total damages. The amount by which specials are multiplied—normally, one-and-a-half to five, and occasionally more—depends on a number of factors discussed in this chapter, including the injuries you have suffered, the type and duration of medical treatment you receive, and the kind of medical providers from whom you receive treatment.

## Types of Injuries

The difficult part of figuring out compensation for someone injured in an accident is how to put a dollar value on pain and suffering. Since that is a large part of what the damages formula attempts to do, it stands to reason that the more painful the injury, the higher the multiplying number that gets plugged into the formula. And the way insurance companies begin looking at pain and suffering is by connecting types of injuries with levels of pain.

Of course, this is not very scientific. A sprained ankle can sometimes be more painful and persistent than a cracked ankle bone. Still, insurance adjusters use the type of injury as a starting place in deciding what numbers to plug into the damages formula. If your injury fits into one of the more serious injury categories described below, this typecasting can work to your advantage. If your injury is normally typecast as less serious, however, then you have to show through other means that your injury did indeed cause significant pain and suffering. (See "Demonstrating Pain and Suffering," below.)

The accident insurance adjusting business divides injuries into two main categories:

1. soft tissue injury, of which the major evidence is the description of discomfort by the patient, and
2. "hard" injury, which is an injury that can be specifically detected through medical examination.

### Soft Tissue Injuries

Injuries such as a sprained or strained back, neck, knee, or ankle are referred to as soft tissue injuries because they involve only muscles and other soft connective tissue. Insurance companies regard them as less serious than hard injuries and usually assign to them a damages formula multiplier of only one-and-a-half to three times specials (unless other factors discussed in this chapter bump that multiplier higher). Insurers reason that soft tissue injuries are usually not permanent or dangerous regardless of how painful they may be. And insurance companies also know that, should a claim ever get to court, it would be difficult for an injured person to prove clearly what the soft tissue injuries were.

### Condition of the Car May Affect Compensation

In determining your compensation for injuries from a traffic accident, an insurance adjuster will likely look at the condition of the cars involved to help gauge the extent of your injuries.

This can help or hurt your claim.

If the car in which you were driving or riding was badly smashed, that supports the idea that your injuries were severe and painful. If you have photographs of the badly damaged car, include them with your demand letter (see Chapter 6) and refer to them during your settlement negotiations (see Chapter 8). Either the size of the repair bill or the fact that the vehicle was totaled can support your claim of painful injuries.

On the other hand, if there is little or no damage to the car you were in, you will have a more difficult time convincing an adjuster that your injuries deserve much compensation. Particularly if the lack of damage is combined with soft tissue injury only, and your treatment consisted only of physical therapy or chiropractic care, an adjuster may well refuse to pay anything other than your medical bills. If you run into this stone wall with an adjuster, your best bet may be small claims court, where a judge is at least likely to award you a small amount of compensation if it is clear that the accident was not your fault. (See Chapter 10.)

### Hard Injuries

Hard injuries are considered more serious and are awarded higher damages—four or five times specials, and sometimes higher—than soft tissue injuries. So if you can point to anything in your medical records identifying an injury actually observed by the doctor by X-ray or by other test, or describing the injury as something other than a strain or sprain (a compressed or pinched nerve, for example, or a joint separation), the value of your claim for damages goes up. Likewise, an injury requiring any physical repair or intrusive examination by a doctor, from stitching a wound to setting a bone to arthroscopic examination of a joint, increases the value of your case regardless of all other considerations.

Categories of hard injuries include:

**Broken bones.** If X-rays show that any bone has suffered even a minor break, including a chip or crack, the numbers in your case will immediately move higher. Of course, insurance adjusters are not robots who simply see "broken bone" and then automatically raise the damage formula. They do distinguish between breaks that are serious and those that are less so. If the break is a fine crack in a tiny bone, for example, and does not require any treatment or affect the way you go about your daily life, the broken bone will not raise the damages formula as much as a more substantial, life-disrupting break that may have permanent consequences. As with all other injuries, the more serious you can show the break to be, the higher you move up the compensation ladder.

> **EXAMPLE 1:** Werner tripped and fell over a hose. At the emergency room, doctors found a small crack in his wrist. The bone required no cast, Werner required no treatment, and he lost no time from work.
>
> Because the doctors found a break, the multiplier in Werner's damages formula would go up from one-and-a-half times medical specials to perhaps three times. But because it involved no treatment, no substantial recovery time, and no permanent effects, it probably would not go any higher than that.

**EXAMPLE 2:** Alicia tripped and fell on a broken stair. Her wrist was fractured badly enough to require a cast for six weeks, another four weeks of physical therapy, and eight more weeks of only light use before it returned to normal.

Because the break required a cast and the time of recovery was relatively long, the damages formula applied to Alicia's injury would probably be about five times medical specials.

**Head injuries.** Any time someone suffers a head injury, there is the possibility that the effects of the injury will be much longer lasting than is obvious at first. What seems like a simple concussion from which you quickly recover can later turn into months or years of recurring headaches and dizziness. And this kind of recurring long-term head injury often does not appear in the original diagnosis because its causes can be detected only by sophisticated and expensive testing.

Insurance adjusters know that head injuries can last a long time and that symptoms can recur after recovery seems to be complete. A head injury usually increases how much the claim is worth. And often it speeds the negotiation process, because the adjuster wants to settle before bigger bills related to the injury are incurred.

If you suffered any kind of head injury, check your medical records for any notation of the injury: concussion, a period of unconsciousness, however brief, or dizziness, disorientation, or nausea. Make specific mention of it in your claim even if other injuries seem more serious. And if you have any long-term effects such as continuing headaches or dizziness, report them to your doctor and emphasize in your claim that you are still suffering from the effects of your head injury.

**Separations, dislocations, and ligament or cartilage tears.** Whenever a doctor describes your injury with a name other than a sprain, strain, or bruise, the injury is considered more serious—that is, given a higher multiplier in the damages formula. Joint dislocation or separation gives the impression of great pain and delicate recovery, whether or not it was actually more serious than something called a sprain. The same thing is true for the word "torn" for a ligament or cartilage. A tear is considered more serious than a stretch or strain or sprain, even though the treatment and healing time may be exactly the same.

## Some Injuries Deserve Special Mention

Anytime you suffer an injury to a joint, there is the possibility of future arthritic problems in the joint. When a joint is injured, blood usually collects there and eventually calcifies, creating a hard and rough surface in the joint that can later—often not until years later—cause pain and difficulty in movement. In your medical records, however, doctors do not normally mention such potential arthritic changes because it is usually not possible to predict whether such changes will later prove troublesome.

If you suffer a joint injury, ask your doctor whether future arthritic change is a possibility. If the doctor makes a note of the possibility in your medical records, it will give you more ammunition in your claim for damages.

Whether or not the possibility of arthritic change appears in your medical records, make sure specifically to mention this possibility in your claim for damages to the insurance company. Such a reminder helps make the insurance adjuster take your injury more seriously and may also help by showing the adjuster that you are organized and have done your medical homework.

**Wounds.** If your injuries include any gash, tear, or cut serious enough to require treatment, that may slightly increase the value of your claim. If the treatment included stitching the wound, the value of your claim goes up slightly more. And if the wound leaves a scar that may be permanent, the value of the case may go up significantly. (See "Demonstrating Pain and Suffering," below.)

**Spinal disk or vertebrae injury.** Movement or displacement of a spinal disk or of the space between vertebrae sounds more serious than "strained neck or back." Insurance adjusters often award more compensation to claimants who describe back or neck injuries in specific medical terms rather than simply saying "strained," even if it is exactly the same injury. Emergency rooms and orthopedists usually take X-rays of the area of the spine—lumbar or lumbosacral (lower), thoracic (middle), or cervical (upper)—in which an injured person complains of pain. Those X-rays may reveal some slight abnormality either in a disk or in the space between vertebrae. Vertebrae are described by reference to the number of the vertebrae in question, such as "slight narrowing in L4-L5 spacing."

If you find any mention in your medical records of such abnormality in a numbered vertebra, repeat that diagnosis word-for-word in your negotiations with the insurance company as a way of demonstrating the seriousness of your injury, regardless of how much or how little treatment you received.

## Nature and Extent of Medical Expenses

According to insurance adjusters, not all medical services are created equal. Both the nature and the duration of a medical service can affect how insurance companies perceive it, as can the type of medical person or facility providing the service.

Some of the variables are discussed here.

**Treatment versus diagnosis.** Before you can be treated for an injury, medical personnel have to diagnose it. In many cases, the diagnostic process is relatively quick, and the charge for it amounts to a small part of your medical bills, as compared with the cost of treatment. In such cases, insurance companies do not usually bother to make any distinction between diagnosis and treatment. They lump all your medical bills together into one medical specials amount.

### You Do Not Have Whiplash

Everyone is familiar with the infamous term "whiplash" used to describe the neck injury and resulting headaches people commonly suffer in auto accidents. Whiplash is not really a medical term, but it has become so widespread that even doctors occasionally use it now, sometimes even in medical records.

Although the term was once a perfectly good one for describing an often very painful and long-lasting neck muscle injury, it has become too much associated with exaggerated insurance claims for you to use it in describing your injuries to an insurance company. If you have a neck injury that might be called whiplash, look in your medical records for some specific medical description of your injury and use that description in all your negotiations with the insurance company. If you cannot find any specific description, then refer to your injury as a severe strain of the cervical spine and supporting musculature, or any other terms that fairly describe your injuries—such as acute neck strain with severe consequent headache. But avoid using that poor old term "whiplash."

Sometimes, though, doctors will put a person through many tests and examinations simply trying to diagnose what is wrong, running up large medical bills in the process. If most of the medical bills are for diagnosis only, and the injury winds up requiring little treatment, an insurance adjuster might not view the total medical specials as accurately reflecting the injured person's pain and suffering. Consequently, the adjuster might use a lower multiplier for those medical bills in arriving at the appropriate range of damages.

**M.D.s and hospitals versus non-M.D.s.** One of the insurance industry's strong prejudices is in favor of mainstream Western treatment by physicians, hospitals, and medical clinics—and against physical therapy, chiropractic, acupuncture, and other nonmainstream medicine. Any medical bill you have incurred at the hands or machines of a medical doctor, hospital, or medical clinic, no matter how outrageously expensive, will be considered legitimate by almost any insurance adjuster and will usually be given a high multiplier in the damages formula. Treatments by nonphysician medical providers are often equally effective and much less costly, but insurance adjusters tend to apply lower multipliers.

For example, in accidental injury claims, physical therapy is a common treatment, yet it is generally considered to be lower in the pecking order than other kinds of medical treatment. If you receive a few weeks of physical therapy prescribed and administered by your doctor's office, an insurance adjuster may lump it in with other medical specials. But if you have physical therapy for months and the therapy accounts for the largest part of your medical bills by far, the insurance adjuster is likely to use a lower multiplier when fitting your medical specials into the damages formula.

Also, where you receive physical therapy may affect how the insurance company views it. If your doctor prescribes physical therapy but you receive the actual treatment outside the doctor's office and beyond the doctor's control, the insurance adjuster might discount the physical therapy bills. That's because insurance companies believe that when left to their own devices, physical therapists tend to treat patients endlessly. And if you seek physical therapy independently, without it having been recommended or prescribed by your physician, an insurance adjuster is likely to discount it even more.

**Treatments by chiropractors, acupuncturists, acupressurists, herbalists, massage therapists, and other nonphysician healers.** Unless bestowed with the rare blessing of a doctor's prescription, other nontraditional treatments are given even less weight than physical therapy. This does not mean that you cannot be reimbursed at all for these treatments by the liable person's insurance company. But it does mean that the insurance adjuster handling your claim will not count these expenses very highly when deciding how to multiply medical specials within the damages formula. Of course, your primary concern should be to obtain the kind of medical care with which you are most comfortable and that you think will help you most. But you should be aware that if you choose services not provided by a physician, an insurance company is likely to compensate you at a lower rate.

**Duration of treatment.** Logic says that if an injury receives a long period of medical treatment, the injury requires a long period to heal, and that translates to a high degree of pain and suffering. So, if you undergo a long period of treatment, you can argue to an insurance adjuster that the long treatment was evidence of the seriousness of the injury. (See "Preparing a Demand Letter" in Chapter 6, and Chapter 8.)

However, insurance adjusters are suspicious of physical therapists and chiropractors, believing that they often give treatment longer than necessary to keep their money rolling in. So, if you have had a long period of physical therapy or chiropractic treatments, an insurance adjuster is less likely to consider that as good evidence of the seriousness of your injury than if you had received a long period of treatment from a physician or medical clinic.

## Demonstrating Pain and Suffering

The type of injury you suffer and the nature and duration of your treatment are the two basic indicators to an insurance company of the degree of pain and suffering you have endured. This section discusses some additional factors you can point out to raise an insurance adjuster's awareness of your pain and suffering caused by the accident.

You can keep a record of these factors by noting them on the Accident Claim Worksheet at the back of this book.

### Do Not Rush to Settle

The seriousness of your injuries, and therefore the amount of compensation you receive, is determined by:
- the exact nature of the injuries
- the amount and type of your medical treatment
- how long your recovery takes, and
- whether you have any residual or permanent pain or disability.

For most injuries, it is impossible to know fully what any of these elements will be until weeks or months after the accident, when treatment has ended and the injuries have healed. If you attempt to settle your claim too early, you may be figuring your compensation based on incomplete information—and you may seriously undervalue your claim.

You may be faced with an urgent need to pay medical bills and to make up for lost income. Therefore you may be tempted to accept an insurance adjuster's attempts to get you to jump at an early offer. But if possible, resist the temptation to settle early. In the long run, you will learn what your claim is truly worth and then be able to collect the full and appropriate amount from the insurance company.

## Medication

The fact that you have been prescribed medication to relieve pain, inflammation, or any other injury symptoms may help to convince an insurance adjuster that your injuries are serious. The stronger the medication and the longer it is prescribed, the greater its influence on your settlement. This is not a very precise measure, of course. Some doctors prescribe medication much more readily than others. And some patients request medication at a certain level of pain while others don't want it or need it. But insurance adjusters are always looking for something concrete indicating that a doctor thought an injury was painful—and a medication prescription serves that purpose.

## Length of Recovery

To an insurance company, the longer the recovery period, the greater an injured person's pain and suffering. The most effective way to let an insurance adjuster know how long your recovery takes is to have that fact indicated in your medical records. Sometimes that task is easy because your doctor has made a notation in your medical chart that recovery is expected to take a certain number of weeks or months, or that you should not engage in certain activities for a certain amount of time.

In many cases, however, the only way your actual recovery time makes it into your medical records is if you report your progress, or lack of it, to the doctor. Many of us get tired of going to the doctor when we know all the doctor will do is nod, write something down, tell us to come back if things don't get better—and then send a bill.

But going to your doctor to report on your recovery can be very important to your claim for two reasons. First, the mere fact that your records show a doctor visit four, six, or 12 weeks after an accident indicates that your injury required ongoing attention. And second, when you visit your doctor and report continuing pain, discomfort, stiffness, or immobility, that specific continuing problem will be noted in the medical records you will later send to the insurance company as part of your claim. (See Chapter 6.) Remarkably, an insurance adjuster will often accept your report of pain and discomfort as true if the doctor writes it down, but the adjuster may discount the very same report of pain and

discomfort you make during the course of your claim if it was not reported to the doctor earlier.

## Residual or Permanent Injury

If you can show that an injury you suffered in an accident has left any long-lasting or permanent effect—referred to as a "residual injury"—such as scarring or back or joint stiffness, the amount of your damages award can go up significantly. The simple and obvious reason that even a relatively small residual disability or disfigurement can greatly increase your award is that you will suffer from it over a long time. And naturally, the more serious the effect on your life—work, home, or recreation—the higher your damages go.

**Scars.** A common permanent residual injury is scarring, from the original injury or from medical repairs. Particularly large and obvious scarring can mean quite a lot in damages, both because of the cosmetic embarrassment it causes and because scar tissue can make an area of flesh less flexible. If there is scarring at any joint or in any other area of the body that flexes—such as the webbing of fingers or toes—it might cause a permanent even though slight loss of mobility, and so might justify higher damages.

The damages for disfigurement go up if the scarred part of the body is normally visible. Scars usually covered by clothes are not considered as important unless they are large enough to cause you embarrassment in your love life or when you want to wear a bathing suit. Scars visible on hands and arms can be considered important if they are large enough that you feel the need to keep them hidden. And any scar on the face and neck—even if small—always increases damages.

Scarring is also one of the few areas in which women sometimes benefit by our society's stubbornly resistant sexism. A woman who receives a permanent scar is normally considered to have been damaged by it far more than a man with an identical scar. Unfortunately, ageism may rear its ugly head here, too. A young single woman is often compensated more for scars than an older married woman, on the assumption that a facial scar may more strongly affect a young single woman's social life. Insurance adjusters are usually socially aware enough to know that they should not openly discuss these biases, especially not directly with the injured person. Nonetheless, you should be aware that these societal prejudices do affect the settlement judgment of most adjusters.

One way to demonstrate to an insurance company how much your scarring is worth is to obtain a medical opinion about the cost of having the scar removed or repaired. Ask your doctor to refer you to a plastic surgeon for an opinion about whether your scar could be removed, and specifically ask how much such a procedure would cost. You can then include both the cost of the examination by the plastic surgeon and the potential cost of repair in the medical costs you use to figure how much your case is worth. Specifically, include the cost of scar removal—whether or not you will actually undergo such a procedure—in your demand letter to the insurance company. (See "Preparing a Demand Letter" in Chapter 6.)

**Back or joint injuries.** In general, if you have an injury to a disk in the spine, or a narrowing, displacement, or other damage to a vertebra, or a dislocation, ligament, or cartilage injury to any joint, you will most likely suffer some permanent effect, even if slight. The pain may subside and the injury may stabilize or "resolve" as the doctors say, but there is a medical likelihood that some pain, discomfort, or lack of mobility will continue or will reoccur as you get older.

If you have had such an injury, your claim for damages should indicate your injury is permanent and therefore deserving higher compensation. And if you can get your doctor to mention in your medical records the possibility of

some permanent or residual effect, you will have documented support for your claim. The simplest way to get your doctor to make a notation about permanent effects is to ask.

Toward the last part of your treatment, ask your doctor's opinion about whether there is a likelihood—doctors rarely speak in anything more definite than "likelihoods"—that you may have recurring or degenerative (showing up later in life) problems as a result of your injuries. If the answer is yes, ask that the doctor note it in your medical records. And if the doctor asks why you want it noted, there is no reason not to say that you want it for an insurance claim you are filing against the person who caused your accident.

**Consult a lawyer if you suffer serious permanent injury.** If you have suffered any injury that is likely to be permanent—such as substantial visible scarring, a limp, bad back, or other disability—you may have a right to very high damages beyond the scope of the damages formula discussed in this book. This is particularly true if you may need future medical treatment to cope with your injury. In such cases, it may be wise to consult with a lawyer who specializes in personal injury cases.

Even if your doctor does not note the likelihood of permanent problems, you are still permitted to raise the possibility in your claim to the insurance company, just as you would mention future problems with any injury to a joint.

## Physical and Emotional Distress

It is not only pain that gives you a right to be compensated, but also any other kind of physical discomfort. Loss of sleep, trouble eating or digesting, stomach upset, and the side effects of medication are just some of the physical miseries in addition to pain for which you have a right to be compensated.

Emotional difficulties, too, can be compensated. Physical injuries can cause stress, embarrassment, depression, or strains on family relationships—for example, the inability to take care of children, anxiety over the effects of an accident on an unborn child, or interference with sexual relations.

As with pain, however, physical or emotional suffering can be difficult to demonstrate. Sometimes the discomforts or disruptions are obvious. If you have a broken arm, you cannot easily care for your small children; if you have a slipped disk in your back, sleeping is going to be a problem. An effective way to show you've suffered physical discomfort is to report it to your doctor, who will then note it in your medical file, which you will eventually show to the insurance adjuster handling your claim. Insurance adjusters more readily accept as true something that appears in a medical record than something that you report directly to the insurance adjuster.

If your discomfort or emotional distress is serious enough that you have to seek assistance from someone other than the doctor treating your original injury—a dietician for eating problems, a psychologist or other therapist to cope with pain or stress—these expenses also become part of your medical special damages, and the records of the person assisting you can serve as proof of the problem.

Offering psychological records may open the door. If you've been seeing a counselor for other reasons, make sure they start a separate set of records related to your auto accident, so that you don't have to send the insurance company your while life story. And be aware that the adjuster may become very interested in your psychological history once you open the door. You are entitled to your privacy, especially when there's only an insurance claim and not a lawsuit, so don't send anything you're not comfortable sending.

## The Proof Is Up to You

Many of the things that can establish the amount of pain and suffering you have experienced and will continue to experience can best be shown if you take charge of documenting them.

- If you have pain or discomfort and are being treated by a physician, make sure you fully report it to the physician so that it will be noted in your medical records.
- If you believe you need medication to control your pain or discomfort, don't be too brave, too shy, or too stubborn to ask for it.
- If you are suffering continued pain or discomfort but do not have any further medical appointments scheduled, consider scheduling one. It makes good medical sense and will document your continued problems.
- If your pain or discomfort is interfering with your ability to lead your normal life, write down any daily activities you are unable to do or that you are having difficulty doing because of your injuries.
- If your injuries can be seen—wounds, swelling, discoloration—photograph them regularly and indicate on each photograph the date on which it was taken.

In addition to taking the steps described above, keeping a contemporaneous log or diary of everything you experience as a result of the accident—missed work, headaches, times of depression, sleepless nights—can be extremely helpful when you have to explain your damages to an insurance adjuster. At the time of the accident, you may feel that you could not possibly forget the details of your injuries and their effects on you. However, many people find that their memories fade quite rapidly. A diary or log can help you to combat this problem.

## Life Disruption

Accident injuries can cause a number of unfortunate results that cannot easily be assigned dollar values but still amount to very real and considerable losses. And since money is the only way these losses can be compensated, they must be figured into your damages compensation. Once again, the damages formula is the way this figuring is done.

Any substantial loss of time, opportunities, pleasures, or effort can be compensated by raising the multiplier used in the formula used to arrive at your general damages, just as the multiplier goes up if you have a serious, long-term, or permanent injury. For example, a claim based on a soft tissue injury that might have a multiplier of one-and-a-half times medical specials could go up to two or three times specials because the injuries caused you to miss a planned vacation or lose out on a special event.

There is no restriction on the types of nonmonetary losses that can increase your general damages. Anything important to you that you missed because of your injuries can be included in a claim for compensation. Here are some of the more common kinds of nonmonetary losses for which compensation is paid:

**Missed school or training.** If your injuries have caused you to miss school or training, or studying for school or training, you will have to make that time up at some point. The difficulty you experience in making up that missed time—perhaps you will have to give up a number of evenings and weekends to catch up, or perhaps you will lose an entire semester of school—will determine how significantly your general damages should be increased.

**Missed vacation or recreation.** If your injuries have caused you to cancel a vacation, family visit, or other trip or event, you are entitled to extra compensation because of it. Similarly, if you have had to give up your regular recreation activities for an extended time—if you are a runner or hiker or other exerciser who has been unable to exercise or someone who regularly takes dance class but has been unable to for some time after an accident—you are entitled to compensation for that loss.

**Canceled special event.** If your injuries made it impossible for you to attend an important or personally meaningful event such as a wedding, funeral, graduation, conference, or reunion, you are entitled to compensation for the loss. Of course, in order to have an insurance adjuster take your claim for compensation seriously, it must have been a onetime event that will not be repeated.

**Loss of consortium.** If you are married or, in a very few states, in a committed unmarried relationship, you may be able to claim damages for loss of consortium—the inability to have sexual relations because of your injuries. The loss of consortium must continue for a significant period of time—probably a few months—before it will be taken seriously, but if that's the case, you should definitely include it in your claim, and the insurance company should take it into account.

## High Multiplier When Many Factors Line Up

As discussed throughout this chapter, in most claims a multiplier of between one-and-a-half to five times medical costs is used to arrive at a base negotiating figure—not including lost income. However, in a few claims, certain factors line up so overwhelmingly for the injured person that the top multiplier of five is simply not high enough. In those claims, the multiplier might move up to six, seven, or even as high as ten times special damages.

Most of us tend to believe that our own pain and discomfort is very bad. But don't quickly jump to the conclusion that your claim is one of those entitled to the highest compensation. In fact, only a few claims justify a multiplier of more than five.

In order to realistically consider a multiplier of more than five, *you must have had a serious injury, and most, if not all, of the following factors must be present:*

- the other party's fault must be obvious and almost total
- your injuries must be unquestionably observed or detected by medical examination
- your injuries must be obviously painful and dramatic—a fracture, or a wound, tear, or displacement that requires surgical treatment, or that cannot be successfully repaired
- diagnosis and treatment must come primarily from physicians and hospitals
- recovery must be prolonged (six months or more)
- you must suffer some permanent consequence—pain, immobility, weakness, discomfort, scarring—that is medically documented
- your physicians must clearly indicate that you will have recurring, degenerative, or future problems as a result of the injuries, even if they have stabilized for the time being.

If all or almost all of these factors are present in your claim, you may be justified in seeking more than five times your medical specials. At least in your formal demand for compensation (Chapter 6) and your early negotiations with the insurance company (Chapter 8), you can begin with an amount that leaves room for a settlement of more than five times specials.

But the fact that you feel justified in initially seeking such an amount doesn't mean that you will receive it. You may find that the insurance adjuster points out weak spots in your claim. (See Chapter 8.) Or you may ultimately find that you have simply inflated in your own mind the seriousness of your injuries, and therefore inflated your expectations. Be aware that if you allow yourself to get carried away with the unjustified hope of a very high settlement when the facts of your case don't support it, you will only prolong what is already a lengthy settlement process, leaving yourself open to great frustration and disappointment. So, make sure that your claim really fits the profile outlined above before you begin thinking of a multiplier of more than four or five times your medical costs.

**EXAMPLE:** Driving her car, Bea was slammed into from behind by a truck. The force of the impact drove her face into the steering wheel, breaking her jaw and driving a tooth through her lip. Her jaw was wired shut for six weeks and she had pain and difficulty eating for over a year. She now has a small scar on her lip and has lost a bit of feeling there. Her medical specials were $8,000. She was retired, so she lost no income.

The accident was entirely the fault of the truck driver. Bea's injuries were dramatic and very painful, requiring over a year's recovery and leaving her with both a scar and some loss of sensation in her lip, which seems to be permanent. Because of all these factors, Bea is likely to receive a settlement of between $40,000 and $60,000.

## Lost Income

You are entitled to reimbursement from the person responsible for an accident for any income you have lost because of the accident or your injuries. This includes both income lost because of time spent unable to work and time missed because you were undergoing treatment for your injuries. The right to be reimbursed applies whether you have a full-time or part-time job, regular or occasional employment, an hourly wage or weekly or monthly salary, or are self-employed.

Income loss is not a part of the amount multiplied in the formula applied to special damages. It is added on after the multiplied amount has been arrived at.

> **EXAMPLE:** After an accident, your medical expenses total $400, and your income loss is $500. Because your injury was soft tissue only, a formula of two times specials is applied. Only your medical expenses of $400 would be multiplied by two, not your $500 income loss. Instead, the $500 income loss would be added on to the multiplied total. In this example, the formula would be 2 x $400 = $800, plus $500 lost income, for a formula total of $1,300.

This total only begins negotiations, and it can go up or down depending on the facts discussed in "Arriving at a Final Compensation Value," below.

### Sick Leave and Vacation Pay

The fact that you were able to take sick leave or vacation pay for the time you missed, and therefore did not directly lose income, does not matter. You were entitled to use that sick leave or vacation time for other periods when you might have needed or wanted it. Therefore, using up

sick leave or vacation pay is considered the same as losing the pay itself.

To be reimbursed for lost income, you must be able to show two things:

- the time you missed from work because of your accident, and
- how much money you would have made during the time you missed.

(See "Documenting Lost Income" in Chapter 6 for a discussion of how to demonstrate these losses.)

## Lost Opportunities

In addition to time lost from work, you are entitled to be reimbursed for work opportunities you lost because of the accident and your injuries. Of course, it's harder to prove you lost income by missing a job interview or a sales meeting than showing you lost income by missing actual work.

But even if you cannot point to specific dollar amounts you lost, the fact that an insurance adjuster knows that lost potential income is a valid part of your claim will move your final compensation amount upward. How much your final compensation is raised will depend on how strong your proof is of lost income opportunity, and how much that lost opportunity might have cost you.

## Property Damage

If someone is liable to you for your personal injuries, he or she is also liable for any damage caused to your property in the same accident. Property damage occurs most frequently in vehicle accidents, not only to the vehicle itself but also to its contents. The value of anything you were carrying in the car or any equipment you were wearing while riding a cycle at the time of the accident should be included in a property damage claim.

Property damage can occur in other types of accidents as well. The clothes, watch, or other jewelry you are wearing, or any object you happen to be carrying, may be damaged.

Property damage claims are not a part of the damages formula for figuring injury compensation. Instead, they are figured separately, and in the case of vehicle damage they are often settled on their own far more quickly than the related injury claims. (See Chapter 7 for a discussion of how much a property damage claim is worth and what is required to settle the claim.)

## Arriving at a Final Compensation Value

Now that you know how the damages formula can be applied to your injuries, and how lost income and property damage are added to the damage formula total, you are more than halfway home to figuring out the total compensation value of your claim. But the remaining parts of figuring out the value of your claim are also important if you want to settle your case for the full amount to which you are entitled—without wasting a lot of time and energy trying to obtain compensation that is unrealistically high.

Basically, the other elements in deciding how much your claim is worth boil down to how the insurance company believes a jury would decide your claim if it were to wind up in court. And in measuring its chances in court, the insurance company has to consider the cost of putting up a legal fight, on top of what a jury might award you, compared with the amount for which your claim could be settled without going to court. To calculate these relevant factors, the insurance company looks at a number of elements.

## Assigning Fault

The degree of fault of each person is the most important factor affecting how much of the damages formula you are likely to receive. The damages formula tells you how much your injuries *might be* worth, but only after you figure in the question of fault do you know how much your claim is *actually* worth—that is, how much an insurance company will pay you.

> **EXAMPLE:** The cracked wrist bone you suffer in a fall results in $2,000 in medical specials, but it heals in a few weeks and you suffer no permanent injury. Applying the damages formula to your injuries might result in a figure of between $7,000 and $10,000, depending on all the other facts previously discussed in this chapter.
>
> If your accident was clearly and completely someone else's fault—a stair crumbled and broke under your foot—then your claim is likely to be worth the full amount of the formula total, that is, around $10,000.
>
> If, on the other hand, the accident was partly your fault, the amount your claim is worth would be reduced by the degree you were to blame—expressed in "percentage" of fault. (See "How Your Carelessness Affects Your Claim," in Chapter 2.) So, if you were 25% at fault for the accident, your claim would be reduced by 25% from a $7,000 to $10,000 range to a range of $3,750 to $7,500.
>
> If it appeared that you were mostly at fault, the value of your claim would be greatly reduced, perhaps to nothing but more likely to a very small amount referred to as "nuisance value." (See below.)

Of course, as discussed, determining fault for an accident is not an exact science. But in most claims, both you and the insurance adjuster will at least have some idea of whether you were entirely at fault, a little at fault, or a lot at fault. And whatever that rough percentage of your comparative fault might be—10%, 50%, 75%—is the amount by which the damages formula total will be reduced to arrive at a final claim figure. (See the examples below to review how degrees of fault are applied in different accident situations.)

In claims negotiations, some insurance adjusters will discuss comparative negligence in terms of specific percentages. Others will discuss who was at fault, or who was negligent, or who violated what rules or laws, but they will never actually put a percentage figure on anyone's degree of fault. Don't worry about it either way. Although it may be useful for you to begin the negotiations by using a specific comparative fault percentage, it doesn't matter how the insurance adjuster phrases things. Just be aware that how much you appear to have been at fault is the crucial element in an insurance adjuster's decision about how much to offer you as a settlement for your injuries.

## The Intangibles

In almost every claim there is at least one thing, in addition to the basic facts of the accident and of your injuries, that might push your settlement toward the higher end of the range of compensation. Usually you will never know whether one of these "intangible" factors has actually increased your settlement. But emphasizing these intangible factors in nego-tiations will at least increase the odds that you will receive as much as possible out of your claim.

### Your Effectiveness as a Potential Witness

One of the most important factors in an insurance adjuster's decision about what your claim is worth is how convincing you are about the accident,

your injuries, and your other damages. An insurance adjuster is more likely to be sympathetic to your claim if he or she believes you are giving an accurate picture of the accident and your injuries. If you are organized and understand how the claims system works, the insurance adjuster will realize you are unlikely to settle the case for less than it is worth. And the insurance adjuster knows that if you are both organized and believable, a jury is more likely to give you a substantial award if your claim should ever go to court.

### An Unfavorable Insured

There may be something about the person who caused the accident that would increase the likelihood that a jury would favor your story over that person's, or would consider the accident or your injuries in a light more favorable to you. And if an insurance adjuster knows that a jury is likely to award higher or lower damages, then the adjuster is likely to increase or decrease your settlement.

For example, if you have had a traffic accident with someone who was driving too fast in a souped-up car, a jury is more likely to be sympathetic to you than to the other driver. The insurance adjuster knows that. And if you show the insurance adjuster that you know it, too—a specific mention of those circumstances in your negotiations would show it—you may get a faster and easier settlement of your claim. (See Chapters 6 and 8.)

Other examples may work either for or against you. If your injury is the fault of a big company or the employee of a big company, chances are a jury would favor you as "the little person." On the other hand, settlement awards against local government entities are usually lower because adjusters for the city or county know that juries do not like to spend taxpayer dollars on high damage awards.

## Witnesses

Having one or more witnesses to corroborate your version of the accident, or to support your contentions about how much your injuries have interfered with your life, can increase your settlement. A witness takes your claim out of the "my word against yours" category.

## Dramatic Advantage

Sometimes something that did not actually affect the amount of fault in an accident or worsen your injuries can increase your settlement because it works emotionally in your favor. If, for example, a police report or a witness says that a person involved in the accident had alcohol on his breath, the odds of your getting a higher settlement go up even though you cannot prove the person was legally intoxicated. Similarly, your seriously damaged car—pictures can be very effective—supports the idea that you were seriously injured even though there might not be any direct relationship between how damaged the car was and how damaged you were.

Another example of a dramatic issue that could increase a settlement is pregnancy. Even if there is no evidence that a fetus has been injured in an accident, and upon delivery it appears that the baby suffered no ill effects, a parent's fear of possible injury can be worth a considerable increase in your settlement. Likewise, the emotional distress caused to you and your small child if the child was riding in the car with you is something to emphasize in your claim for compensation.

If the accident or your injuries have made you fearful of certain situations or concerned about the injured part of your body, you may be able to collect a higher damage award even though there is no medical evidence of permanent injury. This is particularly true if you are an older person, disabled, or otherwise particularly vulnerable.

## Your Patience

Because negotiations about a settlement can take time, your ability to be patient and wait for the best possible offer might affect how much you will receive. Insurance adjusters never immediately offer the full amount they are actually prepared to pay. (See "How the Negotiation Process Works" in Chapter 8.) If you are in a hurry to get your settlement, you might settle for less than you could have gotten if you had been willing to play out your hand as far as it would go.

While patience is paramount, you must also be wary of the time limits within which you must file a lawsuit should your negotiations prove unsuccessful. (See "State Statutes of Limitations" in Chapter 8.)

## Nuisance Value

Insurance adjusters think some claims are worth nothing at all. The reason may be that the person making the claim was completely at fault, or that someone other than the insured person was completely at fault, or that the claimant's injuries were not caused by the accident, or that the claimant had no real injuries at all. In each of these situations, an insurance adjuster may at first completely deny the injured person's claim, saying that the insurance company will not pay any compensation.

In many cases, though, an insurance adjuster's initial refusal to make any settlement will eventually turn into an offer to settle the case for a small amount known as "nuisance value." The term comes from the insurance company's idea that it is better to pay a little bit of money than to have to deal with the nuisance of a claim that will not go away. Insurance adjusters won't usually use the term nuisance value, but when they make a very low offer bearing no relation to the damages formula, that's what they're doing.

As with all other categories in accident settlements, there is no fixed amount for a nuisance value settlement. In claims with medical bills under a thousand dollars, a nuisance value settlement is often equal to the amount of the medical bills—or even half of the medical bills—with nothing for income loss, pain and suffering, general damages, or anything else.

Where the person filing the claim is not able to show any real injuries—small medical bills, soft tissue injury that no doctor has been able to diagnose—an insurance adjuster will often make a nuisance value offer of $500 or $750. On the other hand, if there are medical bills and lost income in the thousands of dollars, and a serious, painful, or permanent injury—all of which would cause the damages formula to come out with a figure of as much as $10,000 to $15,000—a nuisance value settlement could be $2,000 to $3,000.

---

### Even Nuisance Value Is Negotiable

Even when all you will get out of a claim is its nuisance value, remember that any offer of settlement is negotiable. So if you are forced by the circumstances of your accident to settle for some nuisance value amount, you don't have to take the first amount offered. Nuisance value figures probably won't change too much through bargaining, but if you can get an adjuster to move from $500 to $1,000, for example, it certainly will have been worth that extra phone call or two of negotiation.

---

## Examples of How Much Different Claims Are Worth

Several different situations are described below—different accidents, injuries, medical treatments, and intangibles—with an explanation of what the appropriate range of settlement amounts might be in each one.

These examples show how several different factors in any one accident operate together to determine a final compensation amount. Even if a particular example does not apply directly to your circumstances, reading through each of them can help you understand how the different elements in your claim will determine how much it is worth.

### 1. Auto Accident, Short-Term Soft Tissue Injury, Extra Damages for Missed Special Event

A car hits Olly's car from behind at a stop sign. Olly's neck snaps forward, but he is otherwise unhurt.

Olly develops a headache and stiff neck. He is examined, X-rayed, put in a cervical collar, and told to stay in bed until he can move around comfortably.

Olly misses three days' work, as well as his close friend's 50th birthday party in a city a couple of hundred miles away.

The next week, Olly returns to work. His doctor now says Olly can go without the collar. Olly is back to normal in about four weeks.

The cost for Olly's medical treatments—his medical specials—was as follows:

| | |
|---|---:|
| Emergency room/doctor visits | $750 |
| X-rays | 190 |
| Prescription medication | 58 |
| Cervical collar | 65 |
| Total | $1,063 |

Because Olly's injuries were soft tissue—that is, did not involve broken bones, wounds, dislocations, or other medically observable injuries—the damages formula used to figure his claim would be only about 1.5 to 3 times his medical specials of $1,063. This would be between $1,595 and $3,190, plus his lost wages. Olly's pay is $14 per hour; he missed three days (3 x 8 hours) of work for a total lost wages of $392.

Olly would be entitled to the full value of his damages because he was in no way comparatively negligent in the accident. Also, losing something special—going to his close friend's 50th birthday—might boost his settlement toward the upper range of his damages, somewhere between $1,200 and $3,500—including lost wages.

Damage to Olly's car would be settled separately from and in addition to compensation for his injuries.

## 2. Auto Accident, Soft Tissue Injury, Large Amount of Bills for Diagnosis, Extensive Physical Therapy

A car runs through a stop sign and hits another car, driven by Mary. Emergency room X-rays show no broken bones, and she is referred to her own doctor.

Mary develops a bad headache and a very stiff back. An orthopedist takes more X-rays and says Mary has lumbar spine strain but no apparent disk injury. The orthopedist prescribes pain medication, muscle relaxants, and physical therapy.

After four days, Mary returns to work but is in a lot of pain again and so misses two more days. Mary begins physical therapy three days a week for two weeks, then two days a week for two more weeks, and ends therapy altogether after five weeks. The orthopedist now says that after a few months she should be fully recovered.

The cost of Mary's medical treatment is as follows:

| | |
|---|---:|
| Ambulance | $250 |
| Emergency room | 280 |
| Emergency room X-rays | 180 |
| Mary's doctor | 260 |
| Orthopedist | 1,110 |
| Second set of X-rays | 280 |
| Physical therapist | 840 |
| Medications | 70 |
| Total | $3,270 |

Mary missed five days of work—although because she had sick leave, she was not actually out-of-pocket. The value of her missed work is figured by dividing her monthly gross salary of $2,300 by 21 (the number of work days in the month she missed), then multiplying that figure by 5 (the actual number of days she was out). That comes out to $110 per day, for a five-day loss of $550.

Because Mary had only soft tissue injuries—no observable damage to her spine—and no permanent injury, her damages will be calculated using the low end of the damages formula. Also keeping Mary's damages low is the fact that two-thirds of her medical bills were for diagnosis rather than treatment.

On the other hand, Mary's pain and injury were confirmed by two different doctors, she was given prescription medication, and she was told that full recovery would take several months. And since she did not undergo long or unusual treatment, all of her bills would be considered legitimate by an insurance company.

A low formula of roughly two to three times medical specials would bring a figure of about $6,500 to $10,000. Added to this would be the amount of Mary's lost wages (in this case, lost sick leave) of $550, for total damages in the range of $7,000 to $10,500. The other driver was clearly at fault, so Mary's settlement would not be reduced at all by comparative negligence.

## 3. Bicycle-Car Accident, Hard Injury, Long Recovery Period, Extensive Physical Therapy, Lost Unofficial Work Time, Considerable Disruption of Daily Activities

Walter is on a bike when a car switches lanes and pulls in front of him. Walter runs into the back of the car, falls off his bike, and hits the ground.

Hospital X-rays show no fracture of an injured ankle but a cracked left wrist, which is put in a cast. Despite having worn a helmet, Walter has a concussion, so he is kept in the hospital overnight.

An orthopedist diagnoses strained ankle ligaments and advises Walter to begin physical therapy on the ankle the next week and on the wrist as soon as the cast is removed.

Physical therapy for two weeks returns Walter's wrist to normal light use, but two months of physical therapy on his ankle does not seem to help much. Walter's orthopedist does not believe more physical therapy will help, so Walter stops the therapy. Walter doesn't get on a bicycle again for more than six months.

Walter missed eight days of work and after he returned, because of the cast on his wrist, he fell behind in several projects and had to work three straight weekends to catch up.

The cost of Walter's medical specials is as follows:

| | |
|---|---|
| Ambulance | $260 |
| Emergency room | 560 |
| Emergency room X-rays | 260 |
| Hospital room | 840 |
| Orthopedist | 360 |
| Physical therapy (wrist) | 320 |
| Physical therapy (ankle) | 1,600 |
| Total | $4,200 |

Because Walter had several significant injuries—broken wrist, concussion, long-term ligament injury—a formula of four to five times specials might be applied. The long period of physical therapy for the ankle may lessen the value of the claim a bit, because insurance adjusters tend to be mistrustful of extended physical therapy. But the fact that Walter was knocked unconscious and suffered a concussion despite wearing a helmet indicates that the accident was quite serious and may push the formula above five times specials.

Walter's salary is $2,800 per month ($133 per day). He missed eight days of work, for lost income (whether or not he was actually paid sick leave) of $1,064. Walter also "lost" three weekends when he had to work to make up for lost time on the job. That time would also be considered when the settlement amount is calculated.

The amount the insurance company finally pays would also depend on whether it appeared that Walter had been partly at fault for the accident.

Walter's medical specials of $4,200 would be multiplied by at least four or five times, and perhaps slightly higher. That brings the potential settlement to between $16,800 and $21,000. The fact that much of the treatment was physical therapy might reduce this somewhat, but the reduction would be offset by the long recovery time and the long period that Walter was unable or afraid to get on a bike. Added would be the $1,064 in lost income. And increasing that would be compensation for the extra weekends he had to work.

The total value of Walter's settlement, therefore, would be between $14,000 and $20,000, depending on Walter's comparative negligence.

## 4. Non-Auto Accident Caused by Employees, Permanent Hard Injuries

Yolanda parks her car in a lot shared by a shopping center and an office building. Next to the office building, a company softball team is practicing on the building's grassy area, as it regularly does at lunch. One of the players bats a ball into the parking lot where it hits Yolanda in the mouth, breaking her front tooth and pushing it through her upper lip.

Yolanda's tooth requires a permanent cap, and the hole in her lip leaves a small but visible scar. Her medical and dental special damages were as follows:

| | | |
|---|---|---:|
| Emergency room | | $750 |
| Dental work | | 2,400 |
| Doctor | | 520 |
| | Total | $3,670 |

Yolanda's broken tooth and gouged lip are each painful, observable "hard" injuries. That fact alone brings the formula to be applied to her medical costs into the range of three to five times specials. But because the capped tooth and scar are both visible, and since she will require future dental work, the formula would likely go above five times specials. These factors would likely raise the value of her claim to between $15,000 and $25,000.

Yolanda is also entitled to compensation not only for the work she missed after the accident, but also for the time she lost going to the doctor and dentist. These lost wages would be paid on top of the settlement amounts discussed above.

Because Yolanda did not contribute in any way to her injury, her settlement would not be reduced by any comparative negligence.

## 5. Slip and Fall, Commercial Property-Owner Liability, Witnesses, Hard Injury, Surgery Plus Nontraditional Treatments, Long Recovery Period

Seiji works in an office building that has an underground parking garage. One evening, Seiji is walking across the garage floor when he slips on a grease spot and twists his knee badly.

Seiji's doctor advises Seiji to put ice on the knee and rest, which he does. He stays home from work for three days.

Back at work, Seiji finds grease and oil spots all over the garage floor. And several overhead lights are burned out, leaving a dark area where Seiji fell. Seiji takes pictures of the grease spots and burned-out lights. He also finds out that two other people have slipped and fallen in the garage recently.

Seiji continues to have problems with his knee. An orthopedist examines him, takes X-rays, and refers him to a physical therapist. Seiji gets immediate relief after each therapy session, but the knee doesn't get any better, so he stops going to the physical therapist.

Seiji starts going to an acupuncturist who treats him for four sessions, but then advises him to see a body worker who is a licensed chiropractor mixing Eastern and Western techniques. The body worker does eight sessions on Seiji's knee, but then tells Seiji that there might be cartilage damage and that he should see an orthopedic surgeon who is a knee specialist.

The orthopedic surgeon does an arthroscopic examination that reveals torn cartilage. The surgeon repairs the damage by arthroscopic surgery. Seiji misses another week of work, and it is another eight weeks before Seiji can resume the running he did every morning before the accident. Altogether, it takes eight months after the accident for Seiji's knee to return to normal.

The costs for Seiji's treatments are as follows:

| | |
|---|---:|
| Doctor | $360 |
| X-rays (first set) | 220 |
| Physical therapy | 1,040 |
| Acupuncturist | 320 |
| Body worker | 640 |
| Orthopedist (with surgery) | 4,280 |
| X-rays (second set) | 240 |
| Total | $7,100 |

Seiji accompanies his claim with pictures of the oil spots and of the burned-out lights. He informs the insurance company that two other people slipped and fell in the garage before he did. And Seiji demands from the insurance adjuster a copy of the building's schedule for garage cleanup and maintenance. The adjuster soon reports that the company will accept full responsibility for the fall.

However, the insurance company refuses to recognize the acupuncture and body work as legitimate medical treatments. Seiji cannot change the adjuster's mind on acupuncture, but he does show that the body work was just another name for chiropractic and that the body worker is a licensed chiropractor.

Excluding the acupuncture, then, Seiji's medical specials are $6,780. His painful injury that required surgery and a long period of recovery would entitle Seiji to about five times the $6,780 specials, around $30,000 to $35,000. If he had serious permanent problems with the knee, that figure could rise to between $50,000 and $60,000.

## 6a. Slip and Fall on Stairs, Hard Injury, Surgery, Permanent Injury, Large Comparative Negligence

Wanda, 76 years old, goes shopping at Broadmart department store. Coming down some steps from the shoe section, Wanda misjudges an edge and falls. She is taken by ambulance to a hospital, where X-rays reveal a badly broken elbow.

Surgery is performed a week later, and Wanda spends three days in the hospital and the next week in bed, in great pain. After eight weeks, the cast is removed, and the orthopedic surgeon refers her to physical therapy.

Because of Wanda's age, physical therapy goes slowly. At the end of three months, her orthopedist switches her to home exercises. He advises her, however, that she will never recover full use of her arm: she will not be able to twist her elbow or wrist very far in either direction.

The medical costs of Wanda's treatment are as follows:

| | |
|---|---:|
| Ambulance | $320 |
| Emergency room | 510 |
| X-rays (first set) | 190 |
| Orthopedist—X-rays, surgeries, office | 4,860 |
| Hospital surgery, three nights | 5,650 |
| Physical therapy | 1,200 |
| Total | $12,730 |

Broadmart's insurance company denies that it is at all liable for the accident and refuses to pay any settlement to Wanda. Wanda can't remember anything wrong with the stairs that caused her to fall, but she says she wouldn't have fallen if there had been a handrail. The insurance adjuster says that there didn't need to be a handrail because it was only four steps and not a full staircase. Wanda knows she is not very steady on her feet, so she assumes the accident must have been mostly her own fault. When the insurance company offers to settle the case "as a gesture of good will"— meaning "nuisance value"—for whatever amounts Wanda's Medicare coverage did not pay, Wanda accepts the settlement: $2,500.

Now see a different Wanda in the next example.

## 6b. Slip and Fall on Stairs, Hard Injury, Surgery, Permanent Injury, No Comparative Negligence

Everything in this example is the same as in the previous one, except for what Wanda did to investigate the stairs after her accident ... and the large settlement she was able to get because of her investigation.

This time, Wanda went with a friend back to the store as soon as she got out of the hospital. They took a ruler, a measuring tape, a notebook, and a camera. Wanda pointed out where she had fallen, and Wanda's friend took measurements of the stairs and photos of the stairs and of the lights.

At the local library, Wanda looked at a copy of the county's building code. The code said that in any staircase of two steps or more, the risers and runs—the step width and height—had to be within certain measurements and that each step had to be the same as the others. Wanda checked the measurements and found that the store's second step was a different height from the one above it, and the difference was well beyond the building code limit. Also, the building code required stairs of that width in a commercial building to have a handrail in the middle, which the store's stairs did not.

Wanda's claim to Broadmart's insurance company lists these building code violations. Also, Wanda uses the photos to emphasize that spotlights on the upper platform shine right into a shopper's eyes, so that while going down the stairs a person cannot see the steps clearly. She also points out that the all-white carpet that covers the stairs provides no contrast for a person to pick out the edge of one step from the beginning of another.

Because a store must expect elderly people and people with poor eyesight to shop there, stairs have to be safe for them. And if there had been a handrail as the building code required, an accident might not have resulted.

Wanda has established the store's negligence, the seriousness of her injuries, the long time for her recovery, and the permanent residual effects. The damages formula is now four or five times specials. That would make Wanda's settlement about $40,000 to $60,000. ■

# Chapter 6

# Processing Your Claim

## Using This Chapter

This chapter explains what information you should gather to document your accident and injuries and how to put it together into a convincing written claim—known as a demand letter—for a specific amount of compensation.

Your should tailor your demand letter to the specifics of your accident and injuries, and to the information you have to support your claim. "Collecting Information" discusses the various ways to support arguments about liability, injuries, lost income, and property damage; you will be able to use some of these ways in your claim, but not all of them.

"Preparing a Demand Letter" explains how to turn your information into the most effective demand letter—what to include and what to leave out.

"Sample Demand Letters" presents examples of demand letters based on different accidents and injuries that may serve as models for your own demand letter.

# Collecting Information

As soon as you have taken the initial steps to protect your interests (explained in Chapter 3), begin gathering the written records and other information to support your claim.

## Documenting Liability

Gather and organize information concerning who was at fault. Begin as soon after the accident as possible because your memory, and the memories of others who may have information about the accident, will fade with time.

## Police Report of Vehicle Accident

If police responded to the scene and were aware that you or anyone else was injured, they probably made a written accident report. In the report there may be a notation about the location of the cars, a statement by a witness, or some other fact that could prove useful to you. And the insurance company for the other driver will certainly get a copy of the accident report, so you will want to have the same information.

To get a copy of a police report, look in the telephone book for the listings of the police department or highway patrol that responded to your accident. It may have a special number to call just for accident reports. If not, call the central office or a local station and ask how to get a copy of your report. The report will be filed either by date and time, street location, drivers' names, or car description and license plate number, so have that information ready when you call. Three or four days after the accident, you can usually pick up the report in person or request a copy by mail. Call first, though, to find out whether there is any charge—usually you'll pay a couple of dollars to cover copying costs.

Sometimes a police accident report will plainly state the reporting officer's opinion that one driver or another violated a specific Vehicle Code section and caused the accident. It may even indicate that the officer issued a citation to the driver at fault. In other reports, careless driving is mentioned somewhere—not necessarily by specifying a Vehicle Code section—although no citation was issued and the officer does not plainly state that the carelessness caused the accident.

Regardless of how specific a report is, if you can find any mention of a Vehicle Code violation or any other suggestion that the other driver was careless, it can be great support in convincing an insurance company that the other driver was at fault. Naturally, the clearer the officer's statement about fault, the easier your job will be in convincing the insurance company.

An accident claim requires only that you present a reasonable explanation of how an accident happened so that an insurance company sees that it is too great a risk to deny your claim and to try to fight it in court. And when you have the written opinion of a police officer who is a supposed expert in traffic collisions and a representative of the state, you have a powerful ally for the reasonableness of your argument.

Many police officers, however, will not discuss fault in their reports unless they either witnessed the accident themselves or took a statement from an independent witness who saw the accident, or unless the physical evidence at the scene—position of the cars, skid marks, damage—makes the cause of the accident obvious. Even if the report does not mention fault, if there is anything in the report supporting your theory of how the accident happened, focus on that—a comment by the officer, a diagram showing the position of the cars, an estimated speed of the other driver, the reported statement of a witness—in your written compensation demand to the insurance company. (See "Preparing a Demand Letter," below, concerning referring to the police report in your demand letter.)

## Photographs

If you have any photos of the scene of the accident, you may need to explain to the insurance company what the photo shows, what specific part of the photo shows a fact concerning who was at fault, and when the photo was taken. (See Chapter 3.)

## Police Report

An unpleasant surprise may await you in the police report of your accident. The investigating officer may have noted that you appear to have violated a traffic rule or that you were otherwise at fault. One way to try to counteract a bad police report is to telephone the police officer as soon after the accident as possible. Although police do not like to get involved in liability disputes between drivers, the officer who wrote an accident report will probably at least return your phone call.

Politely explain that you are dealing with an insurance company on your own and that you would like to take a couple minutes of the officer's time briefly to discuss the report. Do not try to get the officer to change the report or to say that the other person was at fault. The officer would probably prefer not to take sides, so use this to your advantage by simply asking the officer whether he or she can say for sure who was at fault in the accident. If the officer says that he or she cannot tell who was at fault, you've already helped yourself.

While the conversation is taking place, write down what the officer says, noting the date and time of the call. Later, in your negotiation with the insurance company, if the adjuster mentions the police report, you can say that you have spoken with the reporting police officer and that the officer has specifically said that he or she cannot state who was at fault. You have now accomplished two things: You have neutralized the bad police report; and you have made the insurance company realize that it is dealing with an organized, resourceful claimant who will not disappear easily without a fair settlement.

## Witness Statements

If you know of witnesses but have not spoken with them, or you have supportive information from witnesses but they have not yet given you a written statement, contact them again before too much time slips by. (See "Preserve Evidence of Fault and Damages," in Chapter 3.)

## Applicable Laws

If you haven't yet checked to see whether there are any laws in your state that help to show that another person was at fault, now is the time to do so.

In vehicle accidents, your state's Vehicle Code, also known as the rules of the road, may have a law clearly showing why the other driver was at fault. (See the liability section in Chapter 2.) If so, make a copy of that law to send along with your demand letter. (See "Preparing a Demand Letter," below.)

In staircase or other premises accidents, your local or state building code might contain a rule that has been violated by the other person and that contributed to your accident. (See Chapter 2.)

## Evidence of Prior Incidents

In some states, you are allowed to get a copy of the driving record of a person with whom you have had a traffic accident. Contact the local or central office of your state's department of motor vehicles to find out whether other people's driving records are available. If so, get a copy. The record may show that the other driver has a history of traffic violations or accidents to which you can refer in your negotiations with the insurance company.

If you intend to file a claim against a public entity asserting that a road condition contributed to your traffic accident, you may want to determine whether similar accidents have occurred at the same place. First, return to the scene of the accident and ask people who live or work nearby whether they have seen similar accidents. If possible, get a written statement from anyone who has witnessed a prior accident.

You may also request information about prior accidents from the public agency responsible for the roadway. You may do so by writing to either the public agency in question or to the claims adjuster or public agency representative handling your claim. (See sample request letter, below.) Because the agency or police department that keeps track of accidents is a public entity, most of its records are public documents to which you should be permitted access upon reasonable request.

Such a request can help your claim in several ways. Just asking for the information shows that you are organized and informed, which will help to make the claims adjuster take the claim seriously. It also shows the adjuster that defending the claim will require time and energy, which often results in an earlier fair compensation offer. If you find out from the claims adjuster that similar accidents have indeed occurred at the same spot, this suggests that it was the road that was dangerous, not your driving. It also shows that the public agency knew, or should have known, about the danger and failed to correct it.

What if the public agency or claims adjuster refuses to search for or provide information about prior incidents? You should remind the claims adjuster that if the matter becomes a formal lawsuit, the agency will be legally obligated to produce this information. And you can argue that failing to produce the information suggests either that the agency fails to properly keep track of accidents or that it has the information and is hiding incriminating details.

If the agency or adjuster still won't send the information, you have a decision to make. Sometimes, that information is the only evidence you have to support your version of what happened or to prove the other party's liability. If that's the case, you'll probably need to find an experienced personal injury lawyer and file a lawsuit just to get the information. Chapter 11 tells you how to do that. But if the records you are looking for are only one part of your evidence, you can forget about it for now. In your demand letter, make a note that you requested records and that they weren't given to you, present your other evidence, and see what happens.

If you were injured as the result of an accident caused by a defective product, you may first want to check with *Consumer Reports* magazine to see whether the specific product brand has a history of similar accidents. If so, make a copy of any article that discusses dangers or defects in the product. (See "Dangerous or Defective Products" in Chapter 2.) You can include that article and refer to it your compensation demand letter to the insurance company. (See "Preparing a Demand Letter," below.)

## Safety Inspection Record

Chapter 2 discusses accidents caused by the dangerous condition of business or residential premises; for example, falling on a broken stair, slipping in a supermarket aisle, or tripping over a broken walkway. As explained there, whether the business or property owner is legally responsible for the accident may depend on what steps the owner took to protect the safety of visitors. And that includes whether the owner had the premises inspected regularly and cleaned or repaired.

If you have been injured in a slip and fall or trip and fall accident, you should request

## Sample Letter Requesting Information on Prior Accidents

J.L. Jones
1234 Broadway
Seattle, WA 00000

June 1, 20xx

James T. Smith
Seattle Dept. of Public Works
1000 Main Street
Seattle, WA 00000

Re: Claim No. XXXXX
      Date of Incident: October 10, 20xx

Dear Mr. Smith:

As you are aware, I was injured in an accident on October 10, 20xx at Waterfront Boulevard near 12th Street. At that time, I fell when riding my bicycle across old railroad tracks that cross Waterfront Boulevard.

I believe that the tracks constitute a danger to all bicyclists and that prior, similar bicycle accidents have occurred on those same tracks and on other tracks that cross the road at an angle at other points along Waterfront Blvd. Therefore, I request that you provide me with information concerning any such incidents within the ten years prior to October 10, 20xx in the possession of the Department of Public Works, the Seattle Police Department, or any other City of Seattle agency that maintains records of traffic accidents.

Thank you for your attention to this matter.

Yours sincerely,

*J.L. Jones*

J.L. Jones

information about general inspection and cleaning procedures for the premises. You should ask for any record of the most recent preaccident inspection or cleaning of the spot where you were injured. The request can be directed to the insurance adjuster for the business or property owner. (See sample request letter, below.)

If the business or property owner has no written inspection or cleaning procedures, you might argue that this shows a lack of reasonable safety precautions. If there are procedures but no record of any actual recent inspection or cleaning, you can argue that procedures are worthless if they are not followed. Likewise, you can argue that the owner did not use reasonable care if an inspection revealed a problem but nothing was done to correct it.

How often an owner must "reasonably" clean or inspect differs with the type of premises. It is common for slippery substances to fall on supermarket aisles, so a store should have someone checking the floors several times a day, perhaps hourly. Similarly, oil frequently drips onto a parking lot, so someone should check at least every few days for dangerously slippery patches. On the other hand, a landlord need not check the condition of stairs every day or even every week, but she should have someone check the premises, including stairs, at least monthly for any safety problems.

What if the claims adjuster or the premises or business owner refuses to provide information about inspection procedures and cleaning? Remind the adjuster that if the matter becomes a formal lawsuit, the owner will be legally obligated to produce this information. And you can point out to the adjuster that refusing to produce this information suggests that the owner either fails to properly maintain any inspection procedure or knows that the procedure was not followed before your accident but does not want to admit it.

If the adjuster or the business or property owner still won't send the information, you have a decision to make. Sometimes, that information is the only evidence you have to support your version of what happened or to prove the other party's liability. If that's the case, you'll probably need to find an experienced personal injury lawyer and file a lawsuit just to get the information. Chapter 11 tells you how to do that. But if the records you are looking for are only one part of your evidence, you can forget about it for now. In your demand letter, make a note that you requested records and that they weren't given to you, present your other evidence, and see what happens.

## Documenting Injuries

Although research, photos, and witnesses may be persuasive evidence, the simplest way to show the nature and extent of your injuries is through the records of those who have treated you,

**⚠ Pay attention to the time.** Although in most cases you will finish your medical treatment and recovery before sending a demand letter, be aware that the law sets time limits for when you must file a lawsuit for personal injury.

Most states give you two years or more from the date of your accident within which to file a lawsuit against those you believe responsible for the accident. (See Chapter 8 for a state-by-state list of the legal time limits, called statutes of limitations.)

For most people, the time limit does not present a problem in preparing and negotiating an insurance claim. However, a few states—Kentucky, Louisiana, and Tennessee—allow only one year from the date of the accident to file a lawsuit. So, if you live in one of these states and more than six months have elapsed since your accident but you are not ready to file a demand letter, consider filing a lawsuit

### Sample Letter Requesting Inspection Records

Roberta Thompson
567 Main Street
Atlanta, GA 00000

April 10, 20xx

Abner Jones
All Risk Insurance Company
789 Center St.
Atlanta, GA 00000

Re: Claim No. XXXXX
Date of Incident: October 10, 20xx
Request for Inspection of Records

Dear Mr. Jones:

As you are aware, I was injured in an accident on October 10, 20xx on the premises of your insured, the Lucky Chicken Restaurant, on Downhome Boulevard in Atlanta. I slipped and fell on a substance on the floor in front of the salad and condiments bar.

Lucky Chicken has an obligation to maintain its premises in a manner that reasonably ensures the safety of its customers. That includes keeping the floor dry and free of debris. In that regard, please provide the following information concerning Lucky Chicken's safety practices:

(1) On the date of the accident, whose job was it to keep the floor area clean near the salad bar?

(2) When was the last occasion before the accident that someone inspected and/or cleaned the floor in that area?

(3) Who inspected and/or cleaned the floor in that area on the last occasion before the accident?

(4) What are the written procedures, if any, for maintaining safety on the premises, and in particular for keeping floors clean and free of debris during business hours?

Thank you for your attention to this matter.

Yours sincerely,
*Roberta Thompson*
Roberta Thompson

to protect your rights. (See "Check the Time" in Chapter 8.)

## Medical Records

Doctors, nurses, physical therapists, chiropractors, and other medical providers are all trained to make very detailed notes of everything they observe about your condition and everything they do and say about your treatment. You can usually get a copy of your medical records just by asking—although you may have to pay copying costs.

Even in states where there is no specific law giving patients access to their medical records, most medical providers will provide copies to a patient who wants them for an accident insurance claim. If you meet any resistance to obtaining your records, politely explain that you need them to support your accident claim. If office personnel are not helpful, ask to speak directly with the doctor or other health provider who treated you.

### An Added Boost From X-Ray Reports

Often, a doctor will send you somewhere outside his or her office to get X-rayed. The bill for those X-rays may be included in your own doctor's bill. But your doctor's medical records might not include the notes of the radiologist— the doctor who reads the X-rays. Instead, they might contain only your doctor's summary of what the radiologist saw. If your own doctor's records do not indicate any specific injury shown on the X-ray, request a copy of the radiologist's records, particularly if you had X-rays of any part of your neck or back. A radiologist will often find something slightly wrong with your spine that may be causing you pain but that your doctor doesn't specifically mention. You can ask your doctor's office to obtain the radiologist's records for you, or you can send a medical records request directly to the radiologist's office.

If you still are unable to obtain copies of your medical records, one resource for assistance is a booklet titled *Medical Records: Getting Yours,* published by the Public Citizen Health Research Group. You may order a copy by phone at 800-289-3787, or by mail with a check for $10 to Publications Department, Public Citizen Health Research Group, 1600 20th St., NW, Washington, DC 20009. This booklet explains state and federal laws, how to make a request, and how to interpret your file.

If all your efforts at obtaining your medical records fail, you have two courses of action. If the medical record is for diagnosis or minor treatment and you have your other medical records, submit your claim without the missing records. If the missing records are central to demonstrating your injuries and treatment, consider getting help from a lawyer. (See "What to Do When You Can't Get a Settlement" in Chapter 8.)

Request your records from every hospital, clinic, laboratory, doctor, therapist, chiropractor, or other medical provider who examined or treated you for your accident injuries. But wait until you have finished the treatment before requesting your records; if you don't, you'll have to ask again later for a complete and updated copy.

Call the office of each medical provider and ask what the procedure is for getting a copy of your medical records. Some offices will take the information over the phone, but most require a written request. Your written request should ask for billing records (see "Medical Billing," below) as well as medical records. Give the date of your accident. It will help the office find the correct records and will keep them from sending you and charging you for the records of visits made before the accident.

Some hospitals, clinics, and other medical offices require you to fill out a request on their own forms, or ask that you sign a document called an Authorization for Release of Medical Records, or something similar. Normally there is no reason not to sign such a form, but read it carefully first to make sure that it does not permit your medical information to be released to anyone other than you. Never sign any form authorizing the release of medical records to anyone other than you, your lawyer if you decide to hire one, or your own insurance company if your policy requires it.

## Sample Request for Medical Records and Billing

Augustine Muk
122 Rumblewood Avenue
Coagula, CA 00000
(510) 999-9999

January 13, 20xx

Elizabeth True, M.D.
777 Sunset Street, Suite 666
Coagula, CA 00000

Attention Medical Records
Re: Patient, Augustine Muk
Accident: November 11, 20xx

To Whom It Concerns:

I was treated by Dr. True in November and December 20xx for injuries suffered in an accident on November 11, 20xx. Please provide me with copies of all medical records and billing records concerning my treatment following this accident.

Please contact me at the above phone if you have any questions concerning this request.

Very truly yours,

*Augustine Muk*

Augustine Muk

When you get your medical records, make sure they are complete and include all visits related to your accident injuries. If they are not complete, call the office of the medical provider with the dates of the visits for which the records are missing. Check, too, that the records do not include listings of examinations or treatments unrelated to your accident. Set aside these irrelevant records so that you do not mistakenly send them to the insurance company along with the correct ones.

## Medical Billing

The clearest evidence of what your claim is "worth" is the billing records showing how much it cost to treat your injuries. Make sure you have a copy of a bill for every medical service you received. If any bill was sent directly to a health insurance company, Medicare, or Medicaid, or if for any other reason you do not have a copy, request a copy from the medical provider so that you can include it when you make your demand for compensation.

## Treatment by an HMO or Prepaid Plan

If you belong to a health maintenance organization (HMO) or other prepaid health plan, you are not usually charged a specific sum for visits or treatments, and so there is no actual bill. But every HMO and health plan has a list of charges for each service it provides. If you request it, the business office at your HMO or health plan will give you a list of its charges for each of the examinations, treatments, medicines, and other services provided to you. Insurance companies consider these charges the same as if they were bills you had actually paid.

Most HMO and health plan contracts provide that if you recover compensation from a third person for injuries treated by the HMO or covered by the prepaid health plan, you must repay the amount of the charges. In exchange for giving you a list of charges for your treatment, the HMO or health plan might require you to sign a medical lien against your future compensation. This lien requires that you repay the HMO or health plan when you are compensated for your injuries. However, once you have reached a final settlement of your claim, there are ways to negotiate with the HMO or health plan so that you repay it only a reduced amount of its charges. (See "Reducing Your HMO or Health Plan Repayment" in Chapter 9.)

## Medical Reports

Read copies of your medical records carefully to see that they are accurate and that all your injuries have been mentioned. Unless your medical records show an injury, an insurance company is not going to take the injury very seriously in calculating your compensation. Therefore, if your medical records do not reflect all of your injuries, you may want to contact your doctor about preparing a brief medical report that specifically describes the extent of your injuries, your treatment, and your recovery. And although you may also have been treated by medical providers other than doctors, insurance companies pay much more attention to a report if it comes from a doctor rather than from a nonphysician.

Also, the amount of time you take to recover from your injuries, plus any permanent residual effects, can greatly increase the amount of your compensation. Check whether your medical records accurately reflect these things. If not, ask your doctor to prepare a brief medical report about these aspects of your injuries.

Your medical records may mention what insurance adjusters refer to as a preexisting injury —an injury that already existed in the same area of your body that was injured in the accident. For example, a "bad" knee might have been twisted again in the accident. If so, you have a right to be compensated only for the amount of injury caused by the accident, not for the level of injury that existed before it. However, it is not always easy to tell from medical records alone how much of an injury already existed and how much came from the accident.

Doctors are familiar with the issue of preexisting injuries in accident claims. While it is far from an exact science, they are used to giving an estimate—expressed in percentages—of how much of an injury is preexisting and how much was caused by the accident. If a preexisting injury becomes an issue in your claim, explain the problem to your doctor. If a substantial percentage of your injury was caused by the accident, ask the doctor to prepare a brief report stating that fact.

### Requesting a Medical Report

When you speak with your doctor, explain what you would like the medical report to cover: nature of the injury, length of recovery, inability to perform certain functions, and existence or probability of permanent or disabling effects. Speak to the doctor directly. Most doctors will try to have a nurse or other assistant take nontreatment information, but if you speak only with the assistant, the doctor may not precisely understand what you need, and you will wind up paying for a useless report. Also, explain why you want the report; most doctors are familiar with the accident claim process and will understand.

You will be paying for the report out of your own pocket, so make sure you get your money's worth. A brief report may cost you $50, but some doctors are known to charge $300 to $500 for a full report. Ask the doctor for a brief report only, and find out ahead of time how much the doctor will charge. Unless it seems the doctor can say something useful in a report, don't bother to ask for one.

The report should be addressed "To Whom It Concerns," but it should be given only to you and not sent directly to an insurance company. That way you can make sure it supports your claim, and doesn't say anything that minimizes your injuries, before you make it a part of the negotiating process.

## Medical Reports and No-Fault Insurance

In a number of states, a person covered by no-fault (Personal Injury Protection) automobile insurance can file a claim for compensation if he or she has suffered injuries that go over a certain threshold—defined as either a certain amount of medical bills or a permanent, disabling, or disfiguring injury. If you cannot qualify under your no-fault coverage because the amount of your medical bills does not meet the monetary threshold, you may need to show that your injuries have had some permanent effect. Your medical records alone may do this. But if they do not state clearly that your injury is disabling or permanent as defined by your no-fault policy, a separate statement or report written by your doctor may be your only way of proving that.

### Your Own Medical Research

An inexpensive and sometimes very effective source of information to highlight the seriousness and effects of your injuries can be found in your local library, a nearby law library, or the library of a local hospital. Most local libraries have one or two medical encyclopedias, such as *Current Medical Information and Terminology,* or an illustrated medical dictionary giving both the common and technical names of conditions and parts of the body. A law library will also have a copy of the *Lawyers' Medical Cyclopedia,* which defines medical terms specifically with legal claims in mind.

Check in a medical encyclopedia or dictionary under the medical terms you find in your medical records describing your injuries—for example,

"comminuted fracture" or "root compression." The book may contain information explaining such injuries that was not included in your personal medical records, particularly concerning long-term and permanent effects. If so, copy the information so that you can refer to it in your demand letter.

Another source of medical research is your doctor. Without requesting a costly written medical report, you can ask the doctor questions about the exact extent of your injury and the prognosis for long-term or permanent problems. Often during treatment, a doctor fails to explain in detail the extent of an injury, or will not mention possible long-term effects because they are too uncertain.

However, if you ask—either during a visit or on the phone—the doctor may give you that kind of valuable additional information, which you can then put into your demand letter. The medical details of an injury—and the fact that you know the details—often give the injury more status in the eyes of an insurance adjuster. And the mere mention of possible long-term or permanent residual effects from your injury might increase the compensation you are offered.

### Injury Photos and Witnesses

As suggested, you may have taken photographs of your injuries at different times after the accident. (See Chapter 3.) If so, arrange the photos in chronological order, picking out the four to six photos that most clearly show the extent of your injuries and how long they lasted. Send copies of these photos along with your demand letter.

People other than your doctors may have witnessed your pain and discomfort resulting from the accident. Nonfamily members are particularly useful witnesses because they do not have a direct personal interest in helping your claim. For example, your employer or a coworker might be able to confirm not only how much time you missed but also how much pain and discomfort you were in, and for how long, after you returned to work. If so, a brief note or letter from that witness describing the nature and duration of your pain and discomfort could be useful for your claim negotiations.

Also, there may be witnesses or documents to verify that you have been unable to participate in some family, personal, or social obligation or event, or that you have missed a business or educational opportunity. An invitation to or notice of an event can serve as evidence. If no written evidence exists, a simple letter from anyone involved addressed "To Whom It Concerns" describing the obligation, opportunity, or event would be helpful.

Unlike a special event, the extent to which your injuries have disrupted your regular daily life does not have to be proven by a document or witness. Proof of your injuries and a description in your demand letter of the normal activities you have missed will be enough. (See "Preparing a Demand Letter," below.)

## Documenting Lost Income

If you are regularly employed by someone else, collecting information about your lost income is simple. Ask your supervisor, boss, or personnel office to write a letter on company stationery. The letter should include your name, your position, your rate of pay, the number of hours you normally work, and the number of hours or days you missed following the accident. The letter need not indicate whether you took sick leave, vacation time, or a leave of absence.

If you are irregularly employed or are self-employed, proving lost income is more complicated. You have to show how much work time you lost and what you might have earned had you been able to work. You can use any evidence you have of a drop in billing or invoices, a calendar showing appointments you had to cancel, and any letters or documents showing meetings, conferences, or other appointments you were unable to attend.

After you have demonstrated how much work you missed, you have to show how much you might have earned. If you had been working a relatively steady amount immediately before the accident, you can show an average for the period by putting together copies of your billing, invoices, payments received, or other evidence of money earned. Then, depending on the amount you were working and how much you were earning, you can calculate how much income you are considered to have lost for the time you were unable to work.

If you work sporadically—some weeks or months earning most of your income and other weeks or months earning little or nothing—you can show the value of lost work time through evidence of what you make during an entire year, then dividing that into a weekly or monthly average.

The best evidence of your yearly income is your personal income tax return for the previous year. You need to show only the part of your tax return that gives your year's gross income; the rest of the return—deductions, exemptions—is irrelevant, and an insurance company has no right to see it. If you had particularly low earnings during the previous year, include two or three years of returns to demonstrate how much you usually earn. If you also have some evidence of income for the current year showing a similar earning pattern, include that as well.

## Property Damage

You have a right to be compensated not only for your injuries, but also for any personal property damaged or lost in the accident. This applies most often to traffic accidents, in which vehicles and their contents are damaged or destroyed. But you also have a right to be compensated for damage to your property in any other type of accident. For example, a fall might cause your watch to break, or a piece of your jewelry to be lost, or something you were carrying to be destroyed.

You have a right to compensation for your damaged property even if you suffered no personal injury at all. And if you have also suffered personal injury, you can submit a property damage claim either as part of your demand for personal injury compensation or in a separate, earlier demand. (See Chapter 7.)

## Preparing a Demand Letter

The demand letter is the centerpiece of the negotiation process. In it, you set out to the insurance company your strongest arguments concerning:

- why the other person is legally responsible
- what your injuries were and are
- why you qualify to make a third-party claim under no-fault, if that applies
- what your medical treatment was and how much it cost
- what your income loss was, and
- what other damages you suffered.

The letter concludes with a demand on the insurance company for a lump sum to settle your entire claim.

The insurance company uses this demand letter to compare your claim with the information it has about the case, and then to make a counteroffer of settlement. The process of back-and-forth negotiating from there on—usually a combination of phone calls and letters—will determine the final amount of your settlement. (See Chapter 8.)

Because a demand letter is the beginning of the negotiation process, make your claim as strong and convincing as possible. Even if you know of weaknesses in your argument, do not discuss them in the demand letter. If an insurance adjuster spots a weakness, it will come up during negotiations and you can deal with it then. If the insurance adjuster does not bring up the weakness in your argument, you are under no obligation to do so.

The demand letter sets out your theory of the case and the range of your demand. It can also demonstrate to the insurance company your understanding, organization, and preparation of your claim. In other words, a good demand letter—clear, organized, including all useful information—sets the tone for a good settlement. This section discusses what goes into a good demand letter and how to arrange and forcefully argue the information. (See the sample demand letters below.)

### Letters to More Than One Insurance Company

There may be more than one person or business liable for your injuries, and therefore more than one insurance company that might have to deal with a claim from you. By the time you prepare your demand letter, you will probably have received a notice from one or both insurance companies indicating which company will provide the primary coverage—the one with which you will settle your claim—and which will provide only excess coverage. (See "Getting a Claim Started" in Chapter 3.) You need to send your demand letter only to the primary company.

But if you have not received a notice of primary coverage when you are ready to make your settlement demand, prepare two demand letters—each one tailored to the particular liable conduct of that company's insured. After sending both demand letters, you should receive a response from one or both insurance companies indicating which one assumes responsibility for primary coverage. That insurance company will then be the one with which you negotiate.

If you have not received written acknowledgment of primary coverage by the time you are ready to begin settlement negotiations, you will need to resort to other negotiation tactics. (See Chapter 8.)

## What to Emphasize in Your Demand Letter

Before beginning to write your demand letter, review your notes from the days and weeks following the accident to remind yourself of the details of the accident—your pain, discomfort, inconvenience, disruption of life, and treatments.

Use the "Factors Affecting Compensation" chart, below, to remind yourself of the things that can increase or decrease the amount a claim is worth.

### Liability

A demand letter begins by describing how the accident happened and why the insurance company's insured was at fault. In plain language, briefly describe where you were and what you were doing immediately before the accident, then how the accident took place. For example:

> *"I was driving north in the right-hand lane along 4th Avenue at about three o'clock in the afternoon. When I was more than halfway through the intersection with Broadway, your insured entered the intersection in the center eastbound lane on Broadway and slammed into the passenger side of my car."*

Include all points that might indicate that the insured was at fault for the accident. Put your strongest argument first:

> *"I clearly had the right of way at the intersection. The insured had a stop sign on Broadway, and I had no stop sign on 4th Avenue."*

And add other facts that might lead to an even stronger case against the insured:

> *"Furthermore, since the insured struck my car on the rear side panel, it is obvious that I was already well into the intersection when he entered. Also, the extent of the damage to my car indicates that your insured was moving at a substantial rate of speed, which would mean that he never even stopped at the stop sign."*

If you have any outside support for your theory, make sure to include it here. In a vehicle accident case, repeat any helpful remark in a police report. In a premises liability case, quote a building code section that the owner has violated. Include information received from any source about similar accidents, although you do not have to give the identities of your sources at this stage. If you have information that the other driver has a bad driving record, mention it here.

If you have any witnesses who support your version of the accident, let the insurance company know how many of them back up your story. If you have a good written statement from a witness, quote the best part of the statement. You do not have to reveal the identity of a witness in the demand letter; instead, write that you will make the identity of the witnesses known to the insurance company "at the appropriate time."

Be sure to let the insurance company know that you are aware of other information, or intangibles, that could help you should the case ever get to court. For example, if there was any evidence that another driver's breath smelled of alcohol, or there was an empty beer bottle in the car—even if he or she was not cited for drunk driving—mention it in your demand letter:

*"From the beer cans on the floor of your insured's automobile, observed by my passenger as well as by me, it also appears that your insured may have been drinking and driving."*

## Cyclists, Include Your "Good Conduct" Background

If you are a bicyclist or motorcyclist, some of the intangibles to mention in your demand letter pertain to your general caution and experience as a rider. These aspects of one's riding background are discussed in Chapter 2. For an example of how to include some of these things, see Sample Demand Letter #3 in this chapter.

Another intangible may be how gruesome your damaged car looked. If it was badly smashed, describe that. Include a photo if you have one, to highlight how serious the collision was. If the car was spun all the way around, mention it. If it had to be towed away, mention that. Likewise, if you have a photo of a hole you tripped in or a dangerous-looking object that injured you, include the photo and refer to how obviously dangerous it is just from looking at the picture. If you not only fell but fell down several stairs, mention it.

If property had been in a dangerous condition for a long time, mention that the owner or manager of the property was negligent not only for allowing the danger to occur, but also for failing to inspect or otherwise reasonably look after the property. (See "Accidents on Dangerous or Defective Property" in Chapter 2.)

## Words Can Be Your Best Ally

One of the most important but overlooked effects of language in negotiating a claim is how strong words—instead of merely the most direct words—can get across to an adjuster the emotional impact of the accident and your injuries. The words you use in your claim should highlight the dangerous carelessness of the other person, the pain you suffered, and the seriousness of its consequences. So, for example, a car does not hit another car, it slams into it. Or a car did not merely have the right of way, it clearly or obviously had the right of way. A knee is not merely twisted but has suffered a strained collateral medial ligament. An injury is not just painful, but is extremely painful. A wound doesn't merely leave a scar, but a very disfiguring scar.

Of course, you have to be careful not to get so colorful with your language that an insurance adjuster will mistrust what you say. But bear in mind while you are writing your demand letter that carefully chosen words can be an effective tool for helping an adjuster understand what you have been through.

## Comparative Negligence

In many accidents, there is some question about whether your own carelessness contributed to the accident even though the other person was primarily at fault.

Raise the issue in your demand letter by denying that you were at all comparatively negligent. This denial shows the insurance company that you are aware of the rules and have thought about the issue. It allows you briefly to state your argument in writing so that

## Factors Affecting Compensation

**Factors that signal a higher multiplier to be applied to medical expenses include:**

- hard injury—broken bone, head, or joint injury, wounds, vertebrae injury, nerve damage
- expenses primarily for treatment
- treatment by a medical doctor, clinic, hospital
- prescribed medication
- long treatment
- long recovery
- permanent injury—scar, stiffness, weakness, loss of mobility
- physical or emotional distress resulting from the injury, and
- daily life disruptions—missed school or training, missed vacation or recreation, canceled special event.

**Factors that signal a lower multiplier to be applied to medical expenses include:**

- soft tissue injury—sprain, strain, bruise
- large part of expenses for diagnosis rather than for treatment
- treatment by non-M.D. providers

- no medication prescribed
- brief treatment
- short recovery period
- no residual or permanent injury, and
- no physical or emotional problems other than original injury.

**Factors likely to get you higher compensation after the formula is applied include:**

- no comparative negligence by you
- your organization and calmness
- the insured is not credible or sympathetic
- witnesses in your favor, and
- some "dramatic" advantage.

**Factors likely to get you lower compensation after the formula is applied include:**

- comparative negligence by you
- disorganization or impatience
- a sympathetic insured, and
- no witnesses for you, or witnesses who favor the insured.

All of these factors are discussed in detail in Chapter 5.

you don't have to discuss it for the first time on the phone with the insurance adjuster—a situation that is more difficult for you to control.

Do not admit any fault. Even if you believe that you might have been partly at fault for the accident, do not admit that in your demand letter unless you would lose credibility by failing to do so, such as if you were cited for a vehicle code violation. In that case, acknowledge the issue but insist that your contribution to the accident was minimal. In all other situations, mention only the reasons why you were not at fault. Although you must consider your own negligence in deciding

what a fair settlement is, it is not your job to make the comparative negligence arguments for the insurance company. So, for example, if there was a traffic accident, point out that the police report confirms that you violated no traffic laws and that it mentions no careless driving on your part. If you tripped or slipped and fell on stairs, indicate that you were walking normally, that your shoes had normal heels and soles, and that you were watching your step.

Your discussion of comparative fault should end with a statement that it is clear that the insured was fully liable for the accident.

## Your Injuries and Treatment

In describing your injuries and treatments, do not be too shy. Emphasize your pain, the length and difficulty of your recovery, the negative effects of your injuries on your daily life, and any long-term or permanent injury—especially if it is disabling or disfiguring, such as permanent stiffness, soreness, or scarring.

Of course, do not make things up or be overly dramatic. Insurance adjusters are regular people who are susceptible to the kid-who-cried-wolf phenomenon; they will simply turn a deaf ear to claims they believe are false. To support your claim of injury, pain, and disability, use the words that appear in medical records whenever possible. Choose "official" terms over conversational language; "narrowing of disk spacing" is stronger than "strained back."

The easiest way to describe your injuries, treatment, recovery, and long-term or permanent effects is to go step-by-step chronologically. Proceed from how the injury occurred, to your pain and what you did about it immediately after the accident, through all the medical examinations, diagnoses, and treatments you received, through all the stages of your pain and disability during recovery. End with any long-term or permanent effects. (See examples below.)

## Other Losses

Most of what you recover for your injuries is compensation for pain, discomfort, and disruption in your daily life. But sometimes you suffer extra or unusual discomforts, embarrassments, inconveniences, or losses. (See "Demonstrating Pain and Suffering" in Chapter 5.) Review your notes to remind yourself of the kinds of things you went through, or had to miss or give up, because of your injuries. Mention them in your demand letter, and do not be shy about saying how important those things are to you.

## Medical Expenses

Immediately following your description of all your medical treatments, include in the demand letter a list of each medical provider who treated you and the total amount charged by each. (See examples below.) If you were treated by an HMO or other prepaid plan, list the charges it provided you with in place of actual bills. List all medical costs, regardless of whether you paid them, your insurance or your employer's insurance paid them, or they were part of a health plan. Make sure the list matches your medical billing records, copies of which you will be sending to the insurance company along with the demand letter. (See "Supporting Documents," below.)

If you were in a vehicle accident and your no-fault insurance coverage requires you to meet an expense threshold, include in your demand letter a list of your medical expenses along with copies of the bills. This means you are notifying the insurance company of your right to pursue your claim against its insured.

## Qualifying for a No-Fault Claim

If you are covered by a no-fault (Personal Injury Protection) automobile insurance policy, you may have to meet a qualifying threshold before you are allowed to file a liability claim. (See Chapter 4.) The threshold depends on the state in which you live and the particular provisions of your policy. You may need to have spent a certain amount of money on medical treatment, or your injury may need to be "serious," "permanent," or "disabling" as defined by your state's no-fault law.

Check the listings of no-fault laws in Chapter 4, as well as the terms of your own policy, to see what threshold you must meet in order to proceed with a claim for compensation against the other person's insurance company.

If you are relying on the nature and extent of your injuries—rather than on the cost of your treatment—to get your claim over the no-fault threshold, include in your demand letter a paragraph explaining why you meet the threshold. This explanation should appear immediately after the description of your injuries.

If you are relying on the amount of your medical expenses to get over the threshold, then after you have listed those expenses in the letter you can simply state that the total qualifies you for a third-party claim.

## Lost Income

Make a brief statement of the amount of time you missed from work because of your injuries, and refer to whatever letter you have from your employer verifying your pay and missed time. Then multiply the time missed by your rate of pay to get a total figure for lost income. You do not have to explain why you were unable to work. If the insurance company wishes to challenge your claim that you were unable to work, it will do so during negotiations.

Don't try to convince the insurer in your demand letter that your injuries made you miss work. Lobbying too strongly may signal that this is a subject for disagreement and negotiation. And you do not have to discuss whether you took sick leave, vacation time, or unpaid time off. The time you missed and the amount you are normally paid are the only things that matter.

If you are irregularly employed or self-employed, explain how you arrived at the total figure for lost income. Your income is impossible to predict exactly, so you do not have to claim that the figure you give is exact. Just explain what basis you used for figuring your rate of income—a weekly amount based on your previous year's income as shown on your tax return, for example, or a monthly amount based on the months immediately preceding the accident—and refer to whatever documents you have to back up that income and your missed work.

If the insurance company wants to dispute your figures or the method you used, let it bring up the matter during negotiations. Don't worry about convincing the insurer in your demand letter that the method you are using is the best or only method possible.

## Your Settlement Demand Figure

In the last paragraph of your letter, demand a specific sum of money as total compensation for your pain, suffering, lost income, and other losses. Before naming the amount, very briefly repeat the strongest part of your argument and any special facts—particularly dangerous behavior by the insured, extreme pain, extensive treatment, a long period of recovery and permanent injury—that should increase your compensation.

To arrive at the final number, review how the damages formula works. (See "The Damages Formula" in Chapter 5.) Then plug in the figures for your medical treatment and lost income and choose a higher or lower range of the formula—whichever is more realistic given the nature of your injuries and the difficulty in proving who was at fault. You will arrive at a range of figures that would be a fair settlement amount. Whether you believe your settlement is worth a figure at the higher or lower end of that range depends on several additional facts: how obvious is the other person's fault, your comparative negligence, existence of witnesses, sympathy or dramatic advantage for you or against the other person, and your willingness to be patient through the negotiation period.

In the demand letter, you begin the negotiating process with a request for compensation considerably higher than the amount you would be satisfied accepting in the end. The letter is only the beginning of a negotiation process similar to bargaining at a swap meet. You start too high, the insurance adjuster will start too low, and then you both bluff and counteroffer until you agree on a number somewhere in between. How much bluffing and counteroffering you will do depends on your personality and that of the insurance adjuster you are dealing with, and on how many variables there are in your claim, such as unclear liability or uncertain long-term injury.

Do not make the figure outrageously high, because the insurance adjuster will know that it is a meaningless number. The adjuster will just come back with an equally meaningless low number, and you will be back at square one. The number in your demand letter should be higher than what you think your claim is worth, but still believable. A general rule is 75% to 100% higher than what you would actually be satisfied with. For example, if you think your claim is worth between $1,500 and $2,000, make your first demand for $3,000 or $4,000. If you think your claim is worth $4,000 to $5,000, make your first demand for $8,000 or $10,000.

An insurance adjuster does not know how much you know about what the claim is worth. Making a high first demand announces that you know your claim should not be settled for a small sum. And it also gives the adjuster room to maneuver you downward while keeping the figure within a fair settlement range.

## Supporting Documents

Along with your demand letter, send the insurance company copies of documents, records, letters, bills, and other documentation supporting the things you describe in your letter. Keep the originals for your own files. Although no one's claim has all of the documents listed below, use the following list to remind yourself of the documents you do have that might support your claim. When you send these documents along with your demand letter, arrange them in the same order in which you refer to them to in the letter.

Supporting documents to enclose with your demand letter might include:

- a police report, copy of a traffic law or building code, or any other document supporting your contention that the insured person violated a law or legal rule, such as a statement or report about prior accidents

- photos of the accident scene
- witness statements supporting your description of how the accident happened
- any other document supporting your contention that the other person was at fault in the accident
- photos of your injury
- your medical records, arranged according to each medical provider—that is, all your records from Dr. X together in chronological order, then all records from Dr. Y
- bills, billing records, or lists of charges for all medical treatment—regardless of who paid for it—arranged chronologically by medical provider in the same order as the medical records
- documents showing your income loss, and
- documents showing other losses you suffered, such as the invitation to a wedding you missed, or the schedule of the dance classes you were forced to miss and will not be able to attend for another six months.

## Watch the Time

If more than six months have gone by since your accident, check on the time within which you must file a lawsuit to protect your rights. (See "State Statutes of Limitations" in Chapter 8.) If the time limit for filing a lawsuit is coming up within the next three months or so, remind the insurance adjuster of this in your demand letter. It will signal that you are aware of the time limit, and it might help get you a prompt reply to your demand—insurance adjusters want to settle claims before a lawsuit is filed.

## Sample Demand Letters

In this section are six samples showing the form a demand letter takes and how it can be tailored to different accident and injury situations. There are no special words you have to use, and each demand letter will be a little different. The main thing to remember is to include your strongest arguments that the accident was fully the other person's fault and that your injuries caused you pain, discomfort, inconvenience, perhaps long-term or permanent effects, and income loss, as explained in Chapter 5. Refer to all medical treatments you received for your injuries.

Each demand letter starts with a reference to the name of the insured, followed by your name (as "claimant"), the claim number given by the insurance company when you first notified it of your injuries, and the date of the accident—sometimes called "date of loss." Make sure to include this information at the beginning of all correspondence with an insurance company.

The sample demand letters here are written to support claims for the accidents and injuries described in the examples in Chapter 5. When you read a sample demand letter here, you can refer back to the corresponding example at the end of Chapter 5 to see how the demand letter emphasizes the strongest parts of the injured person's argument. You can also see the relationship between what the claim seems to be worth, as discussed in Chapter 5, and the compensation amount requested at the end of the corresponding sample demand letter.

Within each sample demand letter are explanations highlighted in bold print of why something was included or excluded in the letter, or why certain wording was used to describe one of the elements of the claim. And at the end of each sample letter is a list of the supporting documents the injured person would include with that letter.

## Demand Letters When More Than One Person Is Injured

If you are injured in an accident in which other people were also involved, like family members or friends, each person will have a separate claim against the responsible parties or insurance companies. How many demand letters you have to write depends on the relationships between the people.

If several people in the same family were injured in the same accident, they will all be dealing with the same insurance company for the other party. In that case, it's fine to include information on all the claims in one demand letter. In the letter, describe the accident only once, but then set out each individual's injuries, treatment, medical expenses, and demand for compensation in separate sections of the letter. Usually, the insurance company will want to settle all the claims at the same time.

If two people who are unrelated are injured in the same accident—for example, one person is driving a friend somewhere—they will have to write separate demand letters. Of course, there's nothing to keep them from working together to gather records, decide how much to demand, and prepare their demand letters. But the insurance company will treat the two claims separately. It might decide that one claim is worth considerably more than the other, either because of different long-term effects from the injuries or because of comparative negligence on the part of the driver, but not the passenger.

Also, if the other party doesn't have enough insurance to cover all the damages for both parties, the passenger might have to file a claim against the driver of the car he or she was riding in—this is another reason each person should write a separate demand letter.

## Sample Demand Letter: Auto Accident, Short-Term Soft Tissue Injury, Extra Damages for Missed Special Event

Oliver Simon Ball

135 Southwood Lane

London, CT 12345

March 15, 20xx

Roberta Butler

Claims Adjuster

All Risk Insurance Company

4800 Covent Boulevard

Gainsville, CT 00000

Re:  Your Insured, Matthew White

Claimant: Oliver Simon Ball

Claim No.: G 765-93

Date of Loss: January 13, 20xx

Dear Ms. Butler:

As I informed you by letter of January 17, 20xx, I was injured in an automobile accident with your insured Matthew White on January 13, 20xx in Highgate, Connecticut. I was headed west on Hornsey Lane and stopped at the stop sign at the intersection with Highgate Hill Road. While I was stopped, your insured slammed into the back of my car. *(The words "slammed into" are more dramatic than the simple word "hit" and set the stage for a serious and painful injury.)* The force of the blow threw me forward against my shoulder restraints, and my head snapped forward and back. *(Describing exactly how you were injured makes it easier for the adjuster to understand the injuries that resulted.)*

In the middle of that night, I woke with a severe headache and extremely stiff neck, so in the morning I went to the emergency room of Highgate Medical Center. *(Notice that Olly's headache is "severe" and his neck "extremely" stiff, which sounds more serious than a headache and stiff neck.)* There I was examined, and X-rays were taken of my neck and back. The doctor diagnosed a cervical strain, fitted me with a cervical collar, and advised bed rest. *(Olly describes it here as "cervical strain" even though it could also be called "whiplash.")* Because of the severe pain, he also prescribed pain relief medication. *(The fact that medication was prescribed shows that the treating doctor took the injury seriously.)*

I was in considerable pain for the next five days, and was forced to miss three days of work and the 50th birthday party in Boston of an old and dear friend. On Monday of the next week I returned to work, but still with pain and stiffness and wearing a cervical collar, which made doing my job very difficult. *(Mentioning continued pain shows that even though Olly went back to work, his injury was not yet healed.)* After another week, the doctor advised that I could remove the cervical collar.

I continued to have quite a bit of soreness and stiffness for another two weeks, interfering with my sleep and making it impossible to do any recreation or to drive unless absolutely necessary. *(Mention disruptions in sleep and other daily life matters to show that ability to return to work does not end the effects of the injury.)*

I continue to suffer occasional stiffness and sleep disruptions. *(Mentioning continuing problems may nudge the insurance adjuster to settle the claim quickly rather than risk that Olly will have to return for more medical treatment that would increase his medical specials.)*

The medical expenses for my treatment, as shown in the enclosed medical and billing records, are:

| | |
|---|---:|
| Highgate Med. Center (emergency room) | $750 |
| Highgate Med. Center (X-rays) | 190 |
| Cervical collar | 58 |
| Prescription medication | 65 |
| Total | $1,063 |

As mentioned, due to the accident, I also missed three days of work. As the enclosed letter from the personnel office of Battersea Grocery indicates, my wage loss was $392 (24 hours at $14 per hour).

Because of the negligence of your insured, I went through a period of extreme pain and discomfort that lasted for several weeks. This discomfort continues. Not only was my normal daily life disrupted, but I was forced to miss the 50th birthday party of a very dear friend whom I rarely get to see. *(Mention is repeated of a loss that does not have a dollar value but must be compensated anyway.)* As a result, I demand compensation for my injuries and general damages in the amount of $10,000. *(Olly's claim is probably worth only about $2,000–$3,500, but in his demand letter he begins negotiations by asking for more than twice the amount he would be willing to settle for.)*

I hope to hear from you soon, no longer than 30 days from the date of this letter.

Very truly yours,

*Oliver Simon Ball*

Oliver Simon Ball

**Supporting documents to be enclosed:**

- police accident report
- medical records from the hospital
- bills from the hospital
- receipt from prescription medication
- letter from Olly's job showing income and work days missed, and
- written invitation to his friend's 50th birthday party or other evidence of the event.

## Sample Demand Letter: Auto Accident, Soft Tissue Injury, Large Amount of Bills for Diagnosis, Extensive Physical Therapy

Mary Graham
812 Octavia Street, Apt. #4
Chicago, IL 00000

June 30, 20xx

Oscar Salinas
Claims Adjuster
High Life Insurance Company
1000 Throughway Boulevard
Chicago, IL 00000

RE: Your Insured, Anthony Stacatto
    Claimant: Mary Graham
    Claim No.: 93-8822 TX
    Date of Loss: January 13, 20xx

Dear Mr. Salinas:

As you are aware, I was injured in an automobile accident with your insured Anthony Stacatto on January 13, 20xx at the intersection of 12th Street and Loop Lane, Chicago. I was traveling east on Loop Lane, and as I entered the intersection with 12th Street, your insured came through a stop sign on 12th Street and smashed into my car just behind the driver's seat, barely missing a direct hit on me. ***(Even though a direct hit on Mary did not occur, the near miss increases the sense of emotional trauma Mary suffered.)*** The power of the collision spun my car all the way around and left it facing west almost all the way to the curb. ***(The power of the impact shows how fast the other driver was going, which supports both how negligent he was and how seriously Mary is injured.)*** I have enclosed the police report, which states that I had the right of way, and a diagram that shows where your insured struck my car and the final resting place of the car. The enclosed photograph showing the severe damage to my car indicates how strong the collision was.

In addition to failing to yield the right of way, your insured did not even slow down, let alone stop, at the stop sign. This was apparently due to the fact that your insured was talking on a cell phone. A witness to the accident reported this fact. As you know, if this matter ultimately becomes a lawsuit, I will have access to your insured's cell phone records. As you may be aware, the use of a cell phone while driving quadruples the risk of an accident, making it as dangerous as driving while drunk. (See the study by the University of Toronto in the February 13, 1997, *New England Journal of Medicine.*) This selfish and dangerous conduct by your insured led directly to this serious accident. ***(Emphasizes how bad the other driver would look to a jury if the case ever went to court.)***

I was badly battered by the collision and was taken by ambulance to the emergency room of Providence Hospital. Immediately after the accident, I had severe pain and stiffness in my back and a headache that was rapidly getting worse. After X-rays, I was released and advised to see my private physician. During the night, my headache became more severe and I was unable to move my back. First thing in the morning I was taken to my personal physician, Ann Lindley, M.D., who referred me to an orthopedist, Martin Chuzzlewit, M.D. Dr. Chuzzlewit examined me and discovered an inflammation of the lumbar spine. He prescribed pain and muscle relaxant medication, advised immediate bed rest, and referred me to physical therapy. *(It is important to point out that the orthopedist referred Mary to physical therapy, showing that she did not decide to go on her own. In the mind of an insurance adjuster, that makes the physical therapy treatments more medically legitimate.)*

I was forced by the pain to remain in bed for the next four days. I attempted to return to work the following Monday, but the pain once again forced me to bed for another two days. *(Good to mention that Mary tried to return to work; it shows that she was not just using her injury as an excuse for a holiday.)* I began physical therapy at the Bendright Clinic. I continued in physical therapy for five weeks, during which I remained in considerable pain and discomfort. After completing the physical therapy, I returned for an examination by Dr. Chuzzlewit, who advised me that I would have residual pain and stiffness for another few months. *(The doctor confirms long period of recovery.)*

The medical specials for my treatment are as follows:

| | |
|---|---|
| A-One Ambulance Co. | $250 |
| Providence Hospital | 460 |
| Ann Lindley, M.D. | 260 |
| Martin Chuzzlewit, M.D. | 1,110 |
| Loop Radiology Group | 280 |
| Bendright Physical Therapy | 840 |
| Prescription medication | 70 |
| Total | $3,270 |

As a result of the accident, I missed a total of five days of work as a teacher at Grover Cleveland High School. My monthly gross salary is $2,300, and the number of school days in January were 21, so per diem pay for January was $110. In total, I lost $550 in wages.

Because of the unlawful and dangerous driving *(reminding the insurance company that the insured's driving would look very bad if the claim ever made it to court)* of your insured, I suffered excruciating back pain requiring some five weeks of physical therapy. The pain has taken months to subside. I continue to suffer occasional pain and stiffness now, some six months after the accident. Also, the trauma of so narrowly missing a direct hit by your insured's car has made me fearful of driving and causes me daily anxiety when I have to drive anywhere. *(**Driving is an important part of most people's lives, and being afraid to get in a car may raise the value of the claim.**)* To compensate me for the severity of the shock, the long period of treatment, and the continuing pain and discomfort I suffer, I demand the sum of $18,500.

I look forward to your prompt reply on this matter.

Yours truly,

*Mary Graham*

Mary Graham

**Supporting documents to be enclosed:**
- police accident report and diagram
- photos of Mary's smashed car
- medical records from hospital, doctors, and physical therapists
- bills from ambulance, doctors, hospital and physical therapy, and receipt for prescription medication, and
- letter from the school district showing Mary's employment, wages, and work days missed.

## Sample Demand Letter: Bicycle-Car Accident, Hard Injury, Long Recovery Period, Extensive Physical Therapy, Lost Unofficial Work Time, Considerable Disruption of Daily Activities

Walter Blancmange
666 Crescent View
Palo Alto, CA 00000

June 15, 20xx

Maria Teeuw
Claims Adjuster
Continental Insurance Company
900 Cramer Avenue
San Francisco, CA 00000

Re: Your Insured, Sameer Mehendale
    Claimant: Walter Blancmange
    Claim No.: AQ 65393
    Date of Loss: January 13, 20xx

Dear Ms. Teeuw:

As you have been notified, I was injured in an accident with your insured Sameer Mehendale on January 13, 20xx in the city of Palo Alto, California. On that date, I was riding my bicycle in the right lane of Amstel Road, a four-lane street, when your insured in his large Oldsmobile cut over *("cut over" rather than "changed lanes")* from the middle lane into my lane without properly looking, forcing me into a collision with *("forcing me into a collision" rather than "I ran into the back of")* the rear of his car. As you are aware, the rules of the road in California give a bicyclist the same right to occupy a lane of traffic as an automobile. The accident occurred at about 10:00 on a clear morning. Visibility was good.

I was already in the right lane when your insured moved into it, cutting me off. Therefore he clearly violated my right of way and was fully at fault for the accident. Although I was unable to stop in time to avoid a collision, I was traveling within the speed limit and in a proper position to the right side of the right lane. I am an experienced cyclist who has been using a bicycle for regular local transportation for more than ten years. I ride an average of 100 miles a week, most of that in city traffic. I have ridden on that particular stretch of Amstel Road several times a week for the past seven years, and so I am very familiar with traffic patterns there. I have never before had any problem riding on Amstel Road, and in fact have never had an accident or been issued a traffic citation in all my years of cycling. For all these reasons, it is clear that I was not at all comparatively negligent regarding the accident. *(Details of the accident plus Walter's riding experience combine to show why Walter was not at fault.)*

The collision knocked me off my bicycle, into the car's bumper, and to the ground. Despite wearing a protective helmet, I was knocked unconscious and was taken to the hospital by ambulance. ***(Wearing a helmet is an important point. The fact that Walter was knocked unconscious despite the helmet is a dramatic detail.)*** At the hospital, it was discovered that I had numerous injuries, including a concussion, a fractured left ulna, and damaged ligaments in my right ankle. My injuries were so extensive that I was admitted to the hospital. The staff placed a cast on my left wrist. ***(Walter was probably kept overnight in the hospital more for observation of his concussion than for his other injuries, but it is certainly truthful for him to state that it was the "extensiveness" of his injuries that put him in the hospital.)***

Upon release from the hospital, I was unable to put weight on my right leg, and my broken wrist permitted me to use only one crutch. I was in great pain not only in my ankle and wrist but also in my back and neck. I suffered from severe headaches. I was confined to bed for a week following the accident. ***(Having to spend a week in bed would probably not show up in the medical records, so it is a good idea to mention it here.)***

My broken wrist remained in a cast for three weeks, followed by two weeks of intensive physical therapy as prescribed by my orthopedist, Dr. Kiek Bak. Dr. Bak also prescribed physical therapy for the damaged ligaments of my ankle, but after two months of therapy and four more months of recovery and exercises, the ankle is still stiff and painful when I rotate it or put weight on it. Dr. Bak cannot say whether the ankle will ever return to its preaccident condition. ***(Good to note the doctor's opinion on the likelihood of permanent injury.)***

My medical special damages for the required treatment are:

| | |
|---|---:|
| Lifesaver Ambulance Service | $260 |
| Amstelhof Mem. Hospital | 560 |
| Amstelhof Mem. Hosp. (X-ray) | 260 |
| Amstelhof Mem. Hosp. (inpatient) | 840 |
| Kiek Bak, M.D. | 360 |
| Jolle Demmers (phys.ther./wrist) | 320 |
| Jolle Demmers (phys.ther./ankle) | 1,600 |
| Total | $4,200 |

As a result of the accident and of this complicated recovery, I have been unable to ride my bicycle since the accident. Bicycle riding was not merely an occasional recreation for me—it was both an inexpensive and practical means of transportation and my major source of exercise. Long evening and weekend rides have also, for many years, been a relief from stress. I am now 54 years old. Because of the accident and the fact that I do not know if I will ever be able to ride again, all these important elements of my life are in serious jeopardy.
***(An emphasis here on how life has been seriously disrupted by the injuries.)***

As a further result of the accident, I missed eight days of work in my capacity as an editor for Sunlight Software. As the enclosed letter from the Sunlight personnel office indicates, my salary is $2,800 per month ($133 per day). My lost income, therefore, was $1,064. In addition, I fell behind on a project with a deadline and was forced to work at home for three consecutive weekends for which I received no compensation. At $133 per day, those extra six days of work add a further $798 in lost income. *(Put a specific dollar amount on the makeup work that resulted from the accident.)*

Through the clear negligence of your insured, I suffered serious multiple injuries, including head trauma, a fracture, and ligament damage from which I have not fully recovered six months after the accident. Had I not been wearing a bicycle helmet at the time of the accident, my head injuries might well have been fatal. *(Even though it is not certain, the possibility of permanent or even fatal injury is an important factor and should be emphasized.)* Further, a major source of health and satisfaction in my life, regular and long-distance bicycle riding, may have been permanently taken from me. As a result, I demand the sum of $50,000 in recompense for my injuries and their consequences.

Please respond to this letter by July 15, 20xx. I look forward to hearing from you.

Yours sincerely,

*Walter Blancmange*

Walter Blancmange

**Supporting documents to be enclosed:**
- police accident report
- photo of battered bicycle
- photos of Walter on previous long bicycle trips
- photos of injuries
- medical records from hospital, doctors, and physical therapists
- bills or record of charges from ambulance and hospital, doctors, and physical therapists, and
- letter from employer indicating salary and missed work time, plus extra weekends Walter had to work.

## Sample Demand Letter: Nonauto Accident Caused by Employees, Permanent Hard Injuries

Yolanda Mercurio
24 Park Place
Seattle, WA 00000

October 15, 20xx

Reginald Chen
Claims Adjuster
All-Safe Insurance Company
3400 Salmon Boulevard
Seattle, WA 00000

Re: Your Insured, Gorgon Mortgage Company
     Claimant: Yolanda Mercurio
     Claim No.: 4876-93
     Date of Loss: June 13, 20xx

Dear Mr. Chen:

This letter constitutes a demand for compensation from your insured, the Gorgon Mortgage Company, for serious and permanent injuries I sustained on June 13, 20xx as a result of the reckless behavior of employees of the Gorgon Mortgage Company committed on Gorgon property. **(*"Reckless" behavior sounds worse than "careless" behavior.*)**

On that date at about 1:45 p.m., I had just parked my car in the outdoor parking lot of the Soundbite Shopping Center and had stepped out of the car when I was struck in the mouth by a softball. The softball came from property owned by your insured. It was thrown or batted by employees of your insured during practice of a softball team sponsored by your insured. Because your insured provided a place on its property for its employees to practice softball in a dangerous spot next to a public parking lot, your insured is liable for the consequences.

In addition, your insured is legally responsible for the actions of its employees, who were practicing during the workday with the permission of your insured. **(*These are the reasons why the employer is liable for the acts of the employees even though the accident occurred as the result of activity not normally associated with their work.*)**

When it hit me, the softball was traveling with tremendous velocity. Indeed, it had travelled a full 30 or 40 yards before slamming into my face. The force of the blow directly on my mouth broke my front tooth and drove the broken tooth through my upper lip. **(*A graphic description of a nasty injury.*)** I was knocked to the ground in terrible pain. There was a tremendous amount of blood. A colleague drove me to the hospital emergency room. To close the wound, hospital attendants had to put stitches both in the inside and on the outside of my lip. The enclosed photographs were taken the day after the accident and show the broken tooth, the wound, and the tremendous swelling. *(A picture of the unsightly injury can be very effective.)*

The stitches in my lip were removed by my own doctor after a week, but as the enclosed photograph shows, the wound has left a scar on the outside of my upper lip. My doctor says that although it will reduce somewhat over time, a scar will remain permanently visible. *(Emphasis on the permanent nature of the injury.)*

My broken tooth was treated by my dentist until the lip wound healed, and then a cap was fitted over the tooth. The cap is uncomfortable, and it has affected what I can eat because of my concern for biting into anything hard. Also, it is obvious that the cap is not a real tooth. Because the cap is on my front tooth, the way it looks causes me considerable embarrassment. Every time I start to smile I become self-conscious, thinking about my false tooth as well as my scar. *(Emphasis on the emotional distress caused by the injury.)*

The problem with the false tooth will only get worse over time. It will discolor differently from the normal teeth around it and will have to be replaced at regular intervals for the rest of my life. Also, because it is fit over my broken tooth, there is the potential for movement, gum disease, and other future dental problems that can prove painful, inconvenient, disfiguring, and expensive. That means several future dental bills of around $1,000 each, in current dollars. *(Discussion of future problems suggests to insurance adjuster that claim should be settled sooner rather than later when such long-term problems might actually start to appear.)*

The medical expenses for the treatment of my lip and my tooth, so far, are: *(The words "so far" remind the adjuster that if the claim is not settled soon, more medical bills might have to be put into the formula.)*

| | |
|---|---|
| Puget Sound Medical Center ER | $750 |
| Fiona Brown, M.D. | 2,400 |
| Elton Limpet, D.D.S. | 520 |
| TOTAL | $3,670 |

My injuries also caused me to lose time from work. I am a self-employed graphic artist. For the three months immediately prior to my accident I averaged income of $2,204 per month, as my enclosed billing records indicate. As a result of the accident, I lost a day and a half of work right after the accident, plus another day and a half during medical treatments, for a total of three days. At $105 per day ($2,204 per month divided by 21 work days per month) my income loss for those three days was approximately $315. *(Includes explanation of how self-employment income loss was calculated.)*

Because I was unable to go on any job interviews until my mouth had healed and my tooth was fixed, my income for the following two months dropped to an average of only $850 per month—an additional $2,700 in income loss as a result of the accident.

Through the irresponsible actions of your insured and its employees, I have suffered a painful injury that has left a permanent scar on my face and a permanently disfigured and unstable front tooth. Because of the visibility and permanence of the injuries, and the inevitable future work on the tooth, I demand the sum of $50,000 in compensation.

Please respond to this letter by November 15, 20xx. I look forward to hearing from you.

Sincerely yours,

*Yolanda Mercurio*

Yolanda Mercurio

**Supporting documents to be enclosed:**

- photo of the scene
- photo of Yolanda's injuries immediately after the accident
- photo of Yolanda's scar
- photo of Yolanda's capped tooth
- medical records from hospital, doctor, and dentist
- bills from hospital, doctor, and dentist, and
- Yolanda's business billing records showing her earnings during the months immediately before and after the accident.

## Sample Demand Letter: Slip and Fall, Commercial Property-Owner Liability, Witnesses, Hard Injury, Surgery Plus Nontraditional Treatments, Long Recovery Period

Seiji Kurosawa
236 Sunset Grove
Fontana Beach, FL 00000

September 15, 20xx

William Casey
Claims Adjuster
Atlantic Risk Insurance Company
2400 Causeway Boulevard
Miami, FL 00000

Re:  Your Insured, Medellin Investments
     Claimant: Seiji Kurosawa
     Claim No.: T11889 PX
     Date of Loss: January 13, 20xx

Dear Mr. Casey:

As you are aware, I was injured in a fall on January 13, 20xx in the underground parking lot of a building at 6750 Palm Avenue, Miami, owned by your insured, Medellin Investments. The accident occurred at about 6:00 p.m. when I was heading for my car parked in the garage. I am an employee of the South Florida Import-Export Exchange, which leases offices in the building from your insured. As I crossed the dark garage floor, I slipped on a patch of oil, badly twisting my left knee and falling to the ground.

That night, my knee swelled greatly. In the morning, I went to see my physician, Dr. Rose Parker, who advised that I stay off the leg for the next several days. I went home and rested the leg, missing the next three days of work.

The following Monday, I returned to work and examined the garage where I had fallen. As the enclosed photographs taken that day show, there were grease and oil spots all over the floor, some of which had obviously been there for quite a while. To make matters worse, several of the overhead lights were burned out, leaving dark areas on the floor and hiding the oil and grease spots. Given that there were several lights burned out, it is clear that no one had checked or replaced the bulbs for quite some time. Obviously, your insured fails to maintain the garage in a reasonably safe manner, instead allowing real hazards to exist. *(Seiji demonstrates that he investigated near the time of the accident.)*

The situation in the garage is so dangerous that at least two other people in the building have recently slipped on oil spots in the garage. *(Seiji informs the adjuster that witnesses are available to support his claim of danger in the garage. If he has good written statements from them, he should identify the witnesses here and refer to enclosed witness statements.)* Further investigation may, of course, show that others have slipped in the garage as well.

The swelling in my knee subsided after about a week, but the knee continued to be painful and to catch when bent. I was examined by an orthopedist, Dr. Ralph Brancusa, who began me on physical therapy in his office. Although I obtained some relief from the soreness, the physical therapy did not eliminate the catch inside my knee when I bent or twisted it. Therefore, I ended the physical therapy sessions voluntarily. *("Voluntarily" ended demonstrates that Seiji did not continue treatment any longer than necessary.)*

I received acupuncture treatment from Dr. William Chan, which relieved some of the pain in the knee. *(Shows that nontraditional treatment had positive results.)* I was referred by Dr. Chan to a chiropractor, Lilly Sing Rhee, for manipulation to treat the catch in the knee. Ms. Sing Rhee stopped treatment after a short time and suggested that I return to an orthopedic surgeon.

My physician referred me to Dr. Walter Frisch, an orthopedic surgeon. Dr. Frisch X-rayed the knee and performed an arthroscopic examination, which revealed torn cartilage, which Dr. Frisch repaired arthroscopically.

Following the arthroscopic surgery, I missed another week of work, then resumed walking and began home exercises prescribed by Dr. Frisch. After approximately eight more weeks, I was able to begin running again, my regular daily exercise that I was unable to do for almost eight months because of the accident. *(Emphasizes long time for recovery.)*

My medical expenses for this treatment are:

| | |
|---|---|
| Rose Parker, M.D. | $360 |
| Ralph Brancusa, M.D. (including X-rays) | 1,260 |
| William Chan | 320 |
| Lilly Sing Rhee | 640 |
| Walter Frisch, M.D. (including X-rays) | 4,520 |
| Total | $7,100 |

As the enclosed letter from my employer, South Florida Import-Export Exchange, indicates, I missed eight days of work (three immediately after the accident, five more after surgery), for a total of $1,120 ($140 per day) in lost wages.

Because of the obvious negligence of your insured in failing to properly maintain its building, a dangerous hazard was created that resulted in serious cartilage damage to my knee, requiring surgery and an eight-month period of recovery and rehabilitation. Because of the seriousness of the injury and the long time for its recovery, I demand $80,000 in compensation.

Because the statute of limitations requires me to file a lawsuit against your insured in this matter within three months from now, I look forward to resolving this claim in the near future. Please provide me with a response within 14 days from your receipt of this letter. *(Demands prompt reply.)*

Very truly yours,

*Seiji Kurosawa*

Seiji Kurosawa

**Supporting documents to be included:**

- photos of garage showing grease spots and burned-out lights
- statements of others who have fallen there
- medical records and bills from all doctors and other medical providers, and
- letter from employer stating wages and work time missed.

## Sample Demand Letter: Slip and Fall on Stairs, Hard Injury, Surgery, Permanent Injury, Large Comparative Negligence

Wanda Shore
21566 Riverside Drive
Los Angeles, CA 00000

September 15, 20xx

Roger de la Rue
Claims Adjuster
Twentieth Century Insurance Adjuster
6400 Century Boulevard
Los Angeles, CA 00000

Re: Your Insured, Broadmart Stores
    Claimant: Wanda Shore
    Claim No.: 93-1033 BS
    Date of Loss: January 13, 20xx

Dear Mr. de la Rue:

I was injured on January 13, 20xx in the West Hollywood Broadmart store. I fell coming down some stairs in the women's shoe section where I had been shopping. I landed on my right arm, shattering my elbow. *(Wanda describes her elbow as "shattered" rather than simply broken, establishing the seriousness of her injury.)*

LIABILITY

Two weeks after the accident, I had the stairs on which I fell carefully examined. In at least four separate ways, the stairs present an unreasonable hazard to a customer. First, the lack of handrails is a violation of law. The Los Angeles County Building Code Section 1225 requires that all commercial sets of stairs have handrails every 88 inches. Because this open stairway is more than 11 feet wide, it should have had handrails on each side and one in the middle. It had no handrails at all. At my age, 76, I always use a handrail when one is available, and in this case a handrail would have prevented a serious fall.

Also, the county building code requires that riser heights be the same to within one-quarter inch. The riser heights of the second and third stairs, on which I fell, differ by a full inch (6-1/8 inches to 7-1/8 inches). This violation of the code proved dangerous because when I came down the stairs, the third step down did not meet my foot at the same point as did the previous step, throwing me off balance. *(Wanda specifically explains why the violation of the building code caused her accident.)*

As the enclosed photographs show, the color of the carpeting contributes to the danger. The third step is covered with the same dark red carpet as on the bottom floor, while the platform and the first two steps down are covered in white carpet. Looking down onto the red third step, it is difficult to see that it is a step at all rather than the beginning of the floor. *(Photograph explained instead of merely included.)* The third step should have been white like the other two. And finally, display spotlights set up around the stairs shine directly into your eyes as you come down, making it extremely difficult to see the steps clearly.

For all these reasons, the stairs presented a hazardous condition and caused me to fall. The building code violations alone establish the store's liability. When the other factors are added, it becomes even more clear how dangerous the stairs were.

INJURY AND TREATMENT

Immediately after the fall, I was taken by ambulance to the Mt. Pleasant Hospital emergency room, where they took X-rays and put my arm in a temporary cast. I was in terrible pain and was given a Demerol injection and more Demerol to take orally. *(Mention of the specific strong drug verifies the amount of pain Wanda suffered.)* The next day, I went to see Dr. Barton Groback, an orthopedic surgeon, but my arm was so swollen that he could not examine it. He gave me more prescription pain medication, and for the next several days, I was in so much pain that all I could do was stay in bed. Even the slightest movement brought on excruciating pain. *(Great pain emphasized again.)*

When I returned to Dr. Groback the next week, he took more X-rays and scheduled me for surgery. He operated on January 24, 20xx, and I spent three days in the hospital, then another week in bed, in great pain. I stayed in a cast for eight weeks, during which I required help just to care for myself. For the first two weeks after the operation I was in great pain. And for most of the eight weeks that I was in a cast, I was forced to stay around the house.

After the cast was removed, I began physical therapy treatments to regain movement and strength in my arm. I went to physical therapy for three months, and since then I have been doing daily exercises given to me by Dr. Groback. Despite all the therapy and the exercises, however, I still have much less strength in the arm than before the accident. I cannot bend the elbow much or twist my arm in either direction. Dr. Groback says that I will have to keep doing the exercises just to keep the arm at its present level, but that I will never recover full use of it. He also says that over time I may develop arthritis in the elbow joint, making it even less movable and more painful. *(Mention not only of long recovery and permanent injury but possibility of further problems later on.)*

The costs of my medical treatment are as follows:

| | |
|---|---|
| Osprey Ambulance Service | $320 |
| Mt. Pleasant Hospital (E.R.) | 700 |
| Barton Groback, M.D. | 4,860 |
| Mt. Pleasant Hospital (surgery) | 5,650 |
| Flexall Physical Therapy | 1,200 |
| Total | $12,730 |

Because of the many dangers on the stairs, including two violations of the building code which led directly to my fall, I suffered a shattered right arm. My injury required surgery and many months of rehabilitation, and has resulted in a permanent loss of some use of my arm. Because of the great pain I have suffered and the permanent disability the injury has caused, I demand $120,000 as compensation.

As you are aware, if this matter is not settled before January, I will be forced to file a lawsuit against Broadmart stores to protect my legal interests. *(A reminder to the insurance adjuster that Wanda may file a lawsuit soon, something the adjuster does not want her to do because it would get lawyers involved.)* I hope, therefore, for your prompt attention to this matter.

Very truly yours,

*Wanda Shore*

Wanda Shore

**Supporting documents to be included:**
- a copy of the building code sections that regulate construction of stairs
- photos of the stairs
- photos of Wanda's arm at different stages of treatment and recovery, and
- medical records and bills from ambulance and all hospitals, doctors, and physical therapists.

# Chapter 7

# Property Damage Claims

## Using This Chapter

This chapter discusses claims for compensation for property that is damaged in an accident. These include claims for damage to your vehicle and its contents resulting from traffic accidents, whether or not the other driver is insured or the damage is covered under your own vehicle insurance.

This chapter also covers damage to personal property in other types of accidents—for example, where the injury is caused by a trip and fall or by a defective product. You can usually settle claims for property damage separately from, and often much more quickly than, your injury claim.

M any accidents that cause personal injury also damage property. Both vehicles and contents—things worn or carried inside the car or trunk, or equipment worn or carried while riding a bicycle—are frequently damaged or destroyed in traffic accidents. And given the cost of cars today, a broken axle may pull higher compensation than a broken wrist. In vehicle accidents, the way in which you can be compensated for property damage depends on the type of insurance you and the other driver have—and on who was at fault for causing the accident.

In nonvehicle accidents, the clothes, watch, or jewelry you were wearing or an object you were carrying may have been damaged or destroyed. If you can show that another person was at least partly at fault for such an accident, you may be compensated by the other person's business, homeowner's, or personal liability insurance. (See "Nonvehicle Liability Insurance" in Chapter 4.)

## What Type of Claim to File

You may be compensated for property damage from a vehicle accident through a claim:

- against the liability insurance of another person involved in the accident, called a third-party claim
- under your own uninsured motorist coverage if your uninsured motorist coverage includes property damage and if the other driver was not insured but was at least partly at fault, or
- under your own auto insurance collision coverage, even if you were the one completely at fault.

If you suffered property damage in an accident that did not involve a vehicle, a third-party claim is your only path to compensation.

## What If My Car Is Vandalized?

Collision insurance covers only damage to cars that occurs when they are moving, or are stopped but struck by another vehicle. The same is true for uninsured motorist coverage. Vandalism is covered by a separate coverage known as "comprehensive" or "all risks." Not all people carry this coverage, so an individual's policy determines whether such compensation is available.

Another possible source of insurance coverage is the company's premises liability insurance. If it can be shown that vandalism has been going on for a while in the company lot and the company knows about it but has done nothing to control it, the company might be considered legally responsible for continued acts of vandalism. (See Chapters 2 and 4.)

## Third-Party Claims (Claims Against Someone Else's Insurance Company)

An accident claim against another person's insurance company is known as a third-party claim. The other person and his or her insurance company are considered the first two parties; you are the third party. To receive property damage compensation in a third-party claim, the other person must be at least partly at fault and legally responsible, or liable, for the accident. (See Chapter 2.) If the other person's fault is relatively clear, you can immediately proceed with your third-party property damage claim and usually receive a settlement for property loss or damage—separate from your personal injury claim—within days or weeks. (See "Processing Your Claim," below.) This procedure is also followed in vehicle accidents in states with no-fault auto insurance. No-fault insurance covers personal injury claims, but not property damage, so property claims in no-fault states will always be third-party claims.

In some cases, the insurance adjuster for the other person may dispute the matter of how much—if at all—its insured was at fault. (See Chapter 2.) Until such a dispute is resolved, the other insurance company may delay reaching an agreement with you about who pays how much for damage to your vehicle or other property.

When these negotiations drag on, you may feel stuck. You may need money to get your property repaired or replaced, particularly in the case of a vehicle. Or you may not be prepared to argue the issue of fault with the other insurance company before you have had the chance to look into the matter sufficiently. In either case, instead of a third-party claim, you can file a property damage claim under your own auto insurance collision coverage, if you carry it. (See "Collision Coverage Claims," below.)

## Uninsured Motorist Coverage Claims

Many people carry uninsured motorist insurance coverage to compensate them in case of an accident with another driver who does not carry liability insurance. Some versions of this coverage include a certain amount for property damage.

To be compensated for property damage under uninsured motorist coverage, you must demonstrate that the uninsured driver was at least to some degree at fault for the accident. Whether you can collect the full amount of repair or only a percentage will depend on whether you can demonstrate that the other driver was completely at fault. Your property damage compensation may be reduced by the degree that it appears that you were at fault, called comparative negligence. (See "How Your Carelessness Affects Your Claim" in Chapter 2.)

If you cannot show that the other driver was at fault, or if you can show only that an uninsured motorist was minimally at fault, you may still be able to claim property damage compensation under your collision coverage, because it pays for vehicle property damage regardless of fault.

If you are eligible to collect from both uninsured motorist property damage coverage and collision coverage for the same accident, your uninsured motorist coverage will pay for any deductible you owe under your collision coverage.

## Collision Coverage Claims

Even if you were completely at fault for an auto accident, you may be able to collect compensation for damage to your vehicle if you carry collision coverage in your own auto insurance policy. Also called car damage coverage, collision coverage allows you to make a claim with your own insurance company to pay for repairs to your car regardless of who was at fault for the accident. You can file and collect on your collision claim even though you are still negotiating the question of who was at fault in a third-party claim for injuries with another person's insurance company.

You can file a claim for your property damage under your own collision coverage or under a third-party claim against the other driver, but you cannot collect full compensation from both. Once you settle a claim under your own collision coverage, you give up your right to collect that amount from the other driver's insurance for the same property damage. If you collect from your own insurance company, your company takes over your right to file a damage claim against the other driver's insurance.

> **EXAMPLE:** You are in a car accident with Joseph Blau, who is insured by the Incidental Insurance Company. You are injured in the accident, and your car sustains $3,000 worth of damage. You file a third-party claim against Incidental for injuries to you and for damages to your car.
>
> Incidental argues that the accident was at least half your fault, so it offers only $1,500 for your car damage. You believe that you can show that Joseph was completely at fault, but it will take several weeks to get what you hope will be a helpful police accident report, and the witness who will corroborate what happened is away on a monthlong vacation.
>
> You have $5,000 worth of collision coverage with your own insurer, the New Age Insurance Company. If you do not want to wait to get paid by Incidental, or if you aren't sure Incidental is going to agree that Joseph was at fault and believe it might not pay the full $3,000, you can file a claim with New Age. Collision coverage pays regardless of fault, so New Age must pay you the full $3,000 minus any deductible.

> If you collect from New Age, you give up your right to collect property damage from Incidental—except for your deductible amount. After paying you, New Age will try to get reimbursed by Incidental, but its success or failure in doing so will not affect your right to keep the full $3,000, minus the deductible, you have collected from New Age.

Nothing you do under your own collision coverage affects your right to pursue a personal injury claim against the other driver's insurance company. You are free to go after the other driver's insurance company for any personal injuries and lost income. You are also free to collect whatever property damage your own collision coverage did not pay for—such as your deductible (see below) and any uncovered equipment or property.

## Advantages of Using Your Collision Coverage

There are two main advantages to claiming property damage under the collision coverage of your own policy rather than in a third-party claim.

First, your own coverage is likely to settle with you more quickly. This is because collision coverage pays regardless of fault. A third-party claim is paid only if the other party's fault is shown, and that often takes some time if the other insurance company disputes the degree to which its insured was responsible for the accident. You may have to wait for a police accident report or to contact a witness before you can fully demonstrate the other driver's fault. (See Chapter 2.) Or the other insurance company may simply stall to see whether you will give in on the question of fault.

Second, if you also have a third-party personal injury claim, you simply may not want to discuss the question of fault with the other person's insurance company until you have fully investigated the matter. Until you are certain about the facts and your arguments, it is dangerous to discuss details of the accident with investigators.

The struggle over who was at fault does not come up under your own collision coverage, and so these delays in paying out do not occur. Your own insurance company must reimburse you immediately after you have complied with its rules regarding inspection and estimates and you have agreed on a repair amount.

## Disadvantages of Using Your Collision Coverage

If you collect a claim under your own collision coverage, you are limited to the amount of coverage listed in the policy. If the collision coverage policy limit is less than the cost of repairing the vehicle, you will have to come up with the rest of the repair costs out of your own pocket unless you settle a claim against the other driver's insurance. Also, unlike a third-party claim, your policy may restrict the amount you can collect for items that were inside your vehicle—for example, clothing, luggage, or sound equipment that is not permanently installed—and on rental car and other replacement transportation costs.

In addition, the compensation you collect under your collision coverage will be reduced by the amount specified in your policy as the collision coverage deductible. If the deductible is large and you need the amount to pay for repairs, this can present an added problem in getting your car repaired. For example, most people carry a deductible amount of $500 to $2,000 on their collision coverage. If repairs to your car cost $5,000 and you have a $1,000 deductible, your insurance coverage will pay you $4,000, and you must come up with the other $1,000 out of your own pocket.

Another disadvantage is that the rules set by your insurance policy for processing a claim under your collision coverage may be more restrictive than the process of a third-party claim. For example, your collision coverage may require more bothersome inspections of the car and estimates of the work before you can get approval for repairs. By contrast, the other driver's insurance company has no right to enforce any such specific rules during the course of your claim. That's because your right to compensation from another driver's insurance arises from the other driver's fault and not from any agreement between you and the insurance company. (See "Processing Your Claim," below.)

## Will Your Rates Go Up?

Everyone is painfully aware of the often exorbitant cost of auto insurance. And so people are understandably concerned that if they claim property damage under their own policies, their insurance rates will go up. But while insurance companies often do raise rates after an accident, such increases are not generally based on the fact that you have filed a claim.

Insurance companies base rates on several factors, including location and type of car and age of the primary driver. But it is your driving record that is most likely to affect your rates. If you are involved in an injury accident, your company will look at your overall driving record, including all moving violations and accidents, to determine whether to raise your rates or, if your record becomes bad enough, to cancel your insurance altogether. It is the fact that you have been involved in an accident, rather than the type of property damage claim you file, that may affect your rates.

## Amount of Compensation

You are entitled to compensation for the cost of repair to a vehicle or any other item damaged in an accident, but only up to the actual cash value of the property. Actual cash value, or ACV, is another way of saying market value. It is measured by what the property could have been sold for at the time it was damaged or destroyed. It is usually substantially less than replacement value, or the cost of buying an identical new item.

If a vehicle or other piece of property is damaged so that the cost of repair would be greater than the property's ACV, the property is referred to as a "total" or "total loss." In the case of a totaled vehicle, an insurance company is required to pay you only the vehicle's ACV, not the cost of repair. The same thing is true of property other than a vehicle when the repair cost would be higher than its ACV. The question of how much damaged property is worth can be a sticky one. It involves determining how much similar used property is sold for in your geographic area. (See "Disputes Over Value of Totaled Property," below.)

**EXAMPLE:** Hagatha is in an accident while driving her ten-year-old car, which is in excellent running condition because she has cared for it so well. The accident has cracked the engine block, and the car requires extensive body work. Still, it can be repaired to run as well as it ran before the accident. The bill for the repairs is $5,500. However, the actual current value of a car the make and model of Hagatha's car is only $4,000. The insurance company paying her property damage claim will pay only the $4,000 ACV for the car, not the cost of the repair. Hagatha is left to decide whether to pay the rest of the repair bill out of her own pocket—or junk the car and buy another.

Insurance should also pay for the reasonable cost of temporary replacement property. This could include a rental car or other transportation expense if your car can no longer be driven. In the case of damaged business equipment, it includes any property you need to use until your property is repaired or replaced.

The insurance company is also responsible for vehicle towing and storage costs. Under the collision coverage of your own insurance policy, however, the amount you can collect for towing, alternative transportation, and replacement or repair of the contents of the car may be limited by the terms of the policy.

**EXAMPLE:** After Josh was involved in an auto accident, his car was out of commission for ten days for estimates and repairs. The towing and storage bill was $140, and the cost of repairs was $2,200. He rented a car for $36 per day, using it for work and other transportation.

Also damaged in the collision was Josh's laptop computer he bought a year ago for $1,800 and used for work. He had the computer checked out for repair, which cost $75, but it turned out the computer could not be saved. The newspaper classified ads listed a used computer of the same model and age as selling for between $1,200 and $1,300.

This is the total property damage for which Josh could be compensated by the other driver's insurance or his own collision coverage:

| | |
|---|---|
| Auto towing & storage | $140 |
| Auto repair | 2,200 |
| Rental car | 360 |
| Computer estimate | 75 |
| Computer value (ACV) | 1,250 |
| Total | $4,025 |

⚠ **Watch the deductible.** If you make your claim for compensation under the collision coverage of your own auto insurance policy, the amount of your collision deductible is subtracted from the total amount you are compensated. However, there is no deductible when you make a property damage claim against the other driver in a third-party claim.

---

## No Compensation for a Borrowed Car

Instead of renting a car or taking public transportation while their own vehicles are being repaired, some people borrow cars from friends or relatives and then try to charge the insurance company a "rental" rate for the time the borrowed cars are used.

Although it may be entirely legitimate to pay for using someone else's car, the insurance companies will not foot the bill. The practice is so easily abused that all insurance companies refuse such compensation as a matter of course. If you want to be repaid for alternative transportation, use some official means of transport and save the receipts, tickets, or some other proof that you really have paid to get around.

---

## Processing Your Claim

The process of getting compensation for property damage varies slightly depending on whether there is also a personal injury claim. If the damage was to a car, the process may also vary depending on whether you are filing a third-party claim or a claim under your own auto policy's collision or uninsured motorist coverage. In all of these situations, however, property damage negotiations are almost always carried out soon after the accident. Negotiations are almost always conducted on the phone rather than by formal correspondence as in a personal injury claim. Most often, the only written documents that pass between a property damage claimant and an insurance adjuster are copies of written repair estimates and inspections of the damage, and copies of proof of an item's market value.

## Filing a Third-Party Claim

A third-party property damage claim is usually handled by the other person's insurance company immediately after the accident and separately from the personal injury claim. In vehicle accidents, the two claims—one for personal injury, the other for property damage—are sometimes negotiated by two different insurance adjusters, each of whom specializes in that type of claim.

During your discussions in a property damage claim with another party's insurance adjuster—whether or not the same adjuster handles both personal injury and property damage—follow the general cautions outlined in this book. (See Chapter 3.)

One difference between a property damage claim and a personal injury claim is that with the property damage claim you will be back in contact with the adjuster as soon as you have a repair estimate for your property—whereas with a personal injury claim, you would wait until your medical condition stabilized before speaking again with the adjuster. You may need to speak with the adjuster on the phone several times to set up inspection of your car or other property, or to get a separate insurance estimate of repairs if the adjuster requests it.

In a third-party claim, you are not required to get any particular number of repair estimates. However, if you get more than one written estimate, the insurance company will be less likely to argue with you over the amount of repair costs. The more detailed the estimates you receive—each replacement part and labor specified—the more easily you can argue that they are fair and reasonable.

## Limit Your Conversations With the Adjuster

In many instances, there is a property damage claim to settle quickly and a personal injury claim that will take longer to process and may involve considerably more money.

If you have both types of claims, you will discuss the property damage matters first. Because the facts of the accident or of your medical condition may have a great impact on the outcome of your personal injury claim, do not discuss them in any detail until you are completely prepared to do so.

When initially speaking with adjusters to set up an inspection or repair estimate or to negotiate the amount of your property damage settlement, limit the subject of your conversation to the matter of property damage. Do not give information about your physical injuries, physical condition, or medical treatment. And discuss the cause of the accident in only the most basic terms.

If you are asked about your injuries or treatment, politely tell the adjuster that you are not prepared to discuss those questions until your treatment is complete. (See Chapter 3.) If the adjuster disputes the question of fault and wants to discuss the cause of the accident in detail, consider either collecting under your own insurance collision coverage if you have it or delaying your property damage claim until you are ready to negotiate your injury claim as well.

## Get Quality Estimates

Seek estimates for repairing damage to your vehicle or other property only from places where you would actually go to have the repair work done. Make sure that the repair shop is qualified and thorough enough to find all the damage. And make sure that the estimate quoted will be an amount sufficient to repair the property to the highest standards. If a piece of business equipment or a vehicle is damaged, for example, get your estimate from a factory-authorized repair facility.

If you just get the easiest estimate—taking your car to the corner gas station, for example, or taking your laptop computer to the neighborhood techies—you may find that the amount quoted will not be enough to cover the repairs you eventually have done at a quality repair shop.

The insurance company for the person or business responsible for the accident may simply accept a repair estimate you obtain as a fair settlement amount. But it also has a right to inspect the damage and/or obtain its own estimate of repair costs. The conditions for such inspections and estimates must be reasonable. That means that if the insurer would like to have someone examine the car or other property, it should be at a time and place at your convenience, not theirs. And you should be present at the inspection, according to your schedule. It may be sensible for you and the insurance company to have you take the damaged property to a local inspection site or repair shop. But the emphasis here is on local; you have no obligation to travel any great distance just because the insurance company would prefer to have the inspection done at a particular place. And only one inspection should be needed, unless you or your repair shop later discover some damage you did not discuss with the insurance adjuster originally.

Try to be reasonable with the adjuster about where and when the insurance company is to inspect the property or check it for repair. If you are reasonable, the adjuster is more likely to be reasonable, and the sooner you can agree on an inspection, the sooner you will resolve the matter and receive your compensation.

Once you have obtained your estimates, provided them to the adjuster, and allowed the insurance company to make its own inspection or obtain its own estimate, you will begin to negotiate with the adjuster about how much compensation you should receive for the damage. If the cost of repairs is at all close to the ACV of the property, you should begin to gather information on exactly what the ACV is in the area where you live.

## No Need for Long Delays

Do not allow an insurance company's inspection or estimates to delay repairs unnecessarily. If the insurance company does not inspect the property within a week or so after the accident and you have given it a reasonable opportunity to do so, and if you already have two independent written estimates, then there is no reason to delay getting your property repaired if you can afford to pay from your own pocket. Get the repairs done and then demand reimbursement from the insurance company. Of course, if you get the repairs at the shop that gave the highest estimate, the insurance company might agree to reimburse you only for a lower estimate. Also, be aware that getting car repairs before you agree on an amount removes one of the incentives for the insurance company to settle quickly. Once you have your car back, the insurance company no longer has to pay for alternative transportation.

## Filing Under Your Own Vehicle Coverage

As discussed in "Collision Coverage Claims," above, if you make a property damage claim under your own auto insurance coverage, the terms of your policy may set rules regarding inspections and estimates. And some policies may permit inspections or estimates that you would not have to agree to in a third-party claim. For example, your policy may require vehicle inspections at one of the insurance company's own inspection stations. If you live some distance away from the nearest inspection location, you may have to travel farther than you would to get an estimate for a third-party claim. Or the policy may require that you let the insurer get more than one repair estimate, in addition to any estimates you have already obtained. Moreover, the policy may not permit you to have the car repaired until these extra inspections and estimates are completed.

Generally, though, insurance adjusters don't put you through more than one inspection or estimate. They have to pay their own inspectors and repair shops, and they don't want to spend more money than is necessary. Most important, whatever the specifics of your policy, an insurance adjuster's requests for inspections or estimates always must be reasonable. For example, if you live far from the inspection site, you are perfectly within your rights to request that the adjuster find someplace closer. Likewise, you do not have to follow the adjuster's schedule in setting up an inspection or estimate. If it is inconvenient for you to appear at a given time, ask that the adjuster reschedule the inspection.

Although in general it is a good idea to keep phone conversations with adjusters to a minimum (see Chapter 3) and to put your personal injury settlement arguments in writing (see Chapter 6), estimates and inspections of property damage are almost always arranged over the phone. There are two reasons for this.

First, writing a letter, having it delivered, and receiving an answer can take days. And while letters are preferable for laying out facts and making arguments, they are not nearly as efficient for coming to an agreement on logistical matters such as when and where a car should be inspected. And you probably want to be efficient so that you can have your car repaired as soon as possible.

Second, as long as you confine your discussions to the where and when of inspection and don't discuss the details of the accident or of your injuries, you will not hurt your claim by speaking with an adjuster on the phone. Because the efficiency is high and the risk is low, the phone is the way to go. Email is also effective for logistical discussions, though we don't recommend using it for anything substantive.

If an insurance adjuster continues to insist on inspections or estimates that you consider unreasonable—either because they duplicate other inspections or because they are at times or places that seriously inconvenience you—you may have to try other tactics to get the adjuster to cooperate. (See Chapter 8.)

## Negotiating a Settlement Amount

Often an insurance adjuster will agree with you over the phone that a written repair estimate you obtained is fair—and will quickly send you a check for that amount. If so, you get to decide whether to have the vehicle or other property repaired at the place that gave you that estimate or somewhere else. In fact, you can decide to either repair the property yourself or not at all. The money is yours to do with as you see fit. This is true whether you have settled a third-party claim with another person's insurance company or a claim under your own coverage. The exception is for a claim under your own auto policy when your vehicle has been declared a total.

## A Totaled Car Belongs to Your Insurance Company

If your car is totaled—that is, the cost of repair is greater than the actual cash value—there are limits on your compensation rights. When you file a property damage claim under your own insurance coverage—collision or uninsured motorist—you will be paid the actual cash value of the car. But you must either sign over title to the car to your insurance company or agree on a salvage value, which the company will subtract from your payment. Either way, your insurance company gets the salvage value of the car. But if you're someone who likes to tinker with cars and you don't want to sign over title, you can agree to have the salvage value deducted and tinker to your heart's content.

As you negotiate a settlement figure with the insurance company about your vehicle damage, include your costs of alternative transportation while your vehicle was out of commission. You can prove the amounts of those costs by providing the insurance company with copies of receipts from rental cars and taxis or tickets from public transportation. Also make sure that your negotiations include the value of any damaged or destroyed personal property that you were wearing or that was inside the car.

If you had to rent temporary replacement property other than a vehicle—business equipment, for example—the insurance company must also reimburse you for the rental cost.

## Disputes Over Repair Amount

If the insurance company has conducted its own inspection or obtained its own estimate, the adjuster may dispute the estimates you have obtained. If so, there are several factors to consider in negotiating with the adjuster about the fair amount of a property damage settlement. Before actually negotiating, however, make sure that both you and the adjuster have exchanged written copies of all estimates and inspection reports.

These written estimates will form the basis of your negotiations, so the more detailed your estimates are, the more easily you can argue that they are more complete and accurate than the insurance company's estimates. Discussed below are a number of ways you can argue that your estimate is the correct one.

### Unrealistic Estimates

If the insurance company's estimate of repairs is based on its own inspection rather than on that of a qualified repair shop, you can argue that the estimate is a meaningless figure because it does not reflect what it would actually cost to get the work done competently. Unless the adjuster can guarantee a qualified local repair shop that would thoroughly and expertly repair the property for the amount the inspection has estimated, the inspection figure is just a whistle in the wind.

## Watch Out for Low-Ball Estimates

If a third-party adjuster tells you the company has a repair shop that will fix your car for substantially less than the estimate you got, be cautious. Insurance companies sometimes have sweetheart deals with local repair shops that do cut-rate work for the insurance company in exchange for lots of referrals. But that doesn't guarantee that the inspection for damage is thorough or that the work done is good quality.

The car owner should always get his or her own inspections and estimates from independent repair shops. If two or three independent estimates are higher than the one insurance company estimate, the insurance company's estimate is probably a poor one. Repairs should be made only by a shop chosen by the car owner, regardless of how much money the car owner receives in settlement.

## Incomplete Estimates

If the insurance company's estimate is from a repair shop, make sure that the estimate is thorough and detailed. Particularly with regard to vehicles, these estimates are often made by someone taking a quick overall guess at what repairs would cost rather than taking the time to itemize each part and labor cost. And make sure that the estimate includes any repainting that might be required. Unless the repair estimate has been carefully itemized and can be compared with your own estimate, you can argue that it is too vague or incomplete to be taken seriously.

## Estimates for Improper Repairs

Particularly if the property to be repaired is new, expensive, or rare, an estimate that is not based on factory replacement parts or is not made by a shop that specializes in repairs of that specific make or brand is worthless. You have a right to have your property repaired to the condition it was in before the accident, not merely to have it functional.

If the insurance company's estimate does not spell out all the parts to be used and their cost, and specify that they are to be factory authorized replacement parts, you can explain to the adjuster why that repair estimate is inadequate. Similarly, if the shop that makes the estimate does not specialize in repairing your make or brand of vehicle or other property, its estimate should not be a basis for compensation.

## Beware of Cheap Replacement Parts

In automobile damage claims, it is a shamefully common insurance industry practice to induce repair shops to use cheaper, nonmanufacturer replacement parts—without informing the car owner. These so-called "aftermarket" replacement parts make up 15% to 20% of all repair parts. They save the insurance company money but often do not fit or wear as well as original equipment parts.

If you are negotiating with another driver's insurance company over repairs for your car, make sure that any estimate it provides you includes the cost of original manufacturer's parts. Have the repair shop or other source from which the insurance company obtains its estimate put in writing that the estimate is based upon original—and not aftermarket—parts. If the parts are not original manufacturer parts, they do not fulfill the insurance company's obligation to return your car to its preloss condition.

If you are negotiating with your own insurance company, original equipment rather than aftermarket parts may be more difficult to get. The terms of your policy will determine whether or not you have the right to original parts.

## Disputes Over Value of Totaled Property

You and an insurance adjuster may disagree over the actual cash value (ACV) of property. This could lead to a disagreement over whether the insurance company should pay the cost of repairing the property or total the property. Even if you agree with the adjuster that the property should be totaled, you may disagree over how much you should be compensated for that loss.

### Actual Cash Value of Vehicles

A car or truck's ACV is determined by comparing the current sale price of vehicles in your geographic area of a similar year, make, model, and condition. This comparison can be done in a couple of different ways.

First is by reference to the *Kelley Blue Book,* which is used by all car dealers and auto insurance workers, and is available at your local public library or online at www.kbb.com. The *Blue Book* is a good starting point for determining value, but it is not the only word on the subject. Other valuation methods may show that the Kelley price for your vehicle is too low.

### Remind the Adjuster That the Meter Is Running

If an insurance adjuster is taking too long to offer you a settlement figure for your damaged property, inform the adjuster that you will not get repairs, or replace a totaled vehicle or other property, until a legitimate offer is actually made and you've received the money. Then remind the adjuster that until a settlement offer is made, the insurance company is responsible for your alternative transportation—a rental car, taxis—or temporary replacement equipment, and that those costs are mounting every day. Sometimes, this reminder results in a speedier final settlement.

For example, advertisements in area newspapers for a vehicle similar to yours may show a significantly higher price than in the *Blue Book.* Of course, the price for which a car is advertised is not usually the price at which it is actually sold, but if the advertised prices are consistently and considerably higher than the *Blue Book* prices, you can certainly use that fact to negotiate with the adjuster.

Additionally, special features of your vehicle may indicate a higher market value than that listed in the *Blue Book.* Your car might have had extra nonstandard equipment, or newly replaced and costly parts. Or it may have had very few miles on it given its age. Raise any of these factors with the adjuster to increase the valuation of your vehicle. You can demonstrate these factors by showing written proof of the repairs or added equipment, or by sending photos of the extras to the adjuster.

## Items of Significant Sentimental or Emotional Value

Sometimes an item's actual cash value doesn't truly measure the loss you have suffered. The emotional significance of an item—a family heirloom, for example—cannot be measured fairly by its market value.

In such a case, there are two avenues to pursue. One is to explain to the adjuster the item's significance to you and ask for a settlement amount that takes such value into account.

Alternatively, if the property damage adjuster will not compensate you for your special relation to the item but you also have a separate personal injury loss arising out of the same accident, you may be able to include the loss in your personal injury claim. Laws vary from state to state about whether such a loss is part of general injury damages, part of property damage, or part of a separate legal claim for emotional distress. Regardless of these categories, you can at least include it in your demand for personal injury general damages. Particularly if the emotional loss is an easy one to understand—an engagement ring, for example—you can emphasize the loss in your negotiations, and an adjuster may well consider it when offering to settle your personal injury claim.

### Actual Cash Value of Other Property

Establishing the ACV of motorcycles, bicycles, and property that is not a vehicle can be more difficult than with cars because there are no standard industry guides such as the *Kelley Blue Book* for automobiles.

The first step in demonstrating the value of the loss is to prove what the item was and that you had it in your possession. You can do that by providing identifying information about the item and a photo of it—both before and after the accident, if possible. A receipt, credit card slip, or other proof of purchase identifies the item and establishes that you owned it.

Proof of the original purchase gives a starting price for its ACV. If you have such proof, it also establishes how old the item is, which affects current ACV; older means less value, unless it is the kind of item that maintains its value, such as jewelry or an antique.

The condition the item was in also affects ACV; a stained and worn leather coat is not as valuable as a clean, uncreased one. The adjuster may want to take a look at the actual item before deciding on its ACV.

Once you have established what the item is, what it originally cost, and what shape it was in, you will need to show the price for which people are selling the same used item. Classified ads of any sort—for example, newspapers or computer bulletin boards or auctions—may give an idea of the item's current value. The price of a new replacement item may also be useful in determining ACV, particularly if your item was relatively new. If the item was almost new and its value does not diminish much with careful use—a good camera, for example—the price of a replacement item will give you a reasonable starting place at which to begin negotiating with the insurance company.

### Reducing the Settlement Because of Your Fault

Your right to collect compensation from another person's insurance company in a third-party claim, or from your own insurer in an uninsured motorist claim, depends on the extent to which that person was at fault for causing the damage. Just as in personal injury claims, the amount of your third-party or uninsured motorist compensation for property damage is reduced by an amount related to how much you were also at fault for the accident, measured by degrees of fault called comparative negligence. (See "How Your Carelessness Affects Your Claim" in Chapter 2 and "Assigning Fault" in Chapter 5.)

However, if you make a claim for vehicle property damage under your own auto insurance collision coverage, your degree of fault in the accident does not matter. Collision coverage is paid regardless of fault.

## Final Settlement

Unlike the more complicated and usually higher-value personal injury claims, you can almost always reach a final settlement figure for a property damage claim over the phone, without you or the adjuster having to exchange formal demand letters and replies. Within one to three weeks after you reach your settlement figure, you will receive from the insurance company a check, and often an accompanying document called a release. You must sign the release and return it to the insurance company, after which you are free to deposit the check. Sometimes the release will come first, and you will receive the check only after you have signed and returned the release.

Be careful what you sign. If you also have a personal injury claim arising out of the same accident, be sure to read the documents you are to sign in accepting a property damage settlement. When you receive the check and release document, make sure the words "Property Damage Only" or "Property Damage Claim" are written on both of them. Do not deposit any check or sign any document that reads "General Release" or does not clearly indicate "Property Damage." If you are not certain that either the settlement check or release is properly marked, ask the insurance adjuster to add "Property Damage Only" on the documents and to write you a separate letter confirming that this settlement amount is only for the property damage part of your claim.

### A Release Is Forever

Once you accept a property damage settlement, you are forever prevented from claiming that there is still more damage to your car or other property. The fact that you did not discover the damage until later does not matter. For this reason, it is particularly important that during the course of making estimates the repair people check for possible hidden damage—for example, a cracked engine block or bent watch stem—before you accept a settlement. If they find serious trouble after you have settled your claim, it is too late to collect.

# Chapter 8

# Negotiating a Settlement

## Using This Chapter

This chapter explains how you can take the negotiation process from a first demand for compensation to a settlement of your claim.

- Read the first two major sections to understand how insurance adjusters operate and what you can do and say to ensure fair and speedy negotiations.
- Read "What to Do When You Can't Get a Settlement" for strategies on how to break a negotiating stalemate.

You are now on the verge of settling your claim. If you have presented an organized demand letter and supporting documents (as discussed in Chapter 6), the negotiation process will probably consist of nothing more than a few phone calls with a claims adjuster. During the first of these calls, you and the adjuster will each make your points about the strengths and weaknesses of your claim. Then the adjuster will make an offer to settle your claim for an amount lower than what you asked for in your demand letter. You will counter with a figure higher than the adjuster's offer but lower than that in your demand letter. And after two or three phone calls, you will probably agree on a settlement figure somewhere in between.

Settlement negotiations that begin with a thorough demand letter are often just that simple. Occasionally, though, negotiations take a bit more work. It may be because the adjuster has questions about liability, your injuries, your medical treatment, or your lost income. Or perhaps you have not provided all necessary documents. Or you may just run into a difficult adjuster. This chapter helps you handle any of those situations by explaining who claims adjusters are, how the negotiation process works, and what to do if you cannot get a reasonable settlement offer quickly and easily.

## Adjusters: Who They Are and How They Work

Insurance claims adjusters come with different titles, such as claims specialist, claims representative, or independent claims analyst, but they all do the same job. Understanding who claims adjusters are and how they work lets you see that they have no real advantage over you in the negotiation process. Indeed, by having a good understanding of the facts of your own claim, you may well have an advantage over them.

### Insurance Adjusters

When you have filed a claim against someone you believe was responsible for your accident, normally the negotiation process will be with a claims adjuster for that person's liability insurance company.

Occasionally, a claim is not handled by an insurance company's own adjuster, but instead is referred to a firm of independent insurance adjusters. Insurance companies often do this if they do not have a local claims office in a particular area.

Independent claims adjusters representing an insurance company operate the same as in-house claims adjusters. The only difference is that they may have a lower authority limit within which to settle a case and therefore must have your settlement amount approved by a claims supervisor at an insurance company office. The negotiation process, however, is exactly the same.

Public entities such as state governments or large cities that receive lots of claims often have their own claims adjustment offices. The negotiation process with these government claims adjusters works the same as with private insurance adjusters. The only notable difference in negotiating with a government claims adjuster is that if a claim eventually winds up in court, judges and juries tend not to be overly generous in awarding damages with public money. For this reason, government entity adjusters tend to be tighter with settlement money than private insurance adjusters. If you have a claim against a public entity, expect your settlement to be 10% to 25% lower than if it were against a private party.

It sometimes happens that even though you have not filed a lawsuit, you find an attorney instead of a claims adjuster negotiating with you about your claim. Self-insured corporations and some insurance companies without a local claims office sometimes use either their own staff attorney or a local attorney as a claims adjuster. And government entities sometimes have assistant city, county, or state attorneys who deal directly with accident claims even before they get to court.

If an attorney is handling your claim instead of a claims adjuster, don't panic. In the claims negotiation process, a lawyer cannot do anything different from a nonattorney claims adjuster. A lawyer may bluff a little more than a claims adjuster about the law regarding negligence and liability, but there are easy techniques to call that kind of bluff. (See "Improper Settlement Tactics," below.)

Often, a lawyer handling a claim will actually be easier to deal with than a claims adjuster. Many lawyers realize that in smaller cases, it's better for the company to settle with you promptly than to spend a lot of time, and therefore a lot of the company's money, trying to get you to settle for a little bit less.

If you file a claim under your own automobile collision, uninsured, or underinsured motorist coverage, you do not negotiate a settlement with your own insurance agent. All an agent can do is refer your claim to the claims department—and then it is completely out of the agent's hands. You will then negotiate a settlement with a claims adjuster who will be acting as the company's representative, not yours.

## How Adjusters Settle Claims

The job performance of insurance adjusters is judged not only by how little of the insurance company's money they spend in settlements but also by how quickly they settle claims. Most adjusters get between 50 and 100 new claims a month across their desks. They have to settle that many claims—known as "clearing" or "closing" a claim file—each month just to stay even. Their performance is also rated on how many claims they can personally settle without having to involve supervisors or insurance company lawyers. Once an adjuster knows that you understand the range of how much your claim is worth, the adjuster will not usually stall your claim.

During negotiations, you will find that you know much more about your claim than the adjuster does. Except for those assigned to the largest cases, insurance claims adjusters have no special legal or medical training. And most have neither the time nor the resources to investigate or study your claim very carefully.

The result is that while an adjuster will know more than you about the claims business in general, he or she will not know your particular claim nearly as well as you do. You were there during the accident. You know what your injuries are, how much and where they hurt, and how long they have taken to heal. You have put in the time to understand how the accident happened and to demonstrate through photos and medical records and other documents what your damages were. The insurance adjuster, on the other hand, has only a couple of minutes a week to look at your file. As long as you are organized and understand the process, you are the one with the negotiating advantage.

The adjuster has the authority to come to an agreement with you on the telephone for what the final settlement amount should be. Once you and the adjuster agree on an amount, the adjuster simply sends you the paperwork to finalize the settlement. (See Chapter 9.) But adjusters' authority to settle claims on their own is restricted to certain dollar limits. The limits depend on how much experience the adjuster has. For less experienced adjusters, the limit is between $5,000 and $10,000. For more experienced adjusters, the limit is between $10,000 and $20,000.

An adjuster will not tell you what his or her authority is unless you're going to get an offer higher than that authority. If so, the adjuster will have to ask for approval from a superior—usually called a claims supervisor or claims manager. This is neither unusual nor difficult. But if the adjuster does need to check with a supervisor about your settlement offer, get a date by which you will hear back from either one, and then send a letter to the adjuster confirming that date.

## How the Negotiation Process Works

Negotiating a final settlement is a little like bargaining to buy something at an outdoor market where haggling is commonplace. You and the buyer (the adjuster) both know roughly how much an item (your damages) is worth. You know how much you are willing to take for it, and the adjuster knows how much the insurance company is willing to pay. But neither of you knows how much the other side is willing to pay or receive. So you go through a process of testing each other, a dance of bluff and bluster that goes like this, usually in just two or three phone calls:

- You ask for a high amount in your written demand letter.
- The insurance adjuster tells you what's wrong with your claim—that there is a question about liability, or that your lengthy physical therapy was unnecessary.

- You respond to these arguments.
- The adjuster makes a low counteroffer to feel out whether you are in a hurry to take any settlement amount.
- You concede a little bit concerning the adjuster's arguments and make another demand slightly lower than the one in your demand letter.
- The insurance adjuster increases the company's offer.
- You either accept that amount or make another counterdemand.

It is usually as simple as that. The main facts determining how an accident settlement comes out are how well you have prepared all stages of your claim—investigation, supporting documents, and demand letter—how much you are willing to settle for, and how much of a hurry you are in to settle. The rest of this chapter explains how the unwritten rules of negotiation operate, including some of the legitimate negotiating responses you can expect from adjusters, plus some of the improper tactics a few adjusters might try as a way to get you to settle for less than is reasonable.

### When Negotiating Doesn't Work

Sometimes, despite your best efforts and your diligent attention to the advice in this section, an insurance adjuster will not budge. The adjuster may insist on denying coverage or liability and refuse to make any settlement offer at all, or may make an offer that is so low that you would never consider it. There's a section in this chapter that covers what steps you can take when the negotiating process described here doesn't work. And Chapter 11 deals with how to find and work with a lawyer if you decide you won't be able to get a settlement on your own.

## Keys to Successful Claims Negotiation

How you act during settlement negotiations can go a long way toward making the process run smoothly and quickly, with a minimum of stress or aggravation for you, and with a satisfying settlement as the result. Here are some of the basic rules about dealing with a claims adjuster.

**Be organized.** If you follow the steps mapped out in Chapters 5 and 6, you will already be organized when you begin the negotiation process. Keep up the habits you've already developed. If you have a conversation with the adjuster, make a note of what was said. If either you or the adjuster have said that you will or will not do a certain thing, or that something is to occur by a certain date, write a confirming letter and send it to the adjuster. Keep a copy of everything you send. If you have agreed to provide the adjuster with information, do it promptly.

**Be patient.** Although you may have already had to wait a considerable amount of time to get all your medical and income records, try not to be in too great a hurry to settle your claim. One of the tactics claims adjusters use is to make a low initial settlement offer and see if you are too impatient to continue negotiating. If you can stand to wait, do not jump at a first offer. Holding off for a little while often increases your settlement amount. After some time passes, it will be the adjuster who will want to settle your claim as soon as possible, and then you will be able to get the full value of your claim.

**Be persistent.** The flip side of being patient is being persistent. Don't let the adjuster sit on your claim. If the adjuster has said that he or she will do something—make you another offer, or check with a supervisor—get a specific date by which it will be done. Put everything agreed upon in a confirming letter, and when that date rolls around, call and politely demand a response. If you have asked for information or for a new settlement offer, set a reasonable deadline by which you would like the response. Don't pester an adjuster by calling every day, but make sure the adjuster knows you are out there and that you will be regularly and thoroughly following up on your claim.

**Be calm and straightforward.** Insurance adjusters are overworked and underpaid, and they hear a lot of stories every day. They are also human, which means they don't respond well to abuse or to hysterics. Even if you get an inconsiderate or unsympathetic adjuster, keep your cool and don't get into a personal battle; there are other and better ways to deal with an uncooperative adjuster. (See "What to Do When You Can't Get a Settlement," below.)

Your job is simply to show the adjuster that you know how the process works and that your claim is an honest one. Let the adjuster know you believe in the facts you have presented. Avoid high emotions. If you show the adjuster you are making a good-faith claim, you will likely get a good-faith settlement offer in return.

## Conducting Negotiations

Negotiations with the insurance claims adjuster will begin shortly after the adjuster receives your demand letter. Usually the adjuster will telephone you within a week or two after receiving your demand. The length of time between demand letter and response depends on how busy the adjuster is, and how much time the adjuster needs to go over your claim and perhaps to speak with the insured about the accident.

## Reservation of Rights Letter

The first thing you might receive from an insurance company is called a "reservation of rights letter." This letter informs you that the company is investigating your claim but is reserving its right not to pay anything if it turns out that the accident is not covered under the policy.

A reservation of rights letter is intended to protect the insurance company so that you cannot later claim that because it began settlement negotiations with you, it acknowledged that the policy covers the accident. It also serves to plant the idea that the insurance company might not cover the loss at all, intimidating some people into taking a quick and small settlement.

Do not be intimidated by a reservation of rights letter. The insurance company still must investigate your claim and negotiate with you fairly. Of course, if there is good reason to deny coverage altogether under the policy, the insurer is legally free to do so. But a reservation of rights letter does not change how the insurance company will respond to your claim. That will be determined by the facts of your accident and your injuries.

## Delayed Response From the Insurer

If you do not hear from an adjuster within two weeks after sending your demand letter, call the claims department and ask when you can expect a response. If an adjuster says that he or she hasn't had a chance to review your demand yet, be polite but ask for a specific date—two more weeks, perhaps—by which the adjuster will contact you with a response. Confirm the date with a brief written letter.

If you haven't heard from the adjuster by the date mentioned, telephone or send an email and firmly remind him or her of the promises made. If, after that, you still do not get a prompt response to your demand, you may have to go over the adjuster's head to a supervisor. (See below.)

## Have a Settlement Amount in Mind

In putting together your demand letter, you figured out a range of what you believe your claim is worth. Before you speak to an adjuster about your demand, decide on a minimum settlement figure within that range that you would accept. This figure is for your own information, not something you would reveal to the adjuster. But once the figures and discussions start going back and forth, it helps if you already have your bottom line in mind. That way, you don't have to make a snap decision if an adjuster makes you a take-it-or-leave-it offer on the phone. You will know whether it meets your minimum level or not.

However, you do not have to cling to the figure you originally set for yourself. If an adjuster points out some facts you had not considered but which clearly make your claim weaker, you may have to lower your minimum figure somewhat. And if the adjuster starts

## Sample Confirmation Letter

Allen Wright
345 Tenth Street
Olean, NY 00000

June 15, 20xx

Allison Lavelle
Claims Adjuster
Great Lakes Insurance Co.
Syracuse, NY 00000

Re: Your Insured, Robert Lee
    Claimant: Allen Wright
    Claim No.: 93-HQ1234
    Date of Loss: January 13, 20xx

Dear Ms. Lavelle:

This letter confirms our telephone conversation today during which you agreed to respond by July 1, 20xx to my settlement demand letter dated June 1, 20xx. I look forward to your response by July 1.

Thank you for your attention to this matter.

Sincerely,

*Allen Wright*

Allen Wright

---

### Your Insurer's Deal With Another Party Doesn't Bind You

In addition to your claim against the party who was at fault for your vehicle accident, you may have collected benefits under your own insurance policy's medical payments coverage or collision coverage (see Chapter 4). If so, your insurance company has a right to be reimbursed for those amounts by the other party's insurance company. Your insurance company might negotiate reimbursement with the other party's insurer before you settle your personal injury claim. And that reimbursement deal between the two insurance companies may include an agreed-upon figure for the percentage of your comparative negligence in the accident.

However, nothing that your insurance company agrees to with the other insurer has a binding effect on your claim. Your insurer may have agreed to acknowledge a certain percentage of comparative negligence on your part as a simple way to arrive at a settlement figure. Whatever the reason and whatever the percentage, it was a matter between the two insurance companies only. It has no legal bearing on your own claim negotiations with the other party's insurance company. If you think you were absolutely not at fault or your percentage of fault was much lower than your insurance company conceded, stick to your position for as long as you can.

---

with an offer at or near your minimum—or if you discover evidence that makes your claim stronger—you may want to revise your minimum upward.

## Do Not Jump at a First Offer

It is standard practice for insurance adjusters to begin negotiations by first offering a very low settlement amount—or, sometimes, denying liability altogether. With this tactic, the adjuster is trying to find out whether you understand what your claim is worth and to see if you are so impatient to get some money that you will take any amount.

When a first offer is made, your response should depend on whether it is a reasonable offer but too low or whether it is so low that it is just a tactic to see if you know what you are doing. If the offer is reasonable, you can immediately make a counteroffer that is a little bit lower than your demand letter amount. That shows the adjuster that you, too, are being reasonable and are willing to compromise. A little more bargaining should quickly get you to a final settlement amount you both think is fair. In these negotiations, don't bother to go over all the facts again. Just emphasize the strongest points in your favor—for example, that the insured was completely at fault.

## Get the Adjuster to Justify a Low Offer

If in your first conversation, the adjuster makes an offer so low that it is obviously just a negotiating tactic to see if you know what your claim is really worth, do not immediately lower the amount you put in your demand letter. Instead, ask the adjuster to give you the specific reasons why the offer is so low and make notes of what he or she tells you. Then write a brief letter responding to each of the factors the adjuster has mentioned. A sample letter is shown below. Depending on the strength of any of the adjuster's reasons, you can lower your demand slightly, but before lowering your demand very far, wait to see whether the adjuster will budge after he or she receives your reply letter.

The next time you speak with the adjuster, begin by asking for a response to your reply letter. The adjuster should now make you a reasonable offer upon which you will be able to bargain and arrive at a fair final settlement figure.

### Only You Can Decide How Much Is Fair

There is no rule to go by in deciding whether a particular settlement offer is enough. Some people want to get as much as they possibly can out of a claim no matter how long it takes, and are willing to argue and bargain and bluff on and on and on. Other people want just to get a minimum amount of money as quickly as possible. Most people fall somewhere in between.

Deciding when a settlement offer is acceptable depends completely on your attitude toward both the accident and your injuries, on your tolerance for the claims process, and on your judgment about whether more bargaining is likely to produce a higher offer. Once you are within a certain range that you know is reasonable, how much is enough is completely up to you.

## Emphasize Emotional Points in Your Favor

During negotiations, mention any emotional points supporting your claim. If, for example, you have sent the adjuster a particularly strong photo of a smashed car or a severe-looking injury, refer to it. If there was a bottle of beer found in the other party's car, refer again to the possibility of alcohol use. If similar accidents had occurred in a similar way at that location, remind the adjuster. If your injury interfered with your ability to care for your child, mention that your

## Sample Reply Letter to Unreasonably Low Initial Offer

Angel Ruiz
123 Peach Street
Denver, CO 00000

June 15, 20xx

Victor Rubinion
Claims Adjuster
Rocky Mountain Insurance Company
Denver, CO 00000

Re:  Your Insured, Richard Leonard
     Claimant: Angel Ruiz
     Claim No.: 93-HQ1234
     Date of Accident: January 13, 20xx

Dear Mr. Rubinion:

In our telephone conversation today, you relayed Rocky Mountain Insurance Company's offer to settle my claim for $1,000. However, none of the reasons you gave for such a low offer is supported by the facts.

You claimed that I was as much at fault in the accident as your insured. You assert that I had a duty to avoid hitting him because he was already in the intersection when our cars collided. This assertion is not supported by the facts. Indeed, the police report indicates that your insured had a yield sign, and I had the right of way. Thus, I did not have a duty to avoid hitting your insured and am not at fault in the accident.

In addition, you claimed that I suffered "only a soft tissue" injury, which did not justify either the physical therapy I underwent or my settlement demand. If you look at the record of my X-rays, you will see a narrowing of cervical vertebrae. Therefore, your characterization of my injury as "minor" and as "soft tissue" is completely unjustified.

Because of the slight possibility of some minor comparative negligence in the accident, however, I am willing to reduce by five percent my settlement demand of $15,000. Therefore, I demand the sum of $14,250 as settlement of the claim.

Please provide me with Rocky Mountain's response within 14 days after you receive this letter.

Very truly yours,

*Angel Ruiz*

Angel Ruiz

child suffered as a result. Even though there is no way to put a dollar value on these factors, they can be very powerful in getting an insurance company to settle an accident claim.

⚠️ **Wait for a response.** Do not reduce your demand more than once until you have a new offer from the adjuster. Never reduce your demand twice without an intervening increased offer from the adjuster; it's simply not good bargaining.

If the adjuster comes up with more reasons for a low offer, go over each one. Once you have dealt with all the adjuster's arguments, you will either get a reasonable offer, or you will have found out that no reasonable offer is coming and you will have to try to put some additional pressure on the insurance company. (See "What to Do When You Can't Get a Settlement," below.)

## Put the Settlement in Writing

When you and the adjuster finally agree on a number, immediately confirm the agreement in a letter to the adjuster. The letter can be short and sweet.

## Sample Settlement Confirmation Letter

> Michael Filippi
> 1747 Lemming Way
> Mendota, WI 00000
>
> April 24, 20xx
>
> Esther Berganian
> Claims Adjuster
> All Claims Insurance Company
> Boston, MA 00000
>
> Re: Your Insured, Cynthia Berquette
>     Claimant: Michael Filippi
>     Claim No.: PI-23469
>     Date of accident: April 2, 20xx
>
> Dear Ms. Berganian:
>
> This letter confirms today's telephone conversation in which we agreed to settle my injury claim for $5,000, not including my property damage claim, which was settled previously.
>
> You have informed me that you will prepare and send to me settlement and release documents within 10 days from this date.
>
> With best regards,
> *Michael Filippi*
> Michael Filippi

## The Subjects of Negotiations With an Adjuster

During negotiations, an insurance adjuster has a right to ask questions and dispute facts in an attempt to limit your right to compensation. Questions or disputes might concern:

**Coverage.** Whether the insurance policy in question actually covers the accident.

**Liability.** Who was at fault for the accident and what was the degree of your comparative negligence.

**The extent of your injuries.** Whether an injury was disabling or had a long-term permanent effect.

**The nature and extent of medical treatment.** Whether the type and duration of procedures or therapies were medically necessary, and whether you had preexisting problems that contributed to your damages.

You should meet an adjuster's reasonable questions and inquiries with reasonable answers. But some questions and arguments are not legitimate—and are intended unfairly to influence you to settle the case for less than it is truly worth. (See "Improper Settlement Tactics," below.)

Specific conduct by adjusters, both legitimate and improper, is discussed in this section. But for situations not covered here, there is a simple rule to follow: If the question, request, or argument seems reasonably necessary for the adjuster to get an accurate picture of your claim, be reasonable in your response. And if you are not certain about whether a question, request, or argument is reasonable or not, tell the adjuster precisely that—"I'm not certain that this is a reasonable request"—and allow him or her to explain why it is reasonable.

In deciding the reasonableness of questions or requests for information, consider both sides of the negotiating process. Bear in mind that, except in claims against your own insurance company, a claims adjuster has no legal right either to see or receive anything specific or to get you to answer anything particular, unless a lawsuit has been filed and served on the other party. On the other hand, the claims adjuster is not legally obligated to settle a claim without having sufficient information to understand the accident, your injuries, and your damages. You have to balance your rightful reluctance to give too much information against the insurance company's right to evaluate your claim.

The following discussion of specific arguments, questions, and requests from claims adjusters will give you a feel for what is reasonable and what is not.

## Denying Coverage

A claims adjuster might contend that the insurance policy involved does not cover your accident. The reasons given might be:

- the policy lapsed
- the nature or location of the accident was not covered—particularly if it is a home-owner's policy
- the person who caused the accident is not covered, or
- you do not qualify to make a third-party claim under your state's no-fault vehicle insurance law.

An adjuster's contention that there is no coverage does not end settlement negotiations. Instead, the coverage question simply becomes one more element in your negotiations.

First, ask the adjuster to give you a written explanation of the insurance company's reasons for claiming there is no coverage, including references to the specific policy provisions that limit coverage. This will reveal whether the adjuster is just bluffing and will give you a chance to respond to the reasons more specifically.

If the adjuster does not agree to give you a written explanation, write a letter to the adjuster confirming your conversation, the denial of coverage, and the adjuster's refusal to explain in writing. This letter may pressure the adjuster to give you the information, because an insurance claims supervisor will not like such a letter in the insurance company's file. If you eventually go to the insurance commission or file a lawsuit to pursue your claim, such a letter in the claim file would show the insurance company's lack of cooperation.

Also ask the claims adjuster to provide you with a copy of the insured's policy—or at least the portions on which the adjuster relies in denying coverage—so that you can read it for yourself. If the adjuster refuses, write a letter to the adjuster confirming the refusal so that it becomes a part of your claim file. Then, if the adjuster still refuses to negotiate with you about settlement, you will have to use other pressures to get negotiations moving.

In many cases, an adjuster will initially contend that there is no coverage. As soon as you indicate that you will not abandon your claim, however, the adjuster will begin to negotiate a settlement anyway. If, after that, you cannot reach a satisfactory settlement because of the coverage question—or any other problem— you will have to move into other negotiating strategies. (See "What to Do When You Can't Get a Settlement," below.)

## Don't Be Swayed by a Lawyer's Letter

In claiming that there is no insurance coverage for your accident, an adjuster may tell you that "the lawyers" have said there is no coverage. The adjuster may even send you a copy of a letter from a company lawyer stating that there is no coverage for your accident.

Do not be impressed. A company lawyer's opinion that there may not be coverage for your accident is no more binding than anyone else's opinion. Whether or not there is coverage depends on the terms of the policy, and a policy can often be read in several different ways, depending on the facts. If the matter goes to court, ambiguities in a policy are often resolved in favor of coverage.

So, even if there is a lawyer's opinion, ask to see the language of the policy on which the lawyer and adjuster are relying. You can still dispute the question of coverage under the policy in negotiations with the adjuster; the lawyer's word doesn't resolve the matter.

If the adjuster seems to you to be correct that there is no coverage at all and refuses to negotiate for a settlement, you may be able to turn to insurance that covers someone else responsible for the accident. For example, suppose you tripped and fell on a cracked sidewalk, and the city claims there is no coverage because sidewalk maintenance is the legal responsibility of each property owner. You could then file a claim against the insurance company for the owner of the property fronting the sidewalk. (See Chapter 4.)

## A Claim Beyond Auto Policy Limits

Although most state laws require that automobile liability insurance be sufficient to cover most accidents, in some states the amount of total coverage required by law is quite low—$5,000 or $10,000 total per accident victim; $10,000 to $20,000 total for all injured people per accident. The total amount that can be paid under a given insurance policy coverage is referred to by insurance adjusters as the "policy limits." Per-person and per-accident policy limits are often referred to together as "10-20" or "15-30"—meaning $10,000 per person and $20,000 per accident or $15,000 per person and $30,000 per accident.

Your demand may be for $15,000, for example, but the claims adjuster tells you that the insured's policy limits are only $10,000. If the adjuster tells you that the insured's policy limit are below what you are demanding, request that the adjuster put the policy limits in writing.

Policy limits are the maximum you can recover from that particular insurance company, but low limits may at least make your settlement negotiations simpler. You can demand a policy limit settlement from the insured's company if your claim is worth at least that much—without having to argue with the adjuster about exactly how much more than the limits the claim is worth.

If you accept a policy limit settlement, the insured person's insurance company will require that you release the insured from all liability. (See Chapter 9.) Accepting the policy limits would mean the end of your claim. So, if your claim is worth far more than the insured's policy limits, check with a personal injury lawyer before settling. The lawyer can determine whether the insured has personal assets beyond his or her insurance coverage that might be available to compensate you through a lawsuit. If so, the lawyer can advise you whether it is worth pursuing such a lawsuit.

In a vehicle accident claim, if you have underinsured motorist coverage in your own policy, you can settle with the insured's insurance company for policy limits and then pursue a claim for the rest of your damages under your own underinsurance coverage. You will negotiate with your own insurer about how much your total claim is worth, exactly as you would if it were a third party's insurance company. And when you settle on a full compensation amount, your underinsurance coverage will pay the difference between this total figure and the amount of policy limits you have already received from the other insurance company. (See Chapter 4.)

## No Legal Liability

Occasionally an adjuster will tell you "the law" says that you, and not its insured, are liable for the accident. Most of these adjusters are talking through their hats. They have a general idea of what the law is on certain liability subjects, but rarely do they know the law in any detail.

If an adjuster claims that the law is on the insurance company's side, demand proof. Ask the adjuster to send you the statute, rule, or regulation that the adjuster claims applies to your situation. If the adjuster does not send you any documentation of the law, then tell the adjuster that you cannot consider something that is undocumented. If the adjuster does send you something, make sure it is a copy of an actual legal rule or law and not merely an insurance company's own memo, a letter from a lawyer, or some other unofficial opinion about the law.

When you get a copy of an official rule or law, read it carefully. Often what you will be sent is just a general statement of law that can be applied differently in different situations and does not answer the question of who was at fault for your accident. For example, a traffic law may state that the driver to the right has the right-of-way at a four-way stop intersection, but that doesn't determine whether you got to the intersection first and had the right to go through the intersection before the other car, or whether the other car was careless in failing to stop at the stop sign.

If, despite your arguments, an adjuster continues to rely on an interpretation of a law that denies all liability by the insured, and refuses any settlement at all, you will have to turn to other negotiating options. (See "What to Do When You Can't Get a Settlement," below.)

### Relying on the Police Report

In traffic accident cases, an adjuster will sometimes argue that nothing in the police report confirms your description of how the accident happened. You can point out that nothing in the police report contradicts your version of what happened, either, and that the police officer did not witness the accident, but arrived only after the event.

You have a more difficult problem if the police report specifically contradicts your version of whose fault the accident was. If the claims adjuster points out something in the police report that indicates you were at fault for the accident and suggests you have no claim at all because of it, there are several ways to respond:

- Remind the adjuster that the police report is not actual evidence because the police officer did not see the accident happen.
- Point out that the officer issued you no citation after the accident.
- Note that the reporting officer does not state any opinion about who was at fault.
- Remind the adjuster that the officer's report is based solely on a rough reconstruction of the accident, done without precision, based on limited facts and resting on speculation.

These are all ways of saying to the adjuster that the police officer's accident report is useless as legal evidence of what actually happened. (See "Documenting Liability" in Chapter 6.)

An attack on the legal value of a police report may or may not immediately get the claims adjuster to back off relying on the report in your negotiations. But it will at least let the adjuster know that you know the police report is of limited help should your claim eventually wind up in court. And an adjuster who knows you will not drop your claim just because of a bad police report will get back to bargaining with you. However, you may have to lower your demand somewhat because of the report—even if you think it's wrong, it's strong evidence in favor of the insurance company.

### Request to Examine Evidence

An insurance company against which you have filed a claim has a right to see evidence of yours that shows something about how the accident happened or how badly you were injured. You can either provide a photo of evidence, or if the adjuster requests, arrange for the adjuster or other representative of the insurance company to view the evidence in person. *Do not,* however, let the insurance company take away from you, even temporarily, any piece of evidence you have. Once the evidence is out of your hands, you cannot be sure that it won't be changed, modified, or lost.

If the insurance company says it cannot do the examination while the evidence remains in your possession, tough luck. If the claim ever becomes a lawsuit, the insurance company can go to court to ask for an order entitling it to make such an examination. But until a claim becomes a lawsuit, the insurer has no right to take evidence out of your possession.

## Request to Know Your Witnesses

Simply mentioning in your demand letter that you have supporting witnesses may be enough to convince the insurance company that you can prove the other side was at fault. This is particularly true if you have directly quoted from or sent a written witness statement along with your demand letter.

However, an insurance adjuster may ask you for the names and addresses of your witnesses to speak with them directly. It makes no sense at this point for you to refuse to identify a witness you have already told the insurance company about. Refusing to give the insurance company the name and address of a witness, or refusing to ask the witness to contact the insurance company, will appear to be an unreasonable lack of cooperation. That will create suspicion and lack of cooperation on the insurance company's part, and will also completely undercut the value of having the witness. If you won't let the insurance company verify what the witness says, the insurance company isn't going to be very impressed that you have such a witness.

Nevertheless, a witness who does not want to speak to an insurance company does not have to—not unless there is a formal lawsuit with subpoenas issued by a court. And if a witness has instructed you not to give out his or her identity to the insurance company, tell that to the adjuster. However, if a witness refuses to speak to the adjuster, the adjuster is probably not going to give much weight to what the witness claims to have seen, which makes that witness almost useless for the negotiation process.

A witness who agrees to speak with the insurance company has the right to control where, when, and how that contact takes place. A witness can exercise control in the following ways:

- The witness can contact the adjuster rather than having his or her phone number given out.
- The witness can decline to give a written statement.
- The witness does not have to be interviewed in person.
- The witness does not have to permit the interview to be recorded. (It's usually in your best interest if the interview is not recorded, for the same reasons you wouldn't want your own conversations with an adjuster to be recorded. See Chapter 3.)
- The witness does not have to sign any statement drawn up by the adjuster.
- The witness does not have to return to the scene with the adjuster or anyone else.
- The witness does not have to give any more personal information than he or she wants to.
- Once the witness speaks with the adjuster, the witness does not have to speak with anyone else from the insurance company or to repeat the conversation with the adjuster.

Even though a witness is not legally obligated to speak with the adjuster, you are not permitted to instruct the witness not to speak with the insurance company. That would improperly interfere with the company's right to gather evidence. You can discuss with the witness what is important in the case and stress the points you would like him or her to make clear to the adjuster, but you cannot tell the witness what to say or not say. It is certainly all right for the witness to tell the adjuster that you and the witness have discussed the accident, but the witness should be able to tell the adjuster in all honesty that you have not tried to tell the witness what he or she must say.

## Ask for the Adjuster's Witnesses

If the adjuster asks you to identify your witnesses, ask that the adjuster do the same for you. If the adjuster denies knowing of any witnesses, write a letter confirming that. If the adjuster refuses to discuss witnesses, or to identify them, write a letter confirming the refusal and state that since the adjuster refuses, you must also refuse to reveal your witnesses.

If the adjuster gives you the identities of witnesses you did not previously know about, do not depend on the adjuster's version of what the witnesses say. Contact them directly and find out what they have to say. You may be pleasantly surprised to discover that the witness does not support the insured's version of events nearly as strongly as the adjuster claims. (See Chapter 3.)

### Request for Medical Records

Although you will have sent copies of all your relevant medical records along with your demand letter, the adjuster might ask for some additional record you have not provided. For example, if X-rays were taken but you've provided only the records from your doctor and not from the radiologist, the adjuster might ask for the radiologist's records. Or if there is an indication of a preexisting injury, an adjuster might ask to see medical records concerning that injury.

It is up to you to decide whether the request is reasonable. If it seems to be, tell the adjuster that you will provide the records if the insurance company is willing to pay for them. There is often a small fee from the doctor's office for copying records. If the adjuster agrees to pay for the records, confirm the agreement in writing.

Then request the records yourself and review them before sending them on to the adjuster, removing any records that do not pertain to accident injuries.

Unfortunately, some adjusters like to get additional medical records just to snoop around in your medical history to see if there is anything they can use against you or use to embarrass you. If the request for additional medical records seems unreasonable—that is, is not related to the injuries you suffered in the accident—do not comply. Ask the adjuster to explain why the additional records are needed. If the answer doesn't convince you, politely inform the adjuster that you do not believe the records are relevant to your claim and that providing them would intrude into your privacy. Remind the adjuster that if the claim winds up in court, the lawyers will be able to argue over this issue, but that at this point you can see no reason to allow prying into your personal medical history. Be firm with the adjuster. There is nothing wrong or suspicious about protecting your privacy.

**Do not sign your rights away.** Never sign an agreement authorizing an adjuster to directly obtain any of your medical records, and never give the adjuster verbal permission to obtain them. Always obtain records yourself. Review them to make sure they pertain only to your claim and do not unnecessarily reveal the rest of your private medical history. Then provide the adjuster with those records that pertain directly to accident injuries.

### Request for Medical Report

The records that doctors regularly keep may not explain fully enough some medical issue important to your claim. For example, your medical records may not make it clear how much of your injury is the result of an accident and how much is the effect of a preexisting injury. Or the prognosis for time of recovery may not be included. Or the doctor may have told you something about long-term effects from your injury but not included it in your medical records.

You or the adjuster may want a report from your doctor to clarify some medical issue. If the adjuster asks for a report and the request seems reasonable, do *not* allow the adjuster to contact your doctor directly. Tell the adjuster you will consider the request and will give an answer within a certain amount of time—a week or two. Then contact your doctor and find out whether the doctor would write a report favorable to you. (See "Documenting Injuries" in Chapter 6.) Also find out how much the doctor would charge for the report.

If the doctor indicates that the report might do you some good, you can contact the adjuster and agree to request a report if the adjuster agrees to pay for it. If the adjuster says yes, send a confirming letter.

### Request for Medical Examination

Once in a while, a claimant and an adjuster will have widely different opinions about the seriousness of an injury. Most disagreements arise over long-term or permanent effects that the adjuster does not believe are as serious as you describe them to be. Usually this difference of opinion can be resolved in negotiations. You and the adjuster each compromise and meet at a settlement figure somewhere in the middle. But sometimes the difference of opinion is so wide that the adjuster will ask whether you would be willing to be examined by a doctor, designated by the insurance company, to provide another medical opinion about your injury. Because the insurance company has to pay a doctor for such an examination, cost-conscious adjusters do not request them very often.

Although these second opinions are referred to by insurance people as "independent medical examinations" (IMEs), they are anything but independent. The doctors who conduct the examinations are chosen—and paid—over and over again by insurance companies because they almost never find anything seriously wrong with an insurance claimant.

An IME is usually a bad idea for an insurance claimant. Fortunately, you are not required to submit to an IME, except, sometimes, under your own automobile policy. (See "Special Rules for Negotiating With Your Own Insurer," below.) If an adjuster asks if you are willing to have an IME, politely refuse on the grounds that you do not wish to be examined by a doctor you do not know and whose opinion you have no way of judging. Remind the adjuster that if your claim later winds up in court, the insurance company can then follow the appropriate legal procedures to request an IME.

## Special Rules for Negotiating With Your Own Insurer

A claim filed under the uninsured or under-insured motorist coverage of your own automobile insurance policy is referred to as a "first-party" claim. The rules for proceeding with a first-party claim are determined by the specific terms of your policy. And often your policy requires a bit more from you than a third-party claim.

In general, your own policy will require that you cooperate with your insurance company during the claim. Of course, what cooperation means is subject to different interpretations. It usually comes down to what is reasonable under the circumstances: your right to privacy balanced against the company's right to get enough information to process your claim.

Most policies spell out the main points of cooperation you are required to provide, such as:

**Timely notification.** Your policy may provide a specific time limit within which you must notify the company of your claim. Even if you have missed this time limit, however, your insurance company cannot deny your claim unless it shows that it has been prejudiced—harmed in some way—by the late notice.

**Authorization for release of medical records.** You must sign an authorization permitting your insurance company to obtain medical records concerning your injuries directly from your treaters.

**Authorization for release of personnel and other income records.** If you have claimed income loss, you must sign an authorization permitting the insurance company to obtain directly from your employer information concerning your income and your work record.

**Independent medical examination.** If your insurance company requests that you have an IME, read the policy carefully to see what the terms are. In general, make sure there is only one examination, that the insurance company agrees in writing to pay for it, and that it is arranged at your convenience, not just the doctor's. Also, get a statement from the claims adjuster in writing, in advance, of the limits of the examination. You have to undergo an examination only of the injuries you claim, and not a general physical exam.

If you have any dispute with the adjuster for your insurance company over submitting to a medical examination, providing information, or following policy rules, do not take the adjuster's word as gospel. Read the policy. If you don't have a copy, the adjuster must provide you with one. And if you reach a stalemate with your own company's adjuster about any point of negotiations or about the amount of the settlement offer, you may have to switch negotiation strategies.

## Improper Settlement Tactics

Claims adjusters are hired to save their company's money. And although most adjusters do their jobs within the rules, there are a few who will try to break those rules if they think they can get away with it. This section alerts you to a number of the improper negotiating tactics that some adjusters use and explains how to respond if an adjuster tries one on you.

### "Settle With the Other Company"

When beginning negotiations, an adjuster may tell you to contact the insurance company for another person or business involved in the accident because that other person or business was more responsible than its insured. Politely remind the adjuster that until one company or the other commits itself in writing to be the primary insurance carrier, you are entitled to proceed against either responsible party and that you are doing so against that adjuster's insured. (See Chapter 6.)

### "You Waited Too Long"

If there was any delay between your accident and when you notified the insurance company in writing of your intention to file a claim, an insurance adjuster might try to intimidate you by telling you that you waited too long and that the delay might now disqualify your claim.

In fact, in third-party claims there is no time limit other than the statute of limitations within which you must file a notice of claim. (See "State Statutes of Limitations," below.) The exception is for a claim against the government. (See Chapter 3.) If the adjuster for a third party contends that you delayed "too long" or asks why you waited to file your claim when you are still well within the statue of limitations, remind the adjuster that

## Dealing With an Independent Medical Exam

Your insurance policy may require you to submit to an independent medical examination (IME) if your own insurance company requests it. If the adjuster for your company sets up an IME for you, you can do some things to protect yourself during the exam—and afterward, if the report the doctor submits is inaccurate or harmful to your claim.

**Bring a friend.** See if you can get a friend or family member to go with you. Explain to them ahead of time what the IME is about and what you would like them to do. They can take notes on exactly what time the doctor begins and ends the exam, what medical history or other questions the doctor asked you, what tests the doctor performed and how long they took, and other details that you might not remember. This person can act as a witness if you later have an argument with the adjuster about the fairness or accuracy of the examination (see below). Having another person present also sometimes keeps the doctor from being rude or intimidating with you.

**Counter a bad report.** IMEs are conducted by doctors who regularly work for the insurance company. These doctors want to make the insurance company happy so that they can continue getting these lucrative exams referred to them. That means their reports to the insurance company tend to minimize the extent of accident victims' injuries. If that happens to you, there are several things you can do and say during your negotiations with the adjuster to counter the bad report.

- Ask for a copy of the report. You should refuse even to discuss the report with your adjuster until you have a complete copy—not just portions of it or the adjuster's version of what it says.

- If the examination was in any way unfair— very brief or superficial, or taken without first getting a thorough medical history from you of your symptoms—then point this out

to the adjuster. And tell the adjuster that the friend or family member who attended the IME with you can support your contention.

- Point out to the adjuster any inaccuracy or incompleteness in the report, as an indication of its unreliability as a true measure of your injuries. If possible, use material from your own medical records to point out the problem.

- Contrast for the adjuster the very brief extent of the IME with the much more significant time your own doctors have spent diagnosing and treating your injuries.

- If the IME report is extremely negative and the adjuster is relying on it heavily in denying you a fair settlement, you may want your own doctor—preferably a specialist who has been treating you—to write a response. Show your doctor the IME report and ask if the doctor would be willing to write a letter countering it. Be aware, however, that your doctor is likely to charge you for preparing a response. Find out in advance how much you will be charged so that you can decide whether what your doctor is willing to write seems worth the cost.

- Ask for information about the IME doctor's relationship with the insurance company. Put in writing to the adjuster a request for: the number of IME referrals the insurance company has given the particular doctor over the previous five years; the amount of money the doctor is paid for each IME; how many IMEs the doctor has performed for plaintiffs' attorneys over the same period. There is no way the adjuster will provide you with this information. But refusing to provide it may put the adjuster on the defensive a bit in relying on the report while negotiating a settlement with you.

there is no other time limit for filing a liability claim and politely demand that the adjuster move onto actual settlement negotiations.

If you are filing a claim under your own insurance coverage, your policy may require that a notice of injury be filed within a specific number of days or within a reasonable time after the accident. But even if you have delayed before filing a notice of claim, the insurance company must honor your claim unless the claim was so late that it negatively affected (prejudiced) the insurance company's ability to investigate the claim.

It is up to an insurance company to prove any prejudice caused by the delay—for example, that it was unable to investigate the scene of the accident or that evidence was destroyed. And it is very rarely able to do so. You do not need to prove that there was no prejudice.

Tell the claims adjuster the reasons for the delay in notifying the insurance company: for example, you didn't know who the responsible party might be; you were not provided with adequate insurance information; your injuries made it impossible for you to investigate for a while. But do not concede that the time was unreasonable. And do not permit the adjuster to put you off your claim. This tactic of suggesting that you filed your claim too late is just an attempt to make you so nervous that you will jump at any small settlement offer out of fear of losing your claim entirely.

Unless the adjuster offers to prove specific prejudice to the insurance company, ignore any comments about a delayed claim. If the adjuster continues to deny your claim altogether, you will have to move on to other negotiating tactics. (See below.)

## "You Weren't Out of Pocket"

As mentioned several times, whether you paid for medical care out of your own pocket or it was paid for by your health or other insurance is none of the claims adjuster's business. And it is none of the adjuster's business whether or not your lost time at work was covered by sick leave or vacation pay. Under what is known as the "collateral source rule," it is improper for a claims adjuster to consider other sources of payment in determining a reasonable settlement amount. In fact, the adjuster isn't even supposed to ask you about such other payments.

The reasoning behind the collateral source rule is simple. A person who causes injuries should not benefit because you have taken the precaution of paying for health or other medical insurance coverage—nor by the fact that by working steadily you have earned the right to sick leave or vacation time.

If an adjuster so much as breathes anything about other sources of medical or income payments, remind him or her that the collateral source rule prohibits such questions. Inform the adjuster that you will consider any further reference to collateral payment sources to be bad faith settlement tactics. You are not likely to hear about collateral sources again. But if by some strange chance you do, report the matter to the adjuster's superior and to your state's insurance department, as described below.

## What to Do When You Can't Get a Settlement

Most adjusters want to handle a claim simply and without unnecessary time and energy. But there are always a few adjusters—because of personality, negotiating style, or company policy—

who are willing to bluff or stall well past the time all the documents have been examined and all the arguments have been made on both sides.

These adjusters will often make an extremely low initial offer and then stick to it without giving any justification. They hope that their tactics will either intimidate or frustrate you into accepting a settlement much lower than your claim is worth.

This section suggests several things you might do to get a troublesome adjuster to make you a fair settlement offer. Some of the suggestions involve nothing more than matters to raise in your communications with the adjuster; others involve going over the adjuster's head. And if all else fails, you may have to consider going to court—either on your own to small claims court or with a lawyer through the slow and costly process of standard court litigation. (See Chapters 10 and 11.)

## Persistence

You may be able to move an adjuster off a stubbornly held position simply by regularly—every week or ten days—calling or writing to ask when the adjuster will make a fair and reasonable settlement offer. By reaffirming that you will be both patient and persistent and will not fold up your claim, you may get the adjuster to come up with a fair settlement offer.

## Suggestion of Bad Faith

Key phrases commonly used in the insurance industry sometimes make adjusters sit up and take notice. When you are negotiating a settlement with your own insurance company as part of uninsured or underinsured motorist coverage, "bad faith" can be one such phrase. Because your policy is a paid-for promise by your insurance company to provide you with insurance protection, the company has a duty to provide that protection and to negotiate and settle claims in good faith.

Insurance companies for third parties also have a duty of good faith toward an injured person, but that duty is much less than the duty owed by your own company. A claim of bad faith against a third party's insurance company arises only if the company, through its adjuster, has engaged in outright lies or fraud or has interfered with your ability to pursue the claim (such as by tampering with a witness, withholding evidence, or the like). If you believe a third-party insurer has engaged in such outrageous behavior, contact your state's insurance department (see below) and an experienced personal injury attorney (see Chapter 11).

## Check the Time

Every state has a law, called the statute of limitations, restricting the time a person injured in an accident has to sue. After that time has passed, no lawsuit can be filed by the injured person to seek compensation for his or her injuries.

If the time limit has passed and you have failed to file—or have a lawyer file on your behalf—a lawsuit against the person or business legally responsible for your accident, their legal responsibility ends. And their insurance company will no longer settle a claim with you.

In most states, you have two years or more from the date of the accident to file a lawsuit. And since settling a claim doesn't normally take nearly that long, you don't usually have to be concerned about the timing. However, in Kentucky, Louisiana, and Tennessee, the statute of limitations is only one year from the date of the accident. (See below for a complete listing of state time limits.)

If you have not yet settled your claim by two months before your state's time limit, consider filing a lawsuit. Consult an attorney, who specializes in personal injury cases about getting the formal lawsuit papers filed. Filing the papers does not mean that you have to hire the lawyer to take over your claim. (See "Consult an Attorney," below.) Nor does it necessarily mean you have to move forward right away with an actual court case. You can continue negotiating for a while longer. Filing a lawsuit does, however, protect your right to proceed with your claim and with a court case if that later becomes necessary.

An adjuster for your own insurance company is not negotiating in bad faith just because you and the adjuster have a difference of opinion about how much your claim is worth. However, bad faith may exist if the adjuster for your own company has refused to give you any specific reasons for a very low settlement offer or has said or done something which might amount to an improper settlement tactic. (See "Improper Settlement Tactics," above.)

If you believe the adjuster for your company is negotiating in bad faith, use the term in conversation with the adjuster. If you get no satisfactory response, you may want to put your accusation of bad faith in writing. In a bad faith letter to the insurance company, specifically refer to the conduct of the adjuster that you believe amounts to bad faith.

A written accusation of bad faith often gets prompt attention and, if justified, may rapidly provoke a change in the adjuster's settlement position. If an insurance company is proved to have acted in bad faith, it may be liable to pay damages to the insured well above the injury compensation amount. The rules about what is and is not bad faith vary from state to state, and it is extremely difficult to win bad faith damages in court. Nonetheless, in settlement negotiations, the mere possibility of a fight over bad faith often can help nudge a reasonable settlement offer out of an insurance company.

## Sample Letter Claiming Bad Faith

Alice Mendoza
123 Broadway
Redhook, IL 00000

June 15, 20xx

Ronald Firth
Claims Adjuster
Metropolitan Insurance Co.
St. Louis, MO 00000

Re: Your Insured, Alice Mendoza
Claimant: Alice Mendoza
Claim No.: 93-HQ1234
Date of accident: January 13, 20xx

Dear Mr. Firth:

This letter concerns the discussions you and I have had over the past several weeks concerning settlement of the uninsured motorist claim referenced above. You have made only one offer of settlement in the amount of $500. This offer bears no reasonable relationship to my injuries, since my medical expenses alone total $1,550. Yet you refuse to provide me with any explanation for your position.

The only conclusion I can come to is that Metropolitan Insurance Company is refusing to negotiate in good faith.

If no fair and reasonable settlement offer, or explanation for the lack of such offer, is made by July 1, 20xx, I will be forced to take further steps regarding Metropolitan's apparent bad faith.

Yours truly,

*Alice Mendoza*

Alice Mendoza

## Threat of a Lawsuit

Adjusters do not like lawsuits. A lawsuit usually means that lawyers will soon get involved, costs will go up, and the claim file may be taken away from the adjuster and given to an insurance company lawyer or to another adjuster, which may mean a blemish on the adjuster's work record. Also, a lawsuit can get the insured person upset, which can mean lost business for the insurance company. Since a claims adjuster wants to avoid all this, you might be able to loosen the insurance company's purse strings by suggesting that if a fair offer is not made by a certain date, you will be forced to file a lawsuit and to hire an attorney to handle the claim for you.

### No Lawsuits If Arbitration Is Mandatory

Although the threat of a lawsuit sometimes can be an effective way to nudge an adjuster toward a settlement, it works only if a lawsuit is actually a possibility.

Most uninsured motorist coverages and some no-fault policies require that unsettled claims be submitted to arbitration. (See Chapter 10.) The insured is not allowed to file suit. So make sure you have the legal right to back up your threat before you make it.

## Consult an Attorney

Although most lawyers are paid for handling personal injury cases by taking a percentage of your settlement, some are willing to consult with you on an hourly basis while you continue to handle your claim yourself. If you and a claims adjuster are at an impasse, particularly if there is some legal question about liability over which you and the adjuster disagree, you might want to meet for an hour or so with a lawyer who specializes in personal injury cases.

Bring with you all your papers, documents, notes, and correspondence. After a brief review, the lawyer might be able to point out some particular fact, rule, or tactic you can use in your next contact with the adjuster. The lawyer may also be able to help you file a lawsuit to protect your rights within the limits of your state's statute of limitations. (See below.)

Injecting some new idea or legal theory into the negotiations can sometimes get an adjuster finally to make a serious settlement offer. You may even want to let the adjuster know that you have consulted an attorney and that if a fair settlement offer is not made, you will be forced to let the attorney take over your claim.

If you decide to consult with a lawyer on an hourly basis, make sure you know ahead of time how much the lawyer will charge per hour, and be sure to set a limit, in writing, on the number of hours you want the lawyer to spend reviewing your claim. (See Chapter 11.)

## Speak With the Adjuster's Supervisor

If you are unable to settle your claim with the adjuster assigned to it, there are other people within the insurance company from whom you might get a more reasonable offer. The adjuster has an immediate supervisor, and there is also usually an overall claims manager within the claims department. If you have reached an impasse, or if the adjuster fails to act promptly on your claim, politely suggest that the difficulties might be overcome if you both got another opinion. Ask to speak with the claims supervisor. Merely asking the adjuster to bring the supervisor into the picture may jar the adjuster into changing the settlement offer.

If the adjuster promises to contact the supervisor for a review of the file, allow some time for that. The adjuster may come back with a better settlement offer. But if the adjuster is going to discuss the matter with the supervisor, agree on a specific date by which the adjuster will report back to you on the results.

If the adjuster does not agree to speak with the supervisor, ask for the supervisor's name. Call or write to the supervisor, mention the number of contacts you have had with the adjuster, and explain that the adjuster has yet to make a reasonable settlement offer and has failed to give you satisfactory reasons for the low offer. If the adjuster has delayed or used improper settlement tactics, mention that, too. Then ask that the supervisor review the file and either handle the matter personally or refer it to a new adjuster.

If you cannot get a reasonable settlement offer from the supervisor, ask him or her to write to you the reasons for the insurance company's settlement position. This statement of the company's position may be helpful to you in any further steps you have to take. One of those steps is to contact the claims manager, who is the boss of the adjusters and supervisors. Get the name of the claims manager from the supervisor and repeat the process with the manager, describing the problem you have had with the adjuster and the supervisor. To avoid further hassles with a persistent claimant, the claims manager might authorize an increase in the settlement offer.

## Contact the State Department of Insurance

Every state has a department, commission, or bureau that oversees the insurance industry in the state. And each department has a consumer complaint division that occasionally will get involved when a claimant is having trouble with an insurance company. For the most part, these state departments of insurance are in the pockets of the big insurance companies. And even when they do try to rein in insurance profiteering, they spend far more energy and resources on large matters—like rate increases—than on individual complaints.

Nonetheless, there are a few circumstances in which a complaint to a state department of insurance might bring some results, including when the insurance adjuster:

- has refused to make any offer at all to settle your claim
- has provided false or misleading information, or engaged in pressure tactics or other conduct you believe is unethical, or
- has delayed making an offer or made only a token settlement offer, and has refused to explain why.

When the insurance company has made a settlement offer but you differ on how much the claim is worth, however, filing a complaint with the department of insurance will not bring any results. In those situations, you must depend on the other methods described in this section to reach a settlement.

If your situation seems appropriate for a complaint to the state insurance department, the mere mention to the adjuster of your intent to file such a complaint might bring a new settlement offer. Even though the insurance department is unlikely to get involved, adjusters would rather not have such a complaint on file. Too many of these complaints can result in an insurance department inquiry, and individual adjusters do not want to have these complaints in their own personnel files.

If mentioning the possibility of a complaint to the state department of insurance doesn't get any movement from the adjuster or supervisor, file an actual complaint. Your first step is to call and find out exactly where to send your complaint and whether there is a specific form to use. You can

find the phone number of the state department of insurance by looking in the government section at the front of your telephone directory. You can also find the website for your state department of insurance by using a search engine or by locating the directory at www.insbuyer.com/departmentofinsurance.htm. If you find there's a form, get it and use it. Otherwise, your complaint letter should include the following:

- the date of the accident and people involved in it
- a general description of your claim
- the insurance company's claim number
- details of the difficulties you have had with the claims adjuster—delays, no fair settlement offer, improper settlement tactics
- the number of conversations you have had with the adjuster and supervisors trying to settle the matter, and
- copies of all your correspondence, including your demand letter, so the insurance department investigator will understand exactly what the claim is based on.

The quality, quantity, and speed of response from state departments of insurance varies greatly from state to state. In a few states, every complaint gets at least some attention from the department's consumer affairs office. In other states, however, your complaint may get action only if the office spots obvious and extreme improper conduct, or if it has received numerous other complaints about the same adjuster or insurance company. Most departments of insurance keep a registry of complaints and if any one company has too many, the company may have some trouble with the department or with consumer groups when they try to have new rates or policies approved by the state.

The state insurance department might send a form letter to the insurance company informing

**Sample Letter to the Department of Insurance**

Anton Simchek
2284 West Hawthorne Boulevard
Los Angeles, CA 90000
213-777-0000

November 1, 20xx

Office of Consumer Complaints
California Department of Insurance
66666 Wilshire Boulevard
Los Angeles, CA 90000

Re:  Claimant: Anton Simchek
     Insurance Co.: Pacific All-Risk
     Claim No.: 1X-29987-PI
     Date of accident: January 12, 20xx

To Whom It Concerns:

I was injured in an automobile accident on January 12, 20xx with Corrine Pass, who is insured by Pacific All-Risk Insurance Company. I notified Pacific All-Risk of the accident on January 14, 20xx. On April 22, 20xx, I submitted a demand letter, plus copies of my medical records and billing, to Pacific All-Risk for compensation for my injuries.

On May 28, 20xx, I received a telephone call from John McCarthy, a claims adjuster from Pacific All-Risk. Mr. McCarthy at first denied that Ms. Pass was at all liable for the accident. In a phone call of June 6, 20xx, Mr. McCarthy admitted that Ms. Pass had some liability for the accident and offered to settle my claim for $750, despite the fact that I suffered a broken wrist as well as back injuries and my medical bills were $1,250.

I have had six conversations with Mr. McCarthy and with John Taylor, Mr. McCarthy's supervisor, between June 6 and November 1, 20xx. They have made no other settlement offer and refuse to give any reason for their failure to make a reasonable offer.

I believe that Pacific All-Risk is negotiating in bad faith. I hope that you will investigate this matter and convince Pacific All-Risk to make a good faith offer of settlement.

Enclosed are copies of all correspondence between me and Pacific All-Risk, plus copies of documents supporting my claim.

Yours truly,

*Anton Simchek*

Anton Simchek

it of your complaint. It might require the company to respond in writing.

Your complaint to the state insurance department can accomplish several things. First, someone in the claims department of the insurance company other than the adjuster who handled the claim will become aware that there is a claimant who intends to do whatever it takes to get a fair and reasonable settlement, and that may inspire someone to take another look at your claim and come up with a reasonable settlement offer. Also, because a complaint with the state insurance department adds an extra layer of work for the insurance company, the company will want to try harder to settle your claim.

On rare occasions, an investigator for the state insurance department actually speaks in person to an insurance company on a claimant's behalf. This may get the insurance adjuster to make a more reasonable settlement offer. At the least, it will probably force an explanation of why the insurance company is taking such a hard-line position, an explanation the investigator may pass on to the claimant.

## Mediation

In recent years, there has been slow but steady movement away from the expensive, stressful, and time-consuming adversarial legal system as a way of settling disputes. Instead, people have been taking advantage of different types of alternative dispute resolution—particularly, mediation. Even lawyers and insurance companies now recognize the value of mediation and use it frequently. And in recent years it has become quite common in personal injury cases. If you have reached an impasse in negotiations with an insurance company over settlement of your personal injury claim, mediation may offer a sensible way out.

## The Basics of Mediation

In mediation, the parties involved in a dispute sit down with a neutral third person (the mediator) who is trained to help people come to a mutually satisfactory solution of their conflict. Until a dispute becomes an actual lawsuit, mediation is entirely voluntary; it only happens if both sides request it, and a settlement of the dispute through mediation is reached only if both sides agree to it. The mediator doesn't make decisions or even give opinions. If the parties themselves do not agree to a solution, they go back to where they left off before mediation. Also, nothing either party says during mediation can be used by the other party in later stages of the dispute.

The cost of mediation is usually split equally between the two sides. The process is informal; the purpose is to allow each side to have its say without the burden of special legal procedures, and without fear that if they say the wrong thing they can "lose" in the dispute.

Mediations in personal injury cases follow a basic structure, though they vary slightly among individual mediators. Each party speaks to the mediator in the presence of the other party; each gets to speak directly to the other party with the mediator facilitating the interchange; and each gets to speak alone to the mediator. The mediator then uses the information gathered from the parties—without revealing what either party says in confidence—to coax each side to change position sufficiently so both can reach an agreement. There are no restrictions on what can be said or how facts and opinions are presented, and the parties need no special training to make good use of the mediation.

Mediation may be available from one of several sources:

- **Neighborhood or community dispute resolution centers** can be found in many cities and towns. They are staffed primarily by volunteers who have some training in dispute resolution but who are not professional mediators and do not have legal experience. These centers charge only very small fees, if any. They mostly handle disputes between neighbors or cohabitants, landlords and tenants, and small businesses or contractors and consumers. Most mediators in these centers do not, however, have experience with personal injury claims against insurance companies.

- **Professional mediation services** are staffed by full-time mediators who usually have both mediation experience and a legal background. They are often lawyers or retired judges. They charge substantial fees (often several hundred dollars for each party for a half-day session), and handle many different types of mediation, most often involving business or property disputes. Many of them have experience with personal injury claims.
- **Independent mediators** are practicing or retired lawyers, sometimes retired judges. Some have experience mediating personal injury cases; many of those who do also handle personal injury cases as lawyers, representing either injured parties or insurance companies. Unfortunately, their experience comes with a high pric—$100-$300 per hour, and more.

## Consider Mediation for Your Personal Injury Claim

If you have reached an impasse with the insurance adjuster negotiating your personal injury claim, consider mediation as a way to break the stalemate. Mediation has several potential advantages. It allows you to sit in the same room with the adjuster, which puts a human face (yours) on a claim that is otherwise just a file on the adjuster's desk. An adjuster may be more likely to give you a reasonable settlement when sitting across a table from you than if you remain merely a set of claim documents and a voice on the phone. Mediation also gets the adjuster to put special effort into your claim, which increases the likelihood that the adjuster will try hard to settle the matter. You need no documents or arguments for mediation that you do not already have from the claims process. And you get a third person—the mediator—to encourage a break in the deadlock. And mediation can be much faster, easier, and less expensive that the alternatives of hiring a lawyer or going to small claims court.

There are also barriers to mediating a personal injury claim. Mediation in relatively simple matters, like most personal injury claims, usually lasts only a few hours. But those few hours can be very expensive if you use a professional mediator. And the alternative of an inexpensive community mediation service with experience in personal injury claims may be impossible to find near you. Also, it can be hard to get an insurance adjuster to agree to mediation because of the extra work it requires—including a personal appearance at the mediation session.

Given these benefits and barriers, you might want to consider trying to mediate your claim if:

- you and the insurance adjuster are stalemated more than $2,000 apart in settlement negotiations
- the major sticking point is the extent of your injury and/or what degree each party was at fault for the accident, and
- there don't seem to be any negotiating moves left for you to make, short of going to small claims court or hiring a lawyer.

Under these conditions, it may be worth your while to investigate the mediation process, including whether an appropriate, affordable local mediator is available.

## Finding a Mediator

It's entirely possible that the adjuster might easily agree to mediation and might even suggest a mediator. If the adjuster does propose a particular mediator, make sure you check the mediator out yourself. Contact the mediator and find out whether the insurance company is a client or a frequent user of the mediator's services. And if the mediator is a practicing attorney, find out whether the mediator's experience in personal injury cases is primarily representing claimants, or insurance companies. (These are the same questions you'll ask if you're looking for an independent mediator to propose to the adjuster, as discussed below.) Don't automatically agree to the mediator the insurance company suggests, but don't dismiss that mediator out of hand, either. The adjuster may sincerely want to get the case settled and be willing to hire a neutral mediator. Just do your homework and base your decisions on the facts.

If you're the one who's going to propose mediation or propose the mediator, here are some places to look for a mediator to suggest.

**Community mediation center.** Because of its low cost, a neighborhood or community mediation center might be your first choice. This is especially the case if the difference between what the adjuster has offered you and what you would settle for is only two or three thousand dollars apart—neither you nor the adjuster will want to spend that same money on a mediation. But look only for a local community mediation service that has experience in personal injury claims. Otherwise, the whole process is likely to be a waste of time (assuming you could even get the adjuster to agree to it). The need for an experienced personal injury mediator is particularly great if your claim involves something other than merely arriving at a dollar amount for obvious injuries—for example, some sort of

legal interpretation about responsibility for the accident, or an estimate of how much an injury is likely to affect your daily life in the future.

To find a local community mediation center, look under "Mediation" in the Yellow Pages. Or, call your local bar association (they are listed in the white pages, by city or county name) and ask whether they know of a community mediation service. You can also contact the nonprofit National Association for Community Mediation, 1527 New Hampshire Ave. NW, Washington, DC 20036, 202-667-9700, www.nafcm.org (click on "Locate a Center").

### Find a Mediator Located Near the Adjuster

As discussed below, it can be difficult to get an insurance adjuster to mediate. One of the ways to increase the likelihood of the adjuster agreeing to a mediation is if the adjuster does not have to travel far. An adjuster is less likely to agree to a mediation if merely getting to and from it would take a lot of time. So, check the adjuster's phone number and address, and then try to find an appropriate mediator close to where the adjuster works. Even if there are good mediators closer to where you are, they won't do you any good if the adjuster refuses to travel there.

**Professional mediation services.** If there is no community mediation center near you with experience in personal injury claims, consider using a professional mediator. Dispute resolution companies exist in all major urban areas and many other sites. They all have some mediators experienced in personal injury claims. But they are also likely to be expensive. If there is such a mediation service near you, you need to get as much detail as possible about their rates. They may have a sliding scale, depending on the money involved in the dispute and the experience of the individual mediator to be used. Also, ask whether there are any administrative or other fees on top of the rate (hourly, or by the half-day or day) for the actual mediation session. You can find professional mediation companies by looking in the Yellow Pages under "Dispute Resolution" or "Mediation." You can also get references to dispute resolution companies through the following national mediation organizations:

> Association for Conflict Resolution
> 202-464-9700
> www.acrnet.org
>
> Mediate.com
> 541-345-1629
> www.mediate.com

**Independent mediators.** You might find an independent mediator experienced in personal injury matters—probably a lawyer who handles personal injury cases—whose rates are a bit lower than those of a professional mediation service. An independent might also be more flexible than mediation companies in scheduling and paperwork. You might be able to get a referral to an independent mediator through the organizations listed above. Or, you can go through your local bar association, listed by county or city in the white pages. Bar associations often keep lists of local lawyers available to mediate disputes in specific areas of law, and some have mediator referral programs of their own. Also, if there is a community mediation center near you that does not handle personal injury claim mediations, it might give you a referral to local independent mediators.

Lawyers who handle personal injury cases in their law practice represent either claimants or insurance companies, but rarely both. If you are considering an independent mediator who is a lawyer practicing personal injury law, ask whether the lawyer usually represents injured people or insurance companies. Most insurance defense lawyer-mediators act fairly toward injured claimants. But some may tend (consciously or not) to favor the insurance company, so your odds are better choosing as a mediator someone who usually represents claimants.

## Getting an Adjuster to Agree to Mediation

Even if mediation seems to you a reasonable way to break a deadlock with the insurance adjuster handling your claim, the adjuster may refuse. There are several reasons an adjuster might resist mediation. First, mediation of personal injury claims is a fairly recent phenomenon, so many adjusters have little or no experience with it; like most people, adjusters are wary of the unknown. Also, there is the expense. Particularly if you want to use a professional mediation service or independent mediator, an adjuster may balk at the cost. Then there is the extra time and energy an adjuster would have to spend preparing for and going through the mediation; many adjusters fail to see the potential benefit as worth the effort. Finally, an adjuster may refuse mediation if he or she thinks that mediation is your last resort, and that otherwise you will give up your efforts at increasing the insurance company's settlement offer.

Because of this likely resistance, you may have to do some persuading. Part of that persuasion comes from making the mediation as easy as possible for the adjuster. That may mean using a community mediation service if possible, because the cost will be low. It means finding a mediator close to the adjuster's office so that appearing at the mediation does not cost the adjuster more time than necessary. It also means doing the organizing of the mediation yourself, but showing the adjuster that you are quite flexible with regard to scheduling. Also, you may want to agree to limit the mediation to a half-day, so that the adjuster knows he or she will not be sucked into an open-ended process.

**If you are seriously considering mediating your claim, you can rely on *Mediate, Don't Litigate*, by Peter Lovenheim and Lisa Guerin (Nolo), to help you through the process.** It thoroughly explains mediation, including how to find the right mediator for your dispute, and walks you through both preparation for mediation and the mediation session itself.

The other part of persuasion is putting some pressure on the adjuster. That may include making it clear that if there is no mediation, your next step will be to hire a lawyer. You may even want to let the adjuster know that you have already consulted a lawyer and that mediation is your last chance to avoid lawyer fees. Adjusters know that once a lawyer is involved, costs go up for both sides. If your claim is a smaller one (within your state's small claims dollar limit), you may let the adjuster know that you already have the papers to go to small claims court, which would be your next step if there is no mediation. No adjuster wants a claim to go through the tedious process of small claims court. Finally, you should put your request for mediation—including the specifics of any mediation center or service you have located—in writing and send it to the adjuster. This forces the adjuster to respond, rather than merely ignoring your idea for mediation.

If the adjuster does agree to mediation, confirm the details in a letter. The letter should note who the mediator (or at least mediation service) will be, the fees, and your agreement with the adjuster to split the cost evenly.

Once the adjuster agrees to mediate, the battle is more than half over. An adjuster will not go through a mediation process without increasing the insurance company's settlement offer somewhat—it would be a waste of the adjuster's time to go through mediation simply to see if you will completely give up there when you haven't given up before. The only question will be how much the adjuster will raise the settlement offer, and whether the amount will satisfy you.

## If All Else Fails

If you try the steps suggested here but have no success reaching a settlement with the insurance company, you may be forced to consider other options.

One is to take your claim to small claims court and try to get compensation there. Small claims court is simple, relatively fast, and does not involve lawyers. On the other hand, the amount of money you can recover in small claims court is limited in every state. (See Chapter 10.)

A different option is available—and in some cases, is forced on you—in uninsured motorist and some no-fault claims. These policy provisions do not permit you to go to court, but instead require that you take your claim to arbitration. (See Chapter 10.)

Another option is to hire a personal injury lawyer to represent you in pursuing your claim, with the possibility of taking you through a formal lawsuit. Hiring a lawyer, however, will cost you a lot of your compensation money— usually 33% to 50% of whatever your final settlement or judgment turns out to be. (See Chapter 11.)

## State Statutes of Limitations

Every state has a law called the statute of limitations that sets limits on the time within which a person injured in an accident can file a lawsuit. After that time has passed, no lawsuit can be filed by the injured person to seek compensation for his or her injuries.

In addition, a lawsuit against a government entity can be filed only if a timely formal claim has first been filed. (See Chapter 3.)

The following are the statutes of limitations for personal injury lawsuits in all 50 states and the District of Columbia. The law of the state where an accident happened is the one that controls, regardless of what state you live in. The time begins on the date of the accident.

**Watch the time.** Laws change frequently. If you are getting close to one year from the date of your accident, double-check the statute of limitations in your state to see its latest version. You can find the statute at your nearest law library; ask the law librarian for assistance in finding the latest statute. For your reference, next to each state listed below is the section number of the statute of limitations for personal injury cases. You can also find the statutes by using Nolo's Legal Research Center on Nolo's website at www.nolo.com.

**Alabama**
2 years (Ala. Code § 6-2-38)

**Alaska**
2 years (Alaska Stat. § 09.10.070)

**Arizona**
2 years (Ariz. Rev. Stat. Ann. § 12-542)

**Arkansas**
3 years (Ark. Code Ann. § 16-56-105)

**California**
2 years (Cal. Code of Civ. Proc. § 335.1)

**Colorado**
2 years (Colo. Rev. Stat. § 13-80-102)
3 years (motor vehicle accidents) (Colo. Rev. Stat. § 13-80-101)

**Connecticut**
2 years (Conn. Gen. Stat. Ann. § 52-584)

**Delaware**
2 years (Del. Code Ann. Title 10, § 8107, § 8119)

**District of Columbia**
3 years (D.C. Code Ann. § 12-301)

**Florida**
4 years (Fla. Stat. Ann. § 95.11)

**Georgia**
2 years (Ga. Code Ann. § 9-3-33)

**Hawaii**
2 years (Hawaii Rev. Stat. § 657-7)

**Idaho**
2 years (Idaho Code § 5-219)

**Illinois**
2 years (Ill. Ann. Stat., Ch. 5, § 13-202)

**Indiana**
2 years (Ind. Code Ann. § 34-11-2-4)

**Iowa**
2 years (Iowa Code Ann. § 614.1)

**Kansas**
2 years (Kan. Stat. Ann. § 60-513)

**Kentucky**
1 year (Ky. Rev. Stat. § 413.140)

**Louisiana**
1 year (La. Civ. Code Ann. art. 3492)

**Maine**

6 years (Me. Rev. Stat. Ann. Title 14, Ch. 205, § 752)

**Maryland**

3 years (Md. Ann. Courts & Judicial Proceedings Code § 5-101)

**Massachusetts**

3 years (Mass. Gen. Laws Ann. Ch. 260, § 2A,4)

**Michigan**

3 years (Mich. Comp. Laws § 600.5805)

**Minnesota**

2 years (Minn. Stat. Ann. § 541.07)

**Mississippi**

3 years (Miss. Code Ann. § 15-1-49)

**Missouri**

5 years (Mo. Ann. Stat. Title 35, § 516.120)

**Montana**

3 years (Mont. Code Ann. § 27-2-204)

**Nebraska**

4 years (Neb. Rev. Stat. § 25-207)

**Nevada**

2 years (Nev. Rev. Stat. Ann. § 11.190)

**New Hampshire**

3 years (N.H. Rev. Stat. Ann. § 508:4)

**New Jersey**

2 years (N.J. Stat. Ann. § 2A:14-2)

**New Mexico**

3 years (N.M. Stat. Ann. § 37-1-8)

**New York**

3 years (N.Y. Civ. Prac. R. § 214)

**North Carolina**

3 years (N.C. Gen. Stat. § 1-52)

**North Dakota**

6 years (N.D. Cent. Code § 28-01-16)

**Ohio**

2 years (Ohio Rev. Code Ann. § 2305.10)

**Oklahoma**

2 years (Okla. Stat. Ann. Title 12, § 95)

**Oregon**

2 years (Ore. Rev. Stat. § 12.110(1))

**Pennsylvania**

2 years (42 Pa. Con. Stat. Ann. § 5524)

**Rhode Island**

3 years (R.I. Gen. Laws § 9-1-14)

**South Carolina**

3 years (S.C. Code Ann. § 15-3-530)

**South Dakota**

3 years (S.D. Comp. Laws Ann. §§ 15-2-12.2, 15-2-14)

**Tennessee**

1 year (Tenn. Code Ann. § 28-3-104)

**Texas**

2 years (Tex. Civ. Prac. & Rem. Code, Title 2, § 16.003)

**Utah**

4 years (Utah Code Ann. § 78-12-25(3))

**Vermont**

3 years (Vt. Stat. Ann. Title 12, § 512)

**Virginia**

2 years (Va. Code § 8.01-243)

**Washington**

3 years (Wash. Rev. Code Ann. §§ 4.16.080)

**West Virginia**

2 years (W.Va. Code § 55-2-12)

**Wisconsin**

3 years (Wis. Stat. Ann. § 893.54)

**Wyoming**

4 years (Wyo. Stat. Ann. § 1-3-105)

# Chapter 9

# Finalizing Your Settlement

Once you accept an offer, or a claims adjuster accepts an amount you propose, you have a verbal agreement with the insurance company for a full and final settlement of your claim. This chapter explains:

- how the verbal agreement is processed into a written one by the insurance company
- how and when you will receive your settlement money
- what to do in case of delay, and
- how to deal with a medical plan or insurance company that holds a lien against some of your settlement money.

## Confirming the Offer and Acceptance

As soon as you and an insurance adjuster agree on a settlement amount, you must take two more steps to make it final. First, ask the adjuster to send you a letter confirming the settlement. If you do not receive that letter within a week, call and remind the adjuster to send it. Also, immediately send your own confirming letter to the adjuster.

Although it seems that nothing could go wrong at this point, on rare occasions something does. The adjuster with whom you settled could lose his or her notes about the settlement negotiations. Your claim file could get lost. Or the adjuster may quit or be transferred before preparing the settlement documents. Don't risk having to start the negotiation process all over again. Send the confirming letter—and keep a copy for yourself.

## Formal Settlement Document

Within a couple of weeks after reaching a final settlement amount with the adjuster, you will receive by mail a document entitled Settlement and Release, or Release of All Claims. This release

### Sample Settlement Confirmation Letter

Thomas Tucker
123 Peach Street
Greensville, GA 00000
June 15, 20xx

Elton Jack
Claims Adjuster
Great Southern Insurance Company
Atlanta, GA 00000

Re: Your Insured, Mark deVille
    Claimant: Thomas Tucker
    Claim No.: 9X-HQ1234
    Date of Loss: January 13, 20xx

Dear Mr. Jack:

This letter confirms our telephone conversation today during which you agreed on behalf of Great Southern Insurance Company to settle my claim for the sum of $3,500, excluding property damage amounts previously paid. I agreed to accept that amount in settlement of all personal injury claims I have against your insured, Mark deVille, arising out of an accident on January 13, 20xx.

This letter also confirms that within 14 days you will send me documents reflecting this settlement, and that upon my endorsement and return to you of those documents, Great Southern Insurance Company will send me a check for the agreed amount.

Thank you for your continued cooperation in this matter.

Very truly yours,

*Thomas Tucker*

Thomas Tucker

serves two purposes. First, it puts in writing the insurance company's agreement to pay you a certain amount of money to settle your claim against its insured. Second, it commits you to a final settlement of all claims from the accident. Once you sign this release, you give up your right to seek any additional compensation from this particular insured person—regardless of what you may later discover about how the accident happened or how serious your injuries are.

Because of the slow internal workings of insurance claims departments, the settlement document does not always arrive immediately. Often the adjuster has to have the final settlement figure approved by a supervisor, or the file must be sent to another part of the office to be prepared. And sometimes the delay is due to just plain inefficiency.

Call the adjuster if you do not receive the settlement document within two weeks after your final agreement. If your file has been lost in the shuffle somewhere, ask the adjuster to track it down and let you know that the documents are being processed.

When you receive the settlement document, your check will not be included. You will not receive the money until you sign the settlement document and return it to the insurance company—where it will be processed through the next bureaucratic step. That will probably take another two to four weeks. Before you return the signed release form to the insurance company, make a copy for your files. If there is any delay in processing the settlement and getting your check, you will need a copy of the release as a reference.

## Contents of a Settlement and Release

Although settlement documents differ somewhat in form and language, all releases contain essentially the same things: the names of those involved, the date of the accident (sometimes referred to as date of claim), the settlement amount, and the fact that the settlement fully and finally ends the entire matter.

Most of the legal language in a release serves one purpose: to make clear that no matter what else happens, this settlement completely ends your rights against the insured and anyone else for whom the insured is legally responsible, such as an employee, a child, or another relative. The settlement takes the insurance company off the hook for any further compensation if you later find out something about how the accident happened, or discover that an injury takes longer than expected to heal, or does not heal completely, or some other physical problem develops that may be connected with the accident.

A release also states that the settlement is not an admission of any liability or fault on the part of the insured, that it is intended only to avoid litigation. Although this statement may be a little annoying to you, do not worry about it. These "no admission of liability" clauses came into use in big cases where personal or business reputations were at stake and the individuals or companies did not want to admit publicly that they had done anything wrong. Now they are just a standard part of every release form.

Finally, some insurance companies require that your signature on the release form be notarized. You can find a notary in the Yellow Pages, at your local bank, or in a private mailbox business.

## Sample Settlement and Release

The sample settlement below contains a typical amount of legal lingo to say that this is a final settlement. Thankfully, many releases are simpler than this one. Explanations of legal lingo appear in bold print in parentheses.

If there is something in your release form that you do not understand, do not sign it until you

## Sample Settlement Document

### SETTLEMENT AND RELEASE OF ALL CLAIMS

Claimant RHONDA SIMPSON (hereinafter referred to as Claimant), in consideration of payment of THREE THOUSAND FIVE HUNDRED and no/100ths dollars ($3,500) by Metropolitan Insurance Company (hereinafter referred to as Company), on behalf of MOLLY GARDNER (hereinafter referred to as Insured), does hereby fully, completely, irrevocably, and forever release said Insured, his/her agents, servants, and employees from any and all liability, claims, or causes of action, whether known or unknown, arising out of the matters occurring on or about January 13, 20xx, and as set forth in a claim filed with the company by Claimant and against the Insured, and identified by Company and Claimant as Claim No. 9X-HQ1234. *(This language makes certain that the case is now finished, even if you later discover more injuries or need more treatment.)*

It is understood and agreed that this settlement is the compromise of a disputed claim, and that the payment made is not to be construed as an admission of liability on the part of the Insured hereby released, and that said release denies any and all liability arising out of the matters set forth in the above-described claim and intends merely to avoid litigation in this matter and to buy the Insured his or her peace. *(This is simply a public relations paragraph so that if anyone asks the insured person about who was at fault for the accident, the response can be that fault was never admitted. It does not affect your compensation at all.)*

It is further understood and agreed that all rights under Section 1542 of the Civil Code of the State of California, and any similar law of any state or territory of the United States or other jurisdiction, are hereby waived. Said Section reads as follows:

"Section 1542. Certain claims not affected by general release. A general release does not extend to a claim which the creditor does not know or suspect to exist in his favor at the time of executing the release, which if known by him must have materially affected his settlement with the debtor." *(Some state laws say that a settlement does not necessarily settle a claim for damages if you do not know what all the damages are. This language says that even if you learn of other problems later, you can't rely on these laws to come back and ask for more money—with the release you agree to end the claim forever.)*

Claimant further declares and represents that no promise, inducement, or agreement not herein expressed has been made to Claimant, his agents, servants, or employees, and that this Settlement and Release of All Claims contains the entire agreement between the parties hereto, and that the terms of this release are contractual and not a mere recital. *(This section makes clear that you are not permitted to later claim that you had a different oral agreement with an adjuster or someone else in the insurance company to give you more money or to reopen your claim.)*

THE UNDERSIGNED HAS READ THE FOREGOING SETTLEMENT AND RELEASE OF ALL CLAIMS AND FULLY UNDERSTANDS IT.

Dated: _____

(Signature of Claimant)

get a satisfactory explanation. Call the adjuster and ask what the particular language means. If you get an explanation that satisfies you, ask the adjuster to put the explanation in writing. If you do not get a satisfactory explanation from the adjuster, move up through the ranks of the claims department and then to the state department of insurance. (See Chapter 8.)

**⚠ Make sure the release is only for your bodily injury claim.** If you made a property damage claim against the same insurance company that is paying you for your personal injuries, make sure the release states what you are being compensated for. You don't want to end up reimbursing the company for the amounts it paid you for property damage (as you would for amounts it paid out for medical payments). Usually, there are separate releases for property damage and for bodily injury settlements. A personal injury settlement release should refer to bodily injury and make no mention of property damage. If you haven't yet resolved your property damage claim and your form doesn't refer exclusively to bodily injury, or if it mentions property damage, you should return it to the adjuster. Ask the adjuster to note on the release, and sign the notation, that the release does not involve the property damage claim. Ask the adjuster to return the release to you with a cover letter that says the same thing.

## What to Do If the Check Doesn't Arrive

You should receive your settlement check within two to four weeks after you return the signed release to the insurance company. Ask the claims adjuster how long it usually takes the company to process checks. Some insurance companies have a local office issue the check and do it quickly. Others require that the check be issued by a

regional or home office in another state, which may take a little longer.

All too frequently, however, a settlement check takes longer to arrive than it is supposed to. This usually means nothing more serious than a paperwork logjam in the insurance company office. But there are some things you can do to help speed up the process.

**Call the adjuster.** Although in most companies the adjuster does not prepare the check, if it has not arrived when promised, ask the adjuster to find out what the delay is. The adjuster's job is essentially done, which means you can't expect much motivation to track down the final paperwork. So if you want results, ask politely.

If the check is late, do not let the adjuster put you off simply by telling you that the papers are in the works. Remind the adjuster that the check is already overdue. Ask the adjuster to find out where it is in the process and whether there is anyone else you should contact about speeding things up. Most adjusters will make some effort to find out what is going on—if for no other reason than they know that until the check arrives, you will keep calling.

**Contact the head of the claims department.** If more than four weeks have passed and you still do not have your check, step up the pressure. Call the adjuster, say that your check has still not arrived, and ask for the name of the head of the claims department. Call the head of the claims department and give that person your claim number, the name of the adjuster you dealt with, the amount of your settlement, and the date you returned the settlement document to the company. Then firmly but politely demand that a check be issued immediately.

Whatever the supervisor's response, immediately write a letter that either confirms the supervisor's promise or makes a demand for immediate payment. Send a copy of the letter to the adjuster. After this letter has been received, call the supervisor again to ask the status of your payment.

**Contact the state insurance department.** As discussed, every state has a department or commission or bureau of insurance that oversees insurance companies operating in the state. (See Chapter 8.) And each state has a consumer complaint division that can pressure an insurance company claims department that grossly mishandles a claim. However, a department of insurance will not get involved with a late settlement payment until more than 30 days after you return the completed settlement documents. And the department will intervene only if you have made several unsuccessful contacts with the claims department to find out why the check is delayed.

If you have made several attempts to get your settlement payment but have not received the money after more than 30 days, contact your state department of insurance consumer complaints office. (Chapter 8 tells you how.) Telephone first, so that you can send copies of your papers to the right office and not suffer yet another bureaucratic delay. Then send copies of your settlement confirmation letter, your signed release form, and any follow-up letters you have sent to the insurance company. Also explain in a cover letter how many times you have spoken with the insurance company about receiving your settlement check and what the company has told you about the delay.

If the state department of insurance calls the insurance company to investigate the matter, it shouldn't be long before the settlement check is in your mailbox.

# Liens on Your Settlement Money

A lien is a legal claim against money you might receive from a specific source, such as compensation for your injuries in an accident. Your own auto insurance company might hold a lien against you if it paid you anything for medical bills under your own medical payments coverage. So might the health plan or HMO that covered your medical treatment. Although technically you're required to repay the full amount of these liens as soon as you receive your settlement, sometimes you can negotiate something less than full repayment.

## Lien by Your Own Auto Insurance Company

If you were involved in a vehicle accident and claimed immediate payment of some of your medical bills under the medical payments coverage of your own automobile insurance policy, you may now be obligated to repay that money out of your settlement amount. (See Chapter 4.) Many policies include such a repayment provision.

If you have received a notice of lien or other document from your own insurance company describing its right to reimbursement, you must repay that money as soon as you receive your settlement check. If your policy requires repayment but you have never received a notice of lien from your own insurance company, you can keep all your settlement money and wait to see whether your company requests repayment. But don't think the amount you received is yours to keep just because you don't hear from your insurance company right away. If you do not repay your insurance company and sometime later it requests repayment, you will have to pay the money back even if you have already spent it.

## Lien by an HMO or Other Prepaid Health Plan

If you were treated for your injuries by an HMO or other prepaid health plan, it may have sent you a notice of lien claiming the right to be repaid a certain amount out of your settlement. (See "Treatment by an HMO or Prepaid Plan" in Chapter 6.) Although it never charged you any specific sum for visits or treatments, the HMO or health plan gave you a list of charges for each service it provided—and you used those charges in your claim as the equivalent of a bill showing your medical expenses.

As part of its contract with you, many HMOs and other prepaid health plans provide that if you recover compensation from a third person for injuries treated by the HMO or covered by the prepaid health plan, it has a right to be repaid for its services. And when it provided you with a list of the charges for your medical treatment following the accident, it probably required you to sign—or at least sent you notice of—a lien against your future compensation. This lien now requires that you repay the HMO or health plan the total amount stated in the list of charges.

## Reducing Your HMO or Health Plan Repayment

It is possible, though, for you to negotiate with the HMO or health plan so that you repay only a portion of the lien amount. Most large HMOs and health plans are used to this practice—known as "compromising" a lien. They will understand what you want to do, and most will be prepared to negotiate a compromise with you.

An HMO or other health plan is likely to be willing to compromise with you for a couple of reasons. One reason is that the charge listed for your treatment would not have been collected if you had not filed a claim. Normally, the HMO would have treated you and received nothing beyond the monthly payment you or your employer makes to the health plan. So, by filing a claim and collecting compensation, you are actually giving the health plan a bonus payment. You do not need to remind the health plan office of this fact, but it underlies the willingness to compromise.

A stronger reason for the willingness to compromise is that the HMO or health plan has a right to be reimbursed only to the extent you were compensated for medical treatment from a third party. But your lump sum claim settlement includes payment for your pain and suffering and for general damages—including permanent injuries—as well as for your medical bills. There is no clear-cut way to determine how much of your settlement is for your medical bills and how much is for pain and suffering and general damages, which makes it difficult for the health plan to prove that you were fully reimbursed for all its medical charges. Therefore, it is often willing to be convinced that you received only a partial reimbursement for medical bills and that as a result, it should receive only partial reimbursement of the lien.

The willingness of the HMO or health plan to accept a compromise instead of its entire lien may depend on the total amount of your settlement compared with your total medical bills and the charges made by the HMO or health plan. If your settlement amount is no more than two or three times your total medical bills, you can argue that your settlement only partially paid your medical bills and that the rest of the settlement was general damages. Particularly if your HMO or health plan charges make up a high percentage (25% to 33%) of your total settlement, you can contend that your settlement actually covers only a portion of your HMO or health plan charges.

As soon as you have reached a settlement figure with the insurance company, contact the HMO's or health plan's business office, or whatever office sent you the lien, and ask to speak to someone about compromising a personal injury lien. Explain that your total settlement is only a small amount, and that when general damages are considered, the settlement did not fully cover all your medical costs. If your own comparative negligence reduced your settlement amount, explain that as well. Then offer to pay 50% of the total lien amount. Many HMOs and health plans commonly reduce their liens by 50% if the settlement amount is relatively small; others will reduce the lien by 33%.

## Lien by Medicare or Medicaid

Many people have their medical bills covered by Medicaid (Medi-Cal in California), and most people 65 and over have Medicare coverage. These government insurance programs have lien provisions that require repayment out of a third-party claim settlement. Medicare is not particularly efficient in enforcing such liens, however, and might fail to request repayment. Medicaid, too, is very hit-and-miss in enforcing its lien provisions. And in some states, Medicaid laws automatically reduce (usually by 25%) any lien that is enforced.

## Taxes on Your Settlement Money

Because your settlement amount is for the pain and suffering you endured, it is not technically income, and usually you do not owe any state or federal income taxes on it.

But there are exceptions. If your settlement specifically reimburses you for out-of-pocket lost income, you could be liable for income taxes on that part of your settlement. If your settlement reimburses you for out-of-pocket medical costs for which you took a medical deduction from your income taxes, you could also owe taxes on those amounts. However, if you took no deduction, you owe no taxes on the medical reimbursement part of your settlement.

But as with most tax questions, these are gray areas, subject to interpretation and differing opinions. And because there is no clear or accurate way to separate how much of your lump sum settlement award is for lost income, how much is for reimbursement of medical bills, and how much is for general damages, that interpretation is up to you. If the IRS or state tax people audit you, there is usually no specific basis for an auditor to assign a particular portion of a personal injury settlement to lost income. And in most cases, the auditor will not even bother to look at a personal injury insurance payment unless you previously claimed large medical deductions arising out of the cost of your treatment for accident-related injuries. ∎

*Chapter 10*

# The Last Resorts: Lawyers, Arbitration, and Courts

Despite the most thorough preparation and persistent negotiation, it is possible your claim could reach a dead end. The insurance company might stubbornly deny your claim, contending that its insured was not at fault. Or it may offer you such unreasonably low compensation that you are unwilling to settle without more of a fight. If the negotiating strategies discussed in Chapter 8 have not produced a reasonable settlement and you believe that further negotiations on your own will not bring a better offer, consider taking your claim to small claims court or arbitration. Or, you might find yourself in arbitration if your claim is against your own auto insurance company.

This chapter explains which claims you might be able to take to small claims court without a lawyer. It also discusses whether your claim is likely to end up in arbitration and describes that process. (Chapter 11 shows how to choose and work with a lawyer, if you decide to hire one.)

## Small Claims Court

Every state has a small claims court that provides a simple, quick, inexpensive, and informal procedure for resolving cases that involve relatively small amounts of money. In some states, small claims court is called conciliation court, justice court, or the small claims division or docket of the municipal or district court.

If small claims court turns out to be a practical alternative for you, the documents you have already collected and the work you have already done in presenting your demand to the insurance company will largely prepare you to have your case heard there. Once you get to small claims court, you will make exactly the same arguments you made to the claims adjuster, only this time a neutral judge will be listening. And the value

of your claim—both for personal injury and for any property damage—will be calculated by the judge just as you calculated it using the factors discussed earlier. (See Chapter 5.)

### States With Short Lawsuit Deadlines

As discussed in Chapter 8, each state puts a limit, called the statute of limitations, on the time within which you must file a lawsuit against someone you believe was responsible for your accident. After that time has passed, you are forever barred from filing a lawsuit. If you failed to file a lawsuit within that time, you cannot collect an insurance claim arising out of that accident.

Kentucky, Louisiana, and Tennessee have short time limits: only one year from the date of the accident. So, if your accident was in one of those states, before one year is up you will need either to file a lawsuit in small claims court or regular court on your own, or have a lawyer file a lawsuit in regular court. However, having a lawyer help you file a lawsuit does not necessarily mean giving over your entire claim for the lawyer to handle. (See Chapter 11.)

## Advantages of Small Claims Court

There are at least three advantages of small claims court over regular, more formal courts.

### Simple Rules

Small claims procedures are set up for people to handle their own cases without lawyers. In many states, lawyers are not even allowed in small claims courts. In all states the forms, legal jargon, and courtroom procedure are kept simple enough for anyone to present a case. In other words, it's the one court where regular folks and plain language are not only tolerated but encouraged.

## Low Cost

Getting into and through small claims court is inexpensive. The fees for filing court papers are much less than for filing in regular court. Also, you don't have to go through the expensive investigation and preparation required to bring a case to formal court. And you don't have to pay a lawyer to speak for you in court.

## Efficiency

Small claims court moves quickly. Unlike formal court cases, which can take years, you will get a court hearing in small claims court within a month or two after filing your papers. The hearing itself usually takes no more than 15 minutes, and the judge either announces a decision right there in the courtroom or mails it out within a few days.

## Disadvantage of Small Claims Court

The biggest drawback of small claims court is that, as the name indicates, it is for small cases only. Each state puts a dollar limit on how much you can recover in small claims court—from $1,000 to $15,000. This limit means that regardless of how much your claim might be worth, you can recover only the court's dollar limit amount. And, once you go to small claims court, your claim is finished. Only the defendant has the right to appeal, so for you, whatever happens in small claims court will be the final outcome of your entire claim. By going to small claims court to try to collect up to that court's dollar limit, you forever give up the right to collect any claim value beyond that limit.

Before you can decide whether it makes sense to take your injury claim into small claims court, find out what the dollar limit is in your state (see chart below), then measure it against what you think your claim is worth.

### Lawyers and Small Claims Court

Normally, lawyers are not allowed in small claims court. The people who were actually involved in an accident must speak for themselves. This is one of the things that makes small claims court quick and easy to use. However, there are a few instances when a lawyer or other representative might appear in court in addition to the person who was directly involved in an accident. If you are suing a business, or an employer for injuries caused by an employee, a representative of the business's management would normally be permitted to speak on behalf of the business in small claims court. Similarly, if your claim is against a government agency, the agency may have a representative—sometimes a lawyer—appear in court.

## State Listing of Small Claims Court Limits

The list below gives current dollar limits for each state's small claims court. However, this list is for general reference only. The limit in your state may have changed, or there may be local variances that permit a different limit in certain counties.

Before filing, double-check the latest dollar limits for the small claims court in your county. You will find the court office by looking up small claims court in the government listings of the white pages of your telephone directory. If you

## Small Claims Court Limits: State by State

| | | | |
|---|---|---|---|
| Alabama | $3,000 | Montana | $3,000 |
| Alaska | $10,000 | Nebraska | $2,700 |
| Arizona | $2,500 | Nevada | $5,000 |
| Regular Justice Court | $5,000 | New Hampshire | $5,000 |
| Arkansas | $5,000 | New Jersey | $3,000 |
| California | $7,500 | Special Civil Part, Superior Court | $15,000 |
| Colorado | $7,500 | New Mexico | $10,000 |
| Connecticut | $5,000 | New York | $5,000 |
| Delaware | $15,000 | Town & Village Courts | $3,000 |
| District of Columbia | $5,000 | North Carolina | $5,000 |
| Florida | $5,000 | North Dakota | $5,000 |
| Georgia | $15,000 | Ohio | $3,000 |
| Hawaii | $3,500 | Oklahoma | $6,000 |
| Idaho | $5,000 | Oregon | $5,000 |
| Illinois | $10,800 | Pennsylvania | $8,000 |
| Cook County Pro Se Court | $1,500 | Philadelphia Municipal Court | $10,000 |
| Indiana | $6,000 | Rhode Island | $2,500 |
| Iowa | $5,000 | South Carolina | $7,500 |
| Kansas | $4,000 | South Dakota | $8,000 |
| Kentucky | $1,500 | Tennessee | $15,000 |
| Louisiana (city court) | $3,000 | Shelby and Anderson counties | $25,000 |
| Justice of the peace | $3,500 | Texas | $5,000 |
| Maine | $4,500 | Utah | $7,500 |
| Maryland | $5,000 | Vermont | $3,500 |
| Massachusetts | $2,000 | Virginia | $5,000 |
| Michigan | $3,000 | General District Court | $15,000 |
| Minnesota | $7,500 | Washington | $4,000 |
| Mississippi | $2,500 | West Virginia | $5,000 |
| Missouri | $3,000 | Wisconsin | $5,000 |
| | | Wyoming | $3,000 |

do not find a listing for small claims court, call the justice, municipal, or district court and ask for the number of the small claims court clerk. When you reach the small claims court clerk, ask what the monetary limit is in your state and county for a small claims court lawsuit.

---

### Filing in Small Claims As a Negotiating Tactic

In states with a high dollar limit in small claims court, simply filing a small claims court action and serving the papers on the other side might stimulate the insurance company to raise its settlement offer to you.

If the small claims court dollar limit is significantly higher than what the insurance company has offered, the company has to face the possibility that its insured would lose in small claims court and have to pay you up to the dollar limit. This might prompt a new and higher settlement offer to you. Extra pressure to settle the claim might also come from the insured, who will not be happy about having to go to court.

However, if the small claims court limit in your state is only slightly more than what the insurance company has offered in settlement, a threat to take your claim to small claims court will likely backfire. The only effect of threatening to take the claim to small claims court is that the insurance company will know it doesn't need to offer you anything higher.

---

## Will Small Claims Be Worth Your While?

Once you know what the small claims court limit is in your state and county, you can decide whether that limit compared with the amount of your claim makes small claims court a practical alternative for you.

**EXAMPLE 1:** If your state's small claims limit is only $1,000 and you believe your claim is worth $5,000, small claims court doesn't make much sense. Since you could win only a maximum of $1,000, you would be forever giving up the remaining $4,000 value of your claim. In this case, it would be wiser to consult an attorney about representing you and perhaps taking your claim to a formal court. (See Chapter 11.)

**EXAMPLE 2:** If the small claims court limit in your state is $2,000 and the insurance company has offered to settle the claim for $1,800, small claims court probably isn't worth the effort. Small claims court offers you a chance to get only $200 more than the insurance company has offered. As with any court, there is the possibility that the judge will award you less than the insurance company's offer, or perhaps nothing at all. And the insurance company knows that the small claims court limit is $2,000, so filing a small claims court lawsuit is not likely to induce it to make a higher offer.

**EXAMPLE 3:** If the insurance company has offered only $500 in settlement, you believe your claim is worth $1,500, and the limit permitted by your state's small claims court is $2,000, small claims court may be a sensible way to proceed—and more economical than hiring a lawyer or settling for the insurance company's low offer. Simply filing a small claims action may prompt the insurance company to raise its offer. If not, you can go through with your small claims court case and perhaps win the full amount you believe your claim is worth.

**EXAMPLE 4:** If you believe your claim is worth a bit more than your state's small claims limit—for example, the small claims limit is $2,000 and you think your claim might be worth $2,500—it may make more sense for you to go to small claims court and try for the $2,000 than to settle for an insurance company offer of less than $1,000. Getting $2,000 in small claims court is probably faster, less stressful, and more economical than paying a lawyer the customary cut of up to 33% of whatever you wind up getting from the insurance company.

## One Last Look at Your Odds

Do a final evaluation of your claim. As with any lawsuit, there is always the possibility that in small claims court you will win nothing. Or a judge may award you much less than you think is fair—even less than the insurance company offered to settle your case. Once you take your case through small claims court, you cannot later take the case to another court to try for more money. Nor can you continue negotiations with the insurance company.

Before filing your small claims court case, think once more about how strong your claim is regarding the other party's liability and your own comparative fault. Consider the insurance company's arguments concerning fault and think how those arguments would sound to a judge presented with both sides of the claim in a 15-minute hearing. One way to test your case is to ask a friend or relative to listen to you describe both sides of the story—your claim and the insurance company's response. Your friend or relative can then give you an honest opinion about how your story sounds to someone hearing it for the first time, as a judge will be. And after you have considered the issue of fault, evaluate one more time how much your claim is worth based on the extent of your injuries noted in your medical records.

If you still feel confident that your argument concerning the other party's liability is strong and that your medical records clearly show the injuries for which you are claiming compensation, then small claims court can be a quick and easy place to present your case.

## Getting Tips From a Lawyer

The insurance company may have refused to offer you any settlement, or only a small nuisance value amount, claiming that its insured is legally not at all liable for your injuries. If a small claims court judge accepts this argument, you might get nothing at all out of the court procedure and your claim would be finished.

If the insurance company has totally denied your claim, you may want to consult briefly with an experienced personal injury lawyer before taking the case to small claims court on your own. He or she may be able to come up with a good and simple argument why the insured person is liable. If so, you can then decide whether to pay the lawyer for his or her advice and go to small claims court on your own, or have the lawyer represent you in further negotiations or in formal court. (See Chapter 11.)

## Sources to Help You Through

If you decide to take your claim to small claims court, there are several resources to help guide you through the process. The first is the rules and procedures of the small claims court, available from the small claims court clerk—usually free—and written in straightforward language for nonlawyers.

The second is *Everybody's Guide to Small Claims Court,* by attorney Ralph Warner (Nolo), available in major bookstores or by mail or telephone order. (See the order form at the back of this book.) You can also order it on Nolo's website at www.nolo.com. California residents can use *Everybody's Guide to Small Claims Court in California,* by Ralph Warner (Nolo).

Another source of assistance is the small claims court adviser available in some counties. These advisers are court employees who, free of charge, help people use the small claims court process.

But the best way to learn about how small claims court works is to spend a morning or afternoon sitting in court watching other cases. You can learn how the judge runs a particular courtroom. And you can see the effective and not so effective ways other claimants present their cases.

## Filing and Serving Papers

Before you actually go to small claims court and present your case to a judge, you are required to file with the small claims court clerk a document called a complaint, in which you as the complaining party are called the plaintiff. This complaint must name and be delivered to, or served on, the other people you believe were legally responsible for the accident. In the complaint, these people are referred to as defendants. Along with this complaint, you must serve on the defendants a summons—an official court order to appear in court on the date given to you by the court clerk.

**⚠ Make sure you sue the right people.** The summons and complaint are to be served on the people or businesses actually responsible for the accident, *not* on their insurance company or insurance adjuster.

The rules for how a complaint and summons can be served vary from state to state. Your state's procedures will be spelled out in the official rules available from the small claims court clerk's office. As mentioned above, a small claims court adviser may be available to help explain your local rules about preparing and serving the required papers on the defendant.

## Presenting Your Case

Once you actually go to court, your presentation to the judge can be almost exactly the same as the presentation you made in your demand letter. Small claims courts do not rely on formal rules of evidence that you have seen on television lawyer shows. Instead, a small claims judge will accept as evidence anything that helps to explain what happened in the accident and what your injuries and other damages were.

### Organizing Documents

Because a judge can accept written evidence and all judges like having things on paper to refer to, bring with you to court:

- a copy of the demand letter you sent to the insurance company
- a copy of any police report of the accident
- a copy of any rules or laws you believe have been violated
- a copy of any helpful witness statements, or the witness in person if he or she is willing to come to court
- a copy of any photographs of the accident scene or of your injuries or other damages
- copies of all medical billing
- copies of all medical records
- copies of letters or other documents showing any income loss, and
- copies of letters or other documents that show or help explain other losses you suffered as a result of your injuries.

Organize your papers before you get to court. Put all documents concerning liability together, and all documents concerning medical records and billing together, just as you did when you sent them to the insurance company along with your demand letter. Put a cover sheet on top of the papers with a list showing what the documents are and in what order they are presented. This way you will be able to get the document quickly if the judge asks to see it. And if the judge wants copies of the documents, he or she will also be able to locate specific documents quickly.

### Preparing an Oral Statement

In court, judges want to hear only a brief statement of your claim. And some judges take control immediately and pepper you with questions. Your challenge will be to respond to the judge's questions while making sure you emphasize the important points of your case in the short time you are allotted to speak. Plan on presenting your claim in no more than five minutes. In that time, state as simply as possible:

- what kind of an accident you had
- where and when the accident happened
- how and why you believe the accident happened, including why the other person is responsible
- what your injuries were, emphasizing pain and disability caused by the injuries
- what treatment you received
- how long your recovery took
- how much your medical treatment cost, regardless of whether you paid for it yourself or insurance paid for it
- how much income you lost
- any other damages or inconveniences you suffered as a result of the accident, and
- how much compensation you believe is fair and reasonable.

The amount of compensation you ask the judge to award you should be slightly higher than what you believe the case is actually worth, but not as high as you asked for in the demand letter. If the amount you are seeking is higher than the dollar limit for small claims court, explain to the judge what you believe the case is worth and then state that you are aware of the small claims limit, so you are asking for the maximum allowed.

Your demand letter is the best place to start to put together your statement to the judge. Take the most important points in your demand letter and jot them down in a list. Then think about how you would simply and briefly state each of the points to the judge, keeping in mind that the judge wants to hear only plain language without any legal jargon. Below is a demand letter (based on Example #1 in Chapter 5) followed by a statement to a small claims court judge based on the same facts.

Before your court date, practice telling your story several times, using your list of important points as a reference; you'll also be able to refer to the list in court. You might also have a friend listen to the story and ask you questions as you go along, just like a judge might do. And try to visit a small claims court session to see how other people present their cases and to note the kinds of questions the judge asks.

### The Day of Your Court Hearing

On the day you are scheduled to have your hearing, get to the courtroom early so that you can watch how the judge conducts other cases. Bring to the court with you three complete sets of your demand letter and all your supporting documents: one set for the judge if he or she wants it, one set for the defendant if the judge wants the defendant to have it, and one set for you to refer to as you present your case.

## Demand Letter

Dear Ms. X:

As I informed you by letter of January 17, 20xx, I was injured in an automobile accident with your insured Matthew White on the afternoon of January 13, 20xx in Highgate, Connecticut. I was headed west on Hornsey Lane and stopped at the stop sign at the intersection with Highgate Hill Road. While I was stopped, your insured slammed into the back of my car. The force of the blow threw me forward against my shoulder restraints, and my head snapped forward and back.

In the middle of that night, I woke with a severe headache and extremely stiff neck, so in the morning I went to the emergency room of Highgate Medical Center. There I was examined, and X-rays were taken of my neck and back. The doctor diagnosed a cervical strain, fitted me with a cervical collar, and advised bed rest. Because of the severe pain, he also prescribed pain relief medication.

I was in considerable pain for the next five days, during which I was forced not only to miss work (three days) but also the 50th birthday party in Boston of an old and dear friend. On Monday of the next week, I returned to work with pain and stiffness and wearing my cervical collar, which made doing my job very difficult. After another week the doctor advised that I could remove the cervical collar. I continued to have quite a bit of soreness and stiffness for another two weeks, interfering with my sleep and making it impossible to do any recreation or to drive unless absolutely necessary. I continue to suffer occasional stiffness and sleep disruptions, though the more severe pain and discomfort has subsided.

The medical expenses for my treatment, as shown in the enclosed medical and billing records, are:

| | |
|---|---:|
| Highgate Med. Center (emergency room) | $750 |
| Highgate Med. Center (X-rays) | 190 |
| Cervical collar | 58 |
| Prescription medication | 65 |
| Total | $1,063 |

As a result of the accident, I also missed three days of work. As the enclosed letter from the personnel office of Battersea Grocery indicates, my wage loss was $392 (24 hours at $14 per hour).

Because of the negligence of your insured, I went through a period of extreme pain and discomfort that lasted for several weeks and that continues. Not only was my normal daily life disrupted, but I was forced to miss the 50th birthday party of a very dear friend whom I rarely get to see. As a result, I demand compensation for my injuries and general damages in the amount of $10,000.

I hope to hear from you soon on this matter.

Very truly yours,

*Oliver Simon Ball*

Oliver Simon Ball

## Statement to Court

Your Honor,

I was injured in an automobile accident with the defendant Matthew White on the afternoon of January 13, 20xx in Highgate, Connecticut.

I was headed west on Hornsey Lane and stopped at the stop sign at the intersection with Highgate Hill Rd. While I was stopped, the defendant slammed into the back of my car. The force of the blow threw me forward against my shoulder restraints, and my head snapped forward and back.

That night I had a severe headache and stiff neck, so in the morning I went to the emergency room of Highgate Medical Center. I had X-rays taken, and the doctor diagnosed a cervical strain. The doctor gave me a cervical collar and advised me to stay in bed. He also prescribed pain medication.

I was in a lot of pain for the next five days and had to miss three days of work. I also missed the 50th birthday party in Boston of an old and dear friend.

On the next Monday, I returned to work with pain and stiffness. I wore my cervical collar. I was sore and stiff for another two weeks, sleeping poorly and unable to do anything but work and lie down.

Even now I still suffer occasional stiffness and sleep disruptions.

The medical expenses for my treatment were $1,063, and my lost wages amounted to $392. I have copies for you here of all the medical billing and records. I also have a letter from my employer. I already sent these records to the defendant's insurance company, but I also have more copies here for the defendant.

Because of the defendant's negligence, I endured several weeks of extreme pain and discomfort, and I was forced to miss the 50th birthday party of a very dear friend whom I rarely get to see. Your Honor, I believe that fair and just compensation for my injuries and general damages would be in the amount of $3,000. In addition, I ask that Your Honor also award court costs in this matter.

Sincerely

*Oliver Simon Ball*

Oliver Simon Ball

When your case is called—the name of the case will be your last name versus the other person's last name (*Ball v. White* in our example) —move up to the tables that will be in front of the bench where the judge sits. Because you are the plaintiff—the one who filed the lawsuit—you will be asked to speak first. Begin by letting the judge know what kind of case you have—a car accident in which you were injured, an accident in which you fell at the defendant's store and were injured, etc. Then use your prepared statement to describe the accident, your injuries, your treatment, your recovery, and your damages. End with a request for a specific amount of damages plus your court costs. If you win in small claims court, in addition to the compensation you are awarded, you are entitled to be reimbursed by the defendant for your costs in bringing the lawsuit: the filing fee and the costs incurred in serving the court papers on the defendant. Check your local court rules to see which costs you are entitled to be reimbursed for.

If the judge asks you a question during the course of your statement, answer it as simply and directly as possible. Do not pass over the judge's question in your haste to return to giving your statement.

If you refer to a document you have brought to court—a police report, a medical record, or a bill—offer a copy to the judge. You can also tell the judge that you have a complete set of all your documents with a list of contents on the top. If the judge sees that this is an organized set of documents, he or she may be willing to take the whole thing from you. Also let the judge know that you have another set to give to the defendant if the judge wants you to.

After you have finished your presentation and answered the judge's questions, it will be the defendant's turn to speak. He or she may say

something you think is wrong or improper, but do not interrupt. Wait until the defendant has finished speaking and then ask the judge for permission to respond briefly to what the defendant has said. If the judge lets you speak again, make your comments very brief and to the point. Do not repeat what you have said before. Small claims court judges want to keep cases moving quickly, and they are not pleased when someone in court goes on and on.

Always remain calm and polite with the judge and let your prepared statement do the work for you.

# Arbitration

If you have a vehicle accident injury claim against your own insurance company and all efforts to settle the claim have failed, your policy may require you to take the matter to arbitration instead of to court.

Arbitration is a way to resolve disputes that has the informality of small claims court, but not its dollar limits. Either you or your insurance company can initiate arbitration if it seems that further settlement negotiations would be fruitless.

In arbitration, both sides explain their positions to a neutral person, called the arbitrator. The insurance company must pay any amount the arbitrator determines is fair compensation—and you must accept the arbitrator's decision as final.

## Types of Claims

Only certain types of vehicle accident claims filed under your own insurance policy must go to arbitration rather than to court (there's more about all of these types of claims in Chapter 4):

- most uninsured motorist claims
- most underinsured motorist claims, and

• some claims under Personal Injury Protection (PIP) policies in states with no-fault insurance laws.

To determine whether your claim must head for arbitration rather than court, examine your policy. Look toward the end of the coverage under which you are making your claim to see if there is an arbitration clause. If so, it will read something like this:

> **Arbitration:** If we and an insured person do not agree that the insured person is legally entitled to recover damages from the owner or operator of an uninsured motor vehicle for bodily injury to such insured person, or, if so entitled, do not agree as to the amount, then upon written demand of either party the disagreement shall be submitted to a neutral arbitrator for decision, according to the laws of the state of _____ [*state in which you reside or in which insurance policy was issued*].

> All other issues between us and the insured person, including the existence or limits of coverage, may not be decided by the arbitrator. Any award made by the arbitrator shall be within the terms and coverage limits of this policy.

## Issues to Be Resolved

The arbitrator determines the extent to which each person was at fault for the accident and how much compensation is fair and reasonable for the injuries suffered and income lost. However, the arbitrator can award an amount only up to the limits of the particular coverage in your policy.

### Arbitration Cannot Resolve Coverage Disputes

You and your insurance company may disagree over issues other than who was at fault for the accident and how much your injuries and lost income are worth. For example, the company may dispute whether your coverage was in force at all, contending that your insurance had lapsed or was canceled before the accident.

An arbitrator cannot decide such coverage disputes unless you and the insurer agree in writing to submit them to arbitration. Generally, an insurance company will not agree to do so, and until the matter of coverage is decided, you will not be able to force the claim into arbitration.

If you have a dispute with the insurance company over whether you are covered and the company makes no settlement offer, you may have to hire an experienced personal injury attorney to pursue the matter. If the attorney gets the insurer to agree that you are covered, or to submit the question of coverage to the arbitrator, you can then decide whether to have the attorney represent you in the arbitration or to represent yourself. (See Chapter 11.)

## Basics of Procedure

Who conducts the arbitration and where it is conducted depend on the terms of your policy and on the arbitration laws in the state in which you live. Many arbitration clauses and state laws refer arbitrations to the American Arbitration Association, which has regional offices in many major cities and can arrange for an arbitration almost anywhere. Other laws refer people to a state or county arbitration board or to an arbitration system administered by the state or county bar association. Some of these arbitration systems use three arbitrators to decide the claim, but most use only one.

The arbitration is held in the county in which you live, not where the insurance company has its office. If an insurance company representative initiates arbitration somewhere other than in your county, remind the adjuster that the law requires that the arbitration be conducted where the insured resides. You can then either demand that the insurer change the arbitration or initiate arbitration yourself. (See below.)

If the insurance company has initiated arbitration at a site that is not in your county, you might consider making an offer that could save you money: You agree to the location the insurance company has chosen if it agrees to pay all arbitration fees. Arbitration usually takes only a couple of hours, so you would have to make only one trip, and the fees you save could run to several hundred dollars.

## Starting the Process

Getting the arbitration process going requires a few simple steps. Once you or your insurance company signal that you want the process to begin, you should check on the rules that you must follow to initiate the process.

### Written Demand

Either you or your insurance company can start arbitration proceedings by filing a written arbitration demand. This letter does not need to be in any particular form. It merely needs to state that, as set out in the insurance policy, you demand that the claim proceed to arbitration. Send the arbitration demand letter, by certified mail, to the adjuster with whom you have been dealing.

By this point, the insurance company will already have all the essential information about your claim. But because you must also send copies of your arbitration demand letter to the arbitration association, it must include some basic information to identify the type of claim so that the dispute can be referred to the appropriate arbitrators.

Your arbitration demand letter should include:

- your name, address, and phone number
- the name of the insurance company, the policy number, and coverage limits
- the name of the adjuster and address of the claims office that has handled the claim so far, and the insurance company's claim number
- the date and location of the accident
- a brief description of the accident and, if it is an uninsured motorist claim, of why the other person was at fault
- a summary description of your injuries, treatment, and residual problems
- the amount of your lost income, and
- the total amount you seek in compensation; this should be the amount you requested in the settlement demand letter you sent to the insurance company (see Chapter 6), not merely an amount for which you would settle.

The insurance adjuster will be able to tell you which arbitration association handles vehicle accident arbitration in your state and county. Check with the association to find out:

- where to send your demand
- how many copies of the demand you must submit
- whether you must submit a copy of the provisions of your policy under which you are making your claim, and
- whether there is a filing fee.

## Do You Need a Lawyer in an Arbitration?

The decision whether to handle an arbitration on your own or hire a lawyer to represent you depends on how much money is involved, whether there are technical legal or medical issues on which your whole claim rests, whether the insurance company brings in a lawyer, and how comfortable you are in speaking on your own behalf in a somewhat formal setting.

Because the decision of an arbitrator is final, if there is potentially a large amount of money involved and the insurance company maintains that you are entitled to nothing or very little, you will probably want to hire an attorney. This is particularly true if the insurance company claims you have violated a driving law and are primarily at fault for your accident. It is also true if the insurance company disputes your claim that the injury you suffered is serious or permanent.

You may also want to hire a lawyer if you are not comfortable thinking or speaking on your feet, or if you feel you will be too emotionally involved to keep a clear head and calm demeanor during the arbitration.

Finally, your decision may be affected by whether the insurance adjuster you have been dealing with is going to handle the arbitration or whether, instead, the insurance company will bring in one of its lawyers. You may be uncomfortable facing a lawyer but might feel confident if the insurance company's case were handled by the adjuster with whom you are familiar. On the other hand, if the adjuster has been bullying and intimidating, you may be willing to handle the arbitration yourself only if the adjuster will be replaced by a lawyer. There is no rule about whether lawyers or adjusters are easier to deal with at an arbitration. You will have to base your decision on the individuals involved in your claim.

You can find out who will handle the arbitration by asking the adjuster whether you should continue to contact him or her regarding the arbitration—or whether you need to contact someone else at the insurance company.

### Fees

Payment of arbitration fees is split evenly between the insurance company and the insured person. These fees cover the cost of arbitration, the hearing room, and the paperwork specific to the arbitration. Any additional expenses you or the insurance company run up preparing for the arbitration—such as copying or transportation—must be paid by whoever incurs them.

Vehicle accident arbitrations normally take half a day or less and cost between $750 and $1,500. Many arbitration associations require that the person who initiates arbitration pay half the administrative fees up front, which must be enclosed with the arbitration demand letter. Check the fees procedure with the arbitration association before sending your demand letter.

### Choosing an Arbitrator

Once you have sent in your arbitration demand letter, the arbitration association will provide you with a list of its arbitrators who handle vehicle accident arbitrations. They will all be lawyers experienced in vehicle accident claims, half of them having specialized in representing accident victims, the other half experienced in representing insurance companies. You will be asked either to select two or three, or to eliminate two or three. The insurance company will be asked to do the same. The arbitration association will randomly assign an arbitrator from the selected list and notify you of the choice.

From the list provided, try to choose arbitrators who have represented accident victims, known as plaintiff's personal injury lawyers, rather than arbitrators who regularly represent insurance companies, known as insurance defense lawyers. The easiest way for you to find out what type of law a proposed arbitrator practices is simply to call the lawyer's office and ask. Lawyers who handle accident cases almost always practice exclusively for one side or the other, and they have no reason not to tell you which side they represent.

## The Hearing

Once the arbitrator has been selected, the date, time, and place of the arbitration hearing will be set. The arbitrator will usually schedule the hearing between 30 and 60 days after the date the arbitrator is selected. If you need to change the date for any reason, contact both the insurance company and the arbitrator as soon as possible to work out another date.

### You Can Settle Any Time

The fact that you and the insurance company have been at an impasse for a long time and have now set the matter for arbitration does not mean you can no longer agree to settle the claim yourselves. Anytime you and the insurance company—through the same adjuster or someone else handling the arbitration—want to resume settlement negotiations, feel free to do so. You need not seek the arbitrator's permission.

This may mean settling soon after the insurance company receives your arbitration demand. The fact that you have gone to the trouble of actually beginning the arbitration process, which means the insurance company will have to do more work to prepare for the arbitration, sometimes makes the company more willing to raise the amount of the settlement offer immediately.

You may elect to settle in the days right before arbitration, the day of arbitration before you go in, during a coffee break in the middle of arbitration, or even after arbitration is complete and you are waiting for the arbitrator's decision. Be aware, however, that once the arbitration fees are sent in, you probably cannot get them fully refunded, even if you settle your claim before the arbitration hearing has been completed.

**Sample Arbitration Demand Letter**

Mary Scott
1234 Tenth Street
Jonesburg, WI 00000
999/123-4567

January 10, 20xx

Reginald Thomas
All Risk Insurance Company
2000 Broadway
Smithville, WI 00000

Re: Claim No.: 1234567
Date of loss: March 10, 20xx
Demand for Arbitration

Dear Mr. Thomas:

This letter is my demand for arbitration of the above claim under the uninsured motorist coverage of my All Risk auto policy.

The relevant information concerning my claim is as follows:

Insured: Mary Scott, address and phone as above.

Coverage: Policy number AB 6789-0, uninsured motorist coverage, policy limits $50,000, All Risk's claim number 1234567.

Accident: March 10, 20xx at the intersection of Washington Street and Jefferson Boulevard, Jonesburg, Wisconsin.

Liability: The driver of the other vehicle, Callous McPeak, was traveling east on Washington and failed to stop at the stop sign, entering the intersection with Jefferson Boulevard at the same time I entered from northbound Jefferson. I had arrived at the intersection before Mr. McPeak and had stopped at my stop sign on Jefferson. Mr. McPeak's vehicle struck my car broadside on the driver's side, crushing the driver's side door. Mr. McPeak was uninsured at the time of the accident.

Injuries: I suffered severe lumbar spine strain, requiring medication and treatment by an orthopedist as well as five weeks of physical therapy. I was in pain and discomfort from the injuries for more than three months. The cost of my medical treatment was $1,220.

Lost income: I missed five days of work due to my injuries. Total lost income was $550.

Compensation demand: Based on the above information, a fair and reasonable amount of compensation is the sum of $7,500.

Copies of this letter are being delivered to the regional office of the Big City Arbitration Association at 678 Thomas Street, Big City, WI, for the purpose of initiating arbitration proceedings.

Yours sincerely,

*Mary Scott*

Mary Scott

At the hearing, you will have the chance to present all your documents to the arbitrator and explain in your own words what happened in the accident, what your injuries are, and how they have affected your life. A representative of the insurance company—either an adjuster or a company lawyer—will present the company's side of the story.

## Preparing the Documents

Your success in arbitration depends as much on how you prepare for it as on how you actually perform at the hearing. Half the battle in an arbitration is gathering the necessary documents and presenting them in an organized way.

By this point, you will have put together a package of documents that you sent along with your settlement demand letter to the insurance company, so you should already be well prepared. (For a list of the documents you need to present to the arbitrator, see the discussion of documents accompanying a settlement demand letter in Chapter 6. Also, the advice in the small claims court section of this chapter about how to arrange your documents and provide a cover sheet applies to arbitration as well.)

Some arbitrators want to have copies of all your documents before the arbitration. Others prefer to wait until the arbitration hearing begins. Check with the arbitrator's office well before the date of your hearing to find out how that particular arbitrator wants to proceed. Along with your original settlement demand, you will already have sent the insurance company copies of the documents you will present to the arbitrator. However, if there is any document you intend to give to the arbitrator that the insurance company has not already received, send the company a copy before the hearing date.

## Preparing Your Statement

Technical legal rules do not apply in arbitration. You will be able to speak to the arbitrator informally, explaining your claim in plain language. At the hearing, you will be able to present your original settlement demand letter to the arbitrator as a summary of your claim. But that letter cannot fully substitute for an honest personal presentation to the arbitrator, so you should be prepared to discuss and answer questions about your claim, too.

Your best ally in preparing your statement to the arbitrator is the settlement demand letter you have already written and sent to the insurance company. To prepare for your speaking part of the hearing, make a list of the most important points in your settlement demand letter, including:

- a description of the accident and why you believe the other person was at fault
- a description of your injuries as demonstrated in your medical records
- your medical treatment and the length of your recovery
- the cost of your medical treatment
- the work and income you lost
- any nonmedical losses you suffered— including any social, family, educational, or other matters affected, and
- a total compensation figure you believe is fair and reasonable. This figure should be the same as in the settlement letter you sent to the insurance company and in your arbitration demand.

Be prepared to briefly address each of these points. An arbitrator who wants to hear more about any specific point will ask for more. There is generally no strict time limit placed on your presentation at an arbitration, but it is best to keep it to 15 or 20 minutes.

Before the date of the hearing, practice your presentation with a friend, using the list of points you have developed from the settlement demand letter. Have the friend ask you questions as you go along. That will help you clarify points you may not explain well enough, and it will also help prepare you to answer questions during the arbitration.

You may bring to the arbitration hearing a witness—friend, family member, coworker, bystander at the accident—who can add something to your description and who is willing to come speak on your behalf. This may be particularly useful if the witness can speak about an issue that the insurance company has been disputing, such as how the accident happened, how your injuries affected you, or how much work time you lost. If so, ask the witness to practice with you beforehand. This will help the person prepare and also give you a better idea of exactly what the witness is likely to say.

A witness who cannot or will not come to the arbitration in person may write out a statement describing what the testimony would have been had he or she actually appeared. The written witness statement should include:

- the witness's name and address
- a declaration that: "If present in person at the arbitration, I would testify as follows:"
- a brief description of the point or points the witness can make on your behalf
- a closing statement that: "I declare under penalty of perjury under the laws of the state of _____ that the foregoing is true and correct"
- the date, and
- the witness's signature. It is also a good idea to ask the witness to sign the declaration in front of a notary. However, if the witness will not take the time and trouble to do so, you can still present the

## Sample Witness Declaration

Declaration of Albert McCoy

I, Albert McCoy, declare as follows:

I live at 456 Washington Street in Jonesburg, Wisconsin.

On the afternoon of March 10, 20xx, I was standing on the sidewalk at the corner of Washington Street and Jefferson Boulevard in Jonesburg, Wisconsin, preparing to cross the street. I saw a late-model blue Chevrolet, driven by Mary Scott, arrive at the intersection traveling northbound on Jefferson. The Chevrolet stopped at the stop sign and then moved into the intersection. After the Chevrolet had begun to move into the intersection, a red Ford reached the intersection, traveling eastbound on Washington. The Ford failed to stop at the stop sign on Washington and entered the intersection, colliding with the side of the Chevrolet.

I am unable to appear at the arbitration hearing set for June 1, 20xx, but if I were to appear, I would testify to the facts contained in this declaration.

I declare under penalty of perjury of the laws of the state of Wisconsin that the foregoing is true and correct.

Executed on May 12, 20xx, at Jonesburg, Wisconsin.

*Albert McCoy*
Albert McCoy
NOTARIZED

statement at the arbitration. Most arbitrators will accept it even if it is not notarized.

As with all other documents, if you intend to present a witness statement at the arbitration, make sure the insurance company representative receives a copy before the arbitration date.

## At the Hearing

Arbitration hearings take place at the arbitrator's office, which is usually either an arbitration association or a private law office. You, the arbitrator, and the insurance company representative will sit around a table. Unless the insurance company has hired a stenographic reporter—unusual in most smaller arbitration cases—the three of you will be the only people there. If you or the insurance company has brought a witness, the witness will be asked to sit outside until the arbitrator is ready to hear the testimony.

The arbitrator will explain how the hearing should proceed. Often the arbitrator will first collect any papers you want considered. Even if you have already provided all those documents, bring extra copies with you on the date of the hearing in case the arbitrator or the insurance company representative does not have a particular document in the file.

Because you are making the claim, you will probably be asked to speak first. Generally, you will be asked to begin by giving a statement of your claim. If you have not yet given all documents to the arbitrator, you can do so at the beginning or the end of your statement, whichever the arbitrator prefers.

After your statement, the insurance company representative will have the opportunity to ask you questions. The arbitrator, too, may ask you to clarify some points. In responding to all questions, be clear, polite, and brief. Respond specifically to the question rather than just repeating what you have already said. If the arbitrator asks something, it is likely that it is important to the decision, so answer carefully. If you are asked about something that may seem to weaken your claim, explain it as best you can but do not ignore it or try to cover it up. Being caught in even one falsehood can make an arbitrator doubt everything else you say. It's simply not worth the risk.

### The Importance of Speaking Plainly

Emphasize to the arbitrator the things that most any person would respond to: the pain and discomfort you suffered, the length of time it took you fully to recover, and how your injuries affected your daily life. Do not become melodramatic, but do not be shy about speaking fully and with emotion in describing your injuries and their effects on you.

After you have finished your part of the presentation, the insurance company representative will present the company's side. If the insurance person or its witness says something you disagree with or believe is flat out wrong, do not interrupt. Make a note of the point and when the person has finished, ask for a chance to respond. Then you can either ask questions or simply refute what has been said by presenting your own side of that point.

Occasionally, an arbitrator will ask to see a document that has not been presented at the arbitration. Provide the document as soon as possible and ask the arbitrator not to make a final decision until you have submitted it.

Most arbitrations last between one and two hours, although you will be amazed at how quickly the time goes by.

## Who Will Appear for the Other Side at the Arbitration?

The other person directly involved in the accident will have to appear at the arbitration hearing in order to give his or her side of what happened. But the insurance company representing that person is permitted to have someone there, too. This may be the insurance adjuster you have been dealing with all through your claim. Or, it may be a different insurance adjuster who has more experience in arbitration hearings. It could also be a lawyer for the insurance company. If an insurance company lawyer appears, the arbitrator will make certain that the lawyer does not try to push you around. And if the lawyer does try to intimidate or confuse you, that usually does not sit well with the arbitrator. Most lawyers know this and are careful to be polite to someone who appears at an arbitration *in pro per* (which means self-represented).

### Contacting the Arbitrator After the Hearing

After the arbitration is over, you will no doubt think of something you want to add, or something that you wish you had said differently. In general, however, once the arbitration hearing is over, that's it. You are not permitted to contact the arbitrator again, unless the arbitrator has asked you to provide additional information. If you send additional information on your own after the hearing simply because you did not think of it before, the arbitrator will almost certainly refuse to consider it.

It is possible, though, that there is something crucial to your claim that you were not able to present to the arbitrator through no fault of your own—for example, the statement of a witness who contacts you only after the hearing. If so,

you can attempt to have the arbitrator consider the information by putting it in writing and sending it to the arbitration association through which the arbitrator was chosen. Request that the information be forwarded to the arbitrator. Indicate in your letter why you could not provide the information at the time of the hearing. And state that you have also provided the information to the insurance company, which you must do at the same time you send it to the arbitrator.

### The Decision

Within 30 days after the hearing, you and the insurance company will receive a written copy of the arbitrator's decision. Some arbitrators do a better job of explaining their decisions than others, but generally there will be only a brief statement of the result.

If the arbitrator makes an award in your favor, the insurance company should pay you within two weeks after the arbitrator's decision—and certainly within 30 days. Unless the insurance company intends to go to court to challenge some technical aspect of the arbitration process, it has no reason to delay payment. If payment is slow in coming, politely pester the insurance adjuster and his or her supervisor until you get your check. If you have not received payment within 30 days, get in touch with your state insurance department. (See Chapter 8.) And if that fails, you may want to hire a lawyer to help exact the money due to you.

If you believe there was some kind of technical error in the arbitration process—something fundamentally unfair about the way the arbitration was conducted—there is a slight chance you can have the decision changed in court.

For that, however, you will have to hire an experienced personal injury lawyer. If there was no technical flaw in the process, both you and the insurance company will have to live with the arbitrator's decision. ∎

# Chapter 11

# Working With a Lawyer

Despite your best efforts to settle your insurance claim yourself with help from this book, at some point in the process you might wind up wanting or needing help from a lawyer because of the seriousness of your injuries, complications in your claim, or simply an insurance company refusing to make you a reasonable offer.

This chapter explains how to find the right lawyer to help with your personal injury claim, and whether you need the lawyer to take over handling the claim or just need a couple of hours of advice. And it discusses how you can work with a lawyer without losing control of important decisions regarding your claim.

## Reasons to Use a Lawyer

You might consider consulting with an experienced personal injury lawyer at different points in the claims process, and for several reasons.

### Your Claim Is Too Much to Handle

At the very beginning of the process, or at any point along the way, you might decide that your claim is too big or too complicated to handle without a lawyer. This may be because there are technical or legal complexities that make it very difficult for a nonlawyer to manage. Or it may be that your injuries are severe or permanently disabling, which makes the case more valuable and also means there's a wide range in the amount of money you might recover. In such a case, it becomes worth the cost of a lawyer to make sure that you maximize your compensation. (See Chapter 1.)

It's also possible that even though your claim isn't particularly big or complicated, you still just do not feel comfortable handling it yourself. You might realize this at the beginning of the claim

process. Or, you might begin handling matters yourself but later decide that you would prefer to have a lawyer take over. This happens to many people if their claim is headed to arbitration. (See Chapter 10.) In any of these situations, you are paying a lawyer to relieve your stress in addition to winning more compensation for you.

## You Reach a Stalemate With the Insurance Company

In some cases, you may handle your claim comfortably and competently but still wind up wanting to hire a lawyer because the insurance company refuses to make a fair settlement offer. If you're not willing to settle for a token amount and you believe your claim is worth quite a bit more than the dollar limit of your state's small claims court, you'll need a lawyer to help you—and in these circumstances, the compensation a lawyer might be able to get for you, even considering the lawyer's fee, would be better than settling. There are two main reasons an insurance company might give for refusing to make a reasonable offer.

### Denial of Liability

It is not unusual for an insurance company initially to deny that their insured was in any way at fault for an accident. Often it does this in the hope that you will believe it, or that you will quickly become so frustrated that you give up and drop your claim. Usually, though, after you show that you will not immediately fold up your tent, an insurance company will come around and make a reasonable settlement offer.

However, if an insurance company does not budge from its initial denial of all responsibility, you may need help from a lawyer. You have nothing to lose at that point. If an experienced personal injury lawyer can coax some money out of the insurance company, you will at least have received some compensation. If the lawyer agrees to handle the case for a contingency fee (see "Paying the Lawyer," below) but ultimately gets no compensation for you, you won't have any lawyer's fees to pay and you will at least know you have turned over every stone.

## Denial of Coverage

Another claim the insurance company might make is that the particular accident is not covered by the insurance policy. In this case, your first step should be to demand a copy of the insurance policy and read it carefully to see whether what the insurance adjuster says is true. (See Chapter 4 for guidance.)

Even if you locate in the policy exactly what the insurance adjuster says is there, that does not necessarily end the matter. Most insurance policy provisions can be interpreted several different ways, and courts usually try to interpret them so that injured people are covered. So if an insurance company continues to deny coverage, take your claim to an experienced personal injury lawyer. The lawyer may be able to force the insurance company to provide the coverage it has been paid to provide.

## Government Immunity

The right to sue a government entity—a town, city, county, or state, or a school, transportation, or other local district—for an accident caused by its employee is strictly controlled by specific laws in each state. These laws—known as "sovereign immunity" and the "tort claims act"—establish the rules about when you are allowed to sue the government because of an accident, and the special procedures you have to follow before you may do so. (See Chapter 3.)

Even after completing these procedures, however, the government's response may be to deny you any compensation, arguing that it is immune to claims in your particular kind of accident. Like an insurance company's denial of coverage, a government's claim of immunity is sometimes just a knee-jerk response that disappears after you negotiate for awhile. But claims adjusters for public entities do not give up public money easily, and sometimes they cling to an immunity defense all the way to court. Because of the complexity of the rules involved, if a claims adjuster refuses to make any settlement offer to you because of a supposed government immunity, you will almost certainly have to consult a personal injury attorney about making a legal attack on that immunity claim.

## You Need Advice on a Particular Legal Rule

Occasionally, the success or failure of a claim turns on a specific legal rule. For example, your right to collect insurance from a business might depend on whether its employee was acting within the course of his or her employment when the employee injured you in an accident. The law has technical rules about what is and is not the "course and scope of employment." Or, you might have been injured on a buckled sidewalk, and the question of who is responsible might involve legal rules about water damage, tree roots, or other property law questions.

In one of these situations, you might want to consult with a lawyer on an hourly basis just to get an experienced legal opinion about how the rules of legal responsibility apply in your case. And, if the fate of your entire claim seems to hinge on a legal question, you might want to hire an attorney to take over handling your entire claim.

# Finding the Right Lawyer

Whether you simply want to discuss your claim with a lawyer to get some ideas about how to conduct further negotiations yourself or prepare your case for small claims court or arbitration, or you want to hire a lawyer to completely handle your claim, you don't want to hire just any lawyer. You want an experienced personal injury lawyer. And you want one with whom you are comfortable.

## Finding an Experienced Lawyer

The practice of law has become highly specialized, and most lawyers know less about handling a personal injury claim than you will after you've read this book. So, your first task is to find a lawyer who has experience representing claimants (known as "plaintiffs") in personal injury cases. You do *not* want to be represented by someone who has primarily been a lawyer for insurance companies, even if they're experienced. Such a lawyer may be too accustomed to taking the insurance company's side and might not fight hard enough for your claim.

There are several ways to find experienced plaintiff's personal injury lawyers. The best way to proceed is to comparison-shop. Get the names of several lawyers and meet with each of them to discuss your claim before you decide to hire any one of them.

## Friends and Acquaintances

Contact friends or coworkers who have been represented by a lawyer in their own personal injury claims. If the friend or coworker says good things about the experience, put that lawyer on your list of people with whom to have an initial consultation. But do not make any decision

---

### Lawyers You Already Know

You may already know a lawyer, either personally or because the lawyer has represented you before in some legal matter. And that lawyer may be very good at the job. So, when you consider hiring a lawyer to work on your personal injury claim, it may seem obvious to hire this person you already know.

However, this lawyer might have little or no experience representing plaintiffs in personal injury cases. And instead of immediately referring you to an appropriate personal injury attorney, the lawyer may hang onto your case, either because of a reluctance to disappoint you, or believing that the lack of experience isn't important.

This is a bad idea. Regardless of the good relations you have with a lawyer, that lawyer is not right to handle your claim without having experience in handling personal injury claims for plaintiffs. If the lawyer you know does not qualify, immediately ask that lawyer to refer you to someone—either in the lawyer's same office or elsewhere—who does.

---

about a lawyer solely on the basis of someone else's recommendation. Different people will have different responses to a lawyer's style and personality. Also, at any particular time a lawyer may have more or less energy or interest to devote to a new case. So do not make up your mind about hiring someone until you have met with the lawyer, discussed your case, and decided that you are comfortable entering a working relationship.

## Other Lawyers

Another way to find an experienced personal injury lawyer is through a lawyer with whom you may have had contact. Lawyers commonly refer cases to one another, and most lawyers know someone else who handles plaintiffs' personal injury cases. As with referrals from friends or coworkers, however, do not simply take another lawyer's referral as gospel.

The fact that a lawyer to whom you are referred is in the same office as a lawyer you already know should not be a major factor in your decision. If all other things seem equal, then your familiarity and comfort with a particular law office might properly lead you to choose an experienced personal injury lawyer in that office. But remember that it is a particular lawyer you should be choosing, not the lawyer's associates or officemates.

## Referral Services

Most local bar associations have lawyer referral services through which you can get the name of a lawyer in specialty areas. Call your local bar association referral service and ask for the names of a couple of personal injury lawyers. Unfortunately, bar associations do very little screening concerning the experience of lawyers on their lists. A referral lawyer's experience level can be a hit-or-miss proposition. Make no decision about a bar referral lawyer until you have met and interviewed him or her.

Nolo has a lawyer directory that currently covers only certain geographic areas—but if you live in one of those places, you can look for a lawyer there. The directory, at www.nolo .com, contains extensive information about each lawyer's experience, philosophy, and fee structure.

## A Lawyer Might Not Want Your Case

Finding a lawyer you want to hire is one thing. But that lawyer also has to want your case. And a lawyer could have several reasons for rejecting you as a client.

You may be looking for a lawyer to take on your entire claim on a contingency fee basis, the most common arrangement in personal injury cases. (See "Paying the Lawyer," below.) This arrangement means that the lawyer's fee is a percentage of what you ultimately receive in compensation. And if the amount you are likely to receive is small, most lawyers will not take on the claim. That is because a lawyer's overhead—the cost of operating a law office—is too high to make small cases economically worthwhile. However, even if your case is too small to have a lawyer take over the entire claim, it may still be possible to hire the lawyer on an hourly basis to give you advice on particular parts of your claim that you are unsure of.

Even if your injuries are serious and your potential compensation is high, a lawyer might decline to take your case if the odds of winning full compensation are low. This may be because you were largely responsible for the accident, because it is too difficult to prove that someone else was at fault, or because the person responsible for the accident has little or no insurance coverage.

Finally, a lawyer might refuse to take your perfectly good case for the same reason that you might not want to hire a perfectly good lawyer. That is, the two of you just might not feel comfortable with each other. If a lawyer thinks that you will be more trouble than your case is worth, or if your personality and the lawyer's clash right away, the lawyer may simply decide that handling your claim is just not worth it.

## Small Firm Versus Large Firm

The size of a law firm does not have much to do with how well the office handles your case.

You may have the idea that a large law office will impress an insurance company into giving you a better settlement, but that is rarely true. Large law offices tend to be machines set up primarily to crank out money for themselves, and a small personal injury case can easily get lost in the shuffle. Also, large law offices are in the habit of freely spending money on expenses that may use up much of your potential compensation.

Also, insurance companies know that large law offices often do not put as much time or concern into a standard personal injury case as do smaller law offices. Therefore, insurance adjusters dealing with a large office may find it easier to get away with a lower settlement. You are likely to receive more personal attention from a small law office, and many of the best personal injury lawyers choose to work in a law firm with only a few lawyers.

## Choosing the Right Lawyer for You

To find out whether a lawyer is right for you, sit down with the lawyer to discuss your claim and possible ways of handling it. Bring copies of all the documents you have concerning your claim: police report, medical records and bills, income loss information, and all correspondence with the insurance company, including your demand letter if you have reached that stage.

Most personal injury lawyers do not charge anything for an initial consultation about possibly representing you and your claim. But before you meet with anyone, find out whether you will be charged for an initial interview. If the lawyer wants to charge you just for discussing whether to take your case, go somewhere else.

Of course, a big subject to discuss in your initial interview is what the lawyer's fee would be. That subject is covered separately below. But there are a number of other important matters to discuss with a lawyer before making a decision.

After giving a lawyer a general idea of what your claim is about, there are a few basic things to find out from the lawyer at the outset of your first interview.

### General Experience

Find out a little bit about the lawyer's background and experience. If you're interested in where the lawyer went to school, ask that—although it isn't as important as experience in the real world. Some other questions might be:

- How long has the lawyer been in practice?
- Roughly what percentage of the lawyer's practice involves personal injury cases?
- Does the lawyer most often represent plaintiffs (claimants) or defendants (businesses, insurance companies)?
- Does the lawyer have experience with the insurance company in your case, or even the particular adjuster?

### Who Will Work on Your Case?

In almost every law practice, lawyers work together on cases. Often, less experienced attorneys and paralegals handle routine tasks. This can benefit you if work gets done more quickly than if it had waited for the attention of one of the office's more experienced attorneys. And if you are paying by the hour, it is to your financial advantage not have the more expensive senior lawyer handling routine paperwork.

Make sure, however, that important work on your case is not left to less experienced lawyers or staff. When first interviewing a lawyer, ask which lawyer in the office would have primary responsibility for your case and which lawyer you would be dealing with directly. If more than one lawyer would be working on your case, ask to meet and discuss your case with the other lawyers, too. And ask which specific parts of the case the primary lawyer would handle personally and which would be turned over to a paralegal.

---

## Lines of Communication

How well you and a lawyer will be able to communicate with each other is an important aspect of choosing a lawyer. Does the lawyer listen to you? Is the lawyer willing to follow your wishes about how to approach the case? Does the lawyer explain things well? Do you get the sense that the lawyer will keep you informed and will truly listen to your input before making important decisions in the case?

A lawyer's willingness to listen and ability to understand you may affect how much you can help the lawyer and whether you can control somewhat how the lawyer does the job. A lawyer's willingness and ability to explain what is happening in your case will likewise affect your ability to make good decisions. And your ability to talk to one another may make the entire process much less stressful.

---

### Your Settlement Goal

After you have discussed with the lawyer the facts of your case and the history of your

negotiations with the insurance company, the lawyer may give you a general idea how much he or she thinks your case is worth, and how difficult it may be to get the insurance company to pay something in that range. This is when you should discuss with the lawyer the different ways your case could be approached, and whether the lawyer would be willing to handle it in the way you prefer. These approaches include:

- obtaining a settlement amount for you within a certain range and with as few costs and as little hassle as possible
- obtaining any amount more than what the insurance company has already offered you, as soon as possible, or
- obtaining as much as possible, no matter how long it takes.

Asking to approach a case in a certain way when you first hire the lawyer does not mean that you are stuck with that approach. As the case goes along, you are always free to ask the lawyer to change tack. You may get tired of the whole process and want the lawyer to wrap things up as soon as possible. Or, the cost of taking your case through the lawsuit process may begin to eat up too much of your potential compensation. On the other hand, as the case goes along it may seem to you and you lawyer that the odds have improved of obtaining a higher settlement than you originally anticipated, and so you are willing to have the lawyer fight longer and harder than you were initially.

## Paying the Lawyer

Disagreements over fees are the most frequent sources of friction between lawyers and their clients. You may save yourself considerable grief at the end of your case by getting your fee arrangement, as well as matters relating to expenses, clear at the beginning.

⚠️ **Get your agreement in writing.** A written agreement about fees protects both you and the lawyer in case you have a disagreement later about who gets how much. Most lawyers are careful about putting any fee agreement in writing, and the laws in many states require a lawyer to do so. Both you and the lawyer should sign your written agreement. If it is made on the law office's standard form, make sure that it has been modified to reflect any specific arrangements you have made with the lawyer. The agreement should also address costs— the expenses of conducting negotiations and, if necessary, a lawsuit. Lawyers have a tendency to run up costs without thinking too much about it. And that can be a problem for you, because it is the client who must pay those costs out of the settlement amount.

## Contingency Fee Agreements

It is difficult for most people to come up with a lot of money in advance to pay a lawyer. And most people would find it difficult to pay a lawyer on an hourly basis through the entire pursuit of an injury claim and possible lawsuit. So, lawyers have developed an alternative payment system in which they require no money from a client to begin a case and instead take as their fee a percentage of the client's final settlement or court award. This arrangement, known as a "contingency" fee agreement, can be extremely useful to clients and lawyers alike.

Contingency fees are not cheap—they reflect the fact that the lawyer is taking a risk and that you are not paying anything up front. In personal injury cases, a lawyer's fee is usually 33% to 40% of the amount the lawyer gets for the client. And by the time expenses are also subtracted, the client sometimes takes home much less than the amount the lawyer actually got from insurance company.

**EXAMPLE:** You sign a contingency fee agreement with a lawyer in which you agree to pay the lawyer 33.3% of whatever compensation the lawyer obtains for you. That 33.3% is calculated after the lawyer has been reimbursed for whatever costs were run up processing your case. If the lawyer has spent $1,000 on costs and gets a settlement of $10,000, the $1,000 would first be subtracted from the $10,000, leaving $9,000. The lawyer would then take 33.3% of that remaining $9,000, leaving you with $6,000.

In deciding whether to hire a lawyer on a contingency fee basis, you have to figure out whether the economics of your claim make it worthwhile. For example, if the insurance company has refused to pay you any compensation at all, or only a token "nuisance value" amount, but the potential damages in your case are fairly large, it is probably worth your while to hire a lawyer on a contingency fee basis. You have little to lose and much to gain.

On the other hand, if your claim is relatively small, it may make more sense to continue handling the case on your own, even taking it yourself to small claims court or arbitration. The decision will depend on how comfortable you are going to small claims court or arbitration without a lawyer, on how technical the insurance company's defense is, and on whether a lawyer is willing to take your case and is confident of getting you a certain range of compensation.

And finally, if the insurance company has offered you a substantial settlement amount but you believe it is still too low, you must measure what they have offered against how much more a lawyer could realistically expect to get. If a lawyer can expect to get only an additional 25%, it wouldn't make sense to hire the lawyer and pay out 33% of your settlement. In that case, you might try to negotiate with the lawyer for a reduced contingency or hourly fee arrangement. But if the lawyer believes there's a good likelihood of getting enough added compensation to overcome the lawyer's fee, hiring the lawyer may be a good idea.

In this situation, try to structure a fee arrangement so that whatever the compensation amount, you are guaranteed no less than you would have received had you just settled with the insurance company on your own. The next two sections in this chapter discuss modified fee agreements—and the lawyer's willingness to be flexible about the fee arrangement might be something for you to consider in your decision about which lawyer is right for you.

## Reduced Contingency and Combination Fees

By the time you first consult a lawyer, you may have already investigated your accident, obtained all the documents pertaining to your claim, and negotiated the insurance company into raising their initial settlement offer. If so, you will have done much of the work the lawyer would normally do. Because of this, some lawyers may be willing to accept a lower percentage contingency fee than the normal 33% to 40%.

Be sure to bring all your documents to your initial meeting with the lawyer and show the lawyer the organized file you have put together. If you emphasize how much work the lawyer's office will have been relieved of because of your efforts, the lawyer may agree to some kind of reduced fee arrangement.

Of course, most lawyers will not suggest a reduced fee arrangement; you will probably have to propose it. And many lawyers will be reluctant to agree—in part because they would make less money, but also because they may fear that the

work a nonlawyer has done will not be of much value, and they'll have to do it again. It's your job to show them that your work was useful and that the case is in good shape.

Here are three possible ways to structure fee agreements that take into account the work you've done already:

1. Make an agreement that if the lawyer can settle the case solely by negotiating with the insurance adjuster—that is, without having to go through any of the actual litigation process—then the lawyer will receive a 25% contingency fee. But if pre-lawsuit negotiations alone fail to produce a satisfactory new settlement offer, the lawyer would receive the standard contingency fee of 33% (40% if the case ultimately is formally scheduled for trial). The reason for you to agree to the larger fee if there is no early settlement is that the lawyer would then actually have to begin work litigating the case, filing more complex legal documents, and working to prepare the case for trial.

2. Make an agreement that if you ultimately receive up to a certain amount—say, $5,000 or $10,000 more than what you have already been offered by the insurance company—the lawyer will receive a basic fee of 25% of the settlement. For everything over that amount, the lawyer will receive 33.3%. This structure guarantees that you do not wind up getting less by using a lawyer than you would have if you had accepted on your own the insurance company's earlier offer.

3. Pay the lawyer an hourly fee up to a prearranged limit—say, $2,000. If the claim cannot be settled by the lawyer doing that amount of work, the fee would then switch to a contingency arrangement.

## If a Lawyer Saying "Boo!" Is All It Takes, Don't Overpay

Sometimes, merely having a lawyer enter negotiations on your behalf or file a standard-form lawsuit for you, suddenly gets an insurance company to increase an offer to an acceptable figure. That may happen because the insurance adjuster knows that if the matter is not settled immediately, the insurance company's own legal costs now might rapidly mount.

Such a quick response might seem like good news for you. But if you have agreed to pay your lawyer the standard one-third contingency fee for handling your case, the lawyer will receive that large chunk of your compensation for having done almost no work. This is particularly true if, on your own, you already presented to the insurance company all the significant documents and arguments in the case, as explained in this book.

One way to avoid this windfall for the lawyer is to have your fee agreement cover such a situation. A lawyer might agree to limit the fee if the insurance company makes an acceptable settlement offer after the lawyer has done only a small number of hours work on the case. If the claim is settled within the amount of lawyer-hours you specify, the agreement can provide that you pay the lawyer at an hourly rate rather than the full contingency fee.

## Legal Advice Paid by the Hour

You might consider hiring a lawyer just to give you specific advice—on a technical legal issue, for example—that could help you reopen your negotiations with the insurance company or prepare you for small claims court or arbitration. Or, you might seek a lawyer's help only to prepare and file a lawsuit to protect your rights under your state's statute of limitations. In these situations, you may be able to pay a lawyer by the hour, without having the lawyer take over responsibility for your claim. Because lawyers charge anywhere from $100 to $350 per hour, however, this is not an economical arrangement for you unless you can get useful assistance with only a few hours of the lawyer's time.

In such an advice-only arrangement, the lawyer would not deal directly with the insurance company, put the firm name on any correspondence or legal documents, or appear for you in arbitration or court. You would still officially handle the matter on your own, but you would have the benefit of whatever advice the lawyer has given you. If this advice still does not get you a better offer from the insurance company, you can return to the lawyer to discuss whether it makes sense for the lawyer to take on full representation of your claim.

If you decide to hire an attorney on an hourly basis, set a maximum number of hours the lawyer may spend on your case without your prior approval to do more. Also, know that you will most likely have to pay the lawyer immediately—the lawyer will not wait until you receive your accident compensation.

⚠ **You may have trouble finding a lawyer for advice only.** Hiring a lawyer for an hour or two of advice on your personal injury claim might seem like a fairly easy thing to arrange. But many lawyers do not want to become involved in a case just to give a brief consultation. In part, that is because lawyers are trained to be very thorough, and they are uncomfortable giving limited advice. Also, lawyers become professionally responsible for the consequences of any advice they give. If they cannot control what you do with that advice, many would be reluctant to take on the potentially large responsibility for just a few hundred dollars in fees.

## Costs

In legal parlance, "costs" does not mean fees paid to the lawyer. Instead, costs refer to the expenses paid by the lawyer's office in investigating your claim, conducting negotiations, and pursuing a lawsuit. Depending on the agreement you reach with your lawyer, you will have to repay the lawyer for these costs, usually out of your final settlement amount.

Some costs are unavoidable. For example, if the lawyer must file a lawsuit to protect your rights, the fee for filing that lawsuit is a necessary cost. If your claim does not settle in early negotiations with the insurance company and the lawyer must proceed with a lawsuit, these costs often include the hiring of experts and the expense of recording depositions (see below), and can mushroom rapidly into thousands of dollars.

There are several matters pertaining to costs that you and your lawyer need to discuss and spell out clearly in your written agreement.

### Relation Between Costs and Lawyer Fees

If you are paying a lawyer a contingency fee, the fee agreement must state clearly whether costs are to be deducted from your final compensation amount before or after the lawyer calculates the fee percentage. If the lawyer calculates the fee percentage first and then costs are deducted, the lawyer's fee is larger and the compensation you finally receive is smaller than if the costs are deducted before the lawyer's percentage is calculated.

**EXAMPLE:** A lawyer is to be paid a 33.3% contingency fee in a case with $3,000 in costs and a settlement of $20,000. If costs are deducted before fees are calculated, the $3,000 is first deducted from the $20,000 settlement, leaving $17,000. Out of that the lawyer takes 33.3%, or $5,667, leaving the client with $11,333. On the other hand, if the fee is calculated before costs are deducted, the lawyer first receives 33.3% of the full $20,000, or $6,667. Costs of $3,000 are then deducted from the remaining $13,333, leaving the client with only $10,333. This second method of calculating fees and costs left the client $1,000 poorer.

Obviously, it is to your advantage to have the costs deducted *before* the lawyer's fee is calculated. And many lawyers operate this way as a matter of course. However, a lawyer you are considering hiring might tell you that fees are "always" calculated first. If you hear this, gently tell the lawyer that you know from other lawyers that costs are usually deducted first. And that if this lawyer insists on fees first, you'll insist on taking your case elsewhere.

### Costs You Agree on in Advance

Many costs in a personal injury case are quite standard, and often a lawyer's initial written agreement will include them. These normal and unavoidable expenses are such things as copying, long-distance telephone calls, and court filing fees. Other expenses may not be so crucial—but can be expensive. So, you and the lawyer should spell out what costs the lawyer must ask you about before going ahead and incurring them. These might include such things as depositions, hiring investigators or experts, and scheduling special court proceedings. The simplest way to handle the issue of costs is to set a dollar limit beyond which the lawyer must get your approval for any costs.

### Who Pays Costs If You Lose

While it is important to agree in advance how fees and costs will be deducted from your final settlement amount, what if you don't get any settlement? Or you get a settlement that is less than the combination of lawyer fees and costs? These possibilities should be included in your written agreement with a lawyer. Most of the time, a lawyer will agree not to make you reimburse the lawyer's office for costs if you ultimately don't recover anything. If there is a settlement but the costs plus attorney fees are more than the total recovery, a lawyer might agree to split the costs evenly with the client. However, sometimes at the beginning of a case a lawyer feels that there is only a so-so chance of winning substantial compensation. In that situation, the lawyer might be willing to take the case only if the client agrees to pay some or all costs in the event there is no recovery, or if there is a recovery of less than the amount of costs and fees together. This is something you'll have to negotiate with the lawyer at the outset, based on how much risk you're willing to take and how well the lawyer likes your chances.

## Managing Your Lawyer

As your case proceeds, there will be questions that come up and decisions that need to be made. For example, you and your lawyer may need to decide about:
- ongoing expenses
- the amount of time and hassle you personally give to the case
- how quickly your case gets resolved
- whether to take major lawsuit steps that may cost considerable time and money, and
- when to accept a settlement.

Each of these decisions will depend on your attitude and on how the case is going at the point the question comes up. And although you should participate in these decisions, you will depend a great deal on your lawyer's advice, which is why it is so important to choose a lawyer who explains what is going on and who listens to what you have to say.

Discussed below are some of the most important issues in a lawsuit. We encourage you to continue to exercise some control over these decisions even if you've hired a lawyer to take over your case. Take a few minutes with your lawyer at the beginning of the case and explain that you don't want to limit unnecessarily what the lawyer can do or to tell the lawyer how to do the job. But emphasize that you are concerned about controlling the cost and time of your case, and want to be consulted before major decisions are made. If the lawyer is not sympathetic to this request, perhaps you'd better interview some more lawyers.

## Investigators and Experts

Sometimes it can be useful for a lawyer to hire someone to help figure out and prove what happened in the accident, to find witnesses, or to dig up information about the defendant. This person might be a private investigator or an expert in accident reconstruction. Your lawyer might also want to hire a doctor who specializes in the type of injuries you have sustained, to examine you or your medical records, and to give an expert opinion about the extent of your injuries or your future medical needs and costs.

These experts are not employees of a lawyer's office, so their fees are extra expenses that will be subtracted from your final compensation in the case. And using experts can get very expensive very fast. Ask your lawyer to agree not to use any outside investigators or other outside services unless the lawyer first explains to you the need for such outside help and you agree to it.

## Keeping Your Case Moving

You have a right to have your lawyer and the insurance company process your claim or lawsuit reasonably promptly. Some delay is an unavoidable part of the insurance claims business and an even more common part of the lawsuit game. But you may be able to keep delays to a minimum by regularly monitoring what your lawyer and the other side are doing and gently pressing to keep your case moving.

If you have not heard from your lawyer for a while concerning activity on your case, call and find out what is going on and ask when the next event—a response by the insurance company, a letter or document sent by your lawyer—is supposed to take place. Then follow up to make sure it occurs.

A lawyer, like anyone else, does not like to be pestered. On the other hand, you have a right to know what is going on and to make sure that your case is being handled efficiently. Be reasonable. Don't call every couple of days and demand to know what has happened in the past 48 hours. But do check in regularly to make sure that something is happening and to get a rough schedule from the lawyer about when the next forward movement will occur. (Remember, if you are paying your lawyer by the hour, you will be charged for each phone conversation you and your lawyer have, no matter how brief.)

## When to Settle Your Case

The most important decision you and your lawyer are likely to make together is when to settle your case. As with deciding about whether to accept an insurance adjuster's offer when handling negotiations by yourself, the decision about when to accept a settlement offer your lawyer has obtained depends solely on whether you are satisfied. You must balance what you think the case is worth against the effort and expense it might take to get more than has been offered, plus the likelihood of actually getting more. You also have to consider how quickly you need the money and how weary you are of the whole process.

Of course, you will want and need your lawyer's advice on this important decision. That is part of what you have hired the lawyer to do. But the decision should not depend on what the lawyer wants—for example, to settle quickly because the lawyer is busy with other cases or no longer wants to put in work to try to raise the offer, or not to settle because the lawyer wants to go for a jackpot and is willing to take the risks with your time and money. The final decision must be yours. It should be made after full discussion with your lawyer about the possibilities and risks of going forward, measured against the offer of settlement currently on the table.

## Deciding When to Begin Lawsuit Activity

Until a lawsuit actually begins, your lawyer can keep a lid on the claims process. For example, the insurance company has no right to interview you directly unless an actual lawsuit is underway. And the insurance company cannot speak to your doctors. Nor can it force your lawyer to do any more work, or run up more in expenses, than the lawyer decides is necessary to investigate and prepare your claim. Once a formal lawsuit begins, however, your lawyer may have to do considerably more work, responding to procedures initiated by the insurance company's lawyers. This can run up both stress and expenses that you and your lawyer cannot completely control.

A lawsuit technically begins when a complaint —a legal document setting out the facts and legal basis for your claim against the defendant—is filed in court. This complaint must be filed within the time limit set by your state's statute of limitations. But the real action of a lawsuit does not begin until the defendant and his or her lawyer are formally brought into the case when your complaint is served on—formally delivered to—the defendant.

The decision of when to serve the defendant, and therefore when to start the expensive and stressful activity of a lawsuit, depends on whether settlement negotiations are making any progress. If they are not, your lawyer may feel that proceeding with a formal lawsuit is the only way to pressure the insurance company enough to get a reasonable settlement offer. A decision about beginning the lawsuit process should be made jointly by you and your lawyer after a thorough conversation about the pros and cons.

## Conducting Discovery

The legal process used to get information from the other side in a lawsuit is called discovery. Discovery can involve the relatively simple exchange of written questions and answers called interrogatories, as well as other exchanges of documents. But it can also include expensive procedures called depositions—in which lawyers from both sides get together and question you,

the defendant, or a witness in person, under oath, while a court reporter records the answers (and then later prepares a written transcript).

Although depositions are a basic part of most lawsuits, the number of depositions scheduled in a case can vary considerably. In a case involving huge amounts of money, lawyers take the deposition not just of the plaintiff and defendant but of every conceivable witness, hoping to turn up even a single crumb of information. However, this is not the way to run a lawsuit in which smaller amounts of money are involved. Your lawyer needs to bear in mind the expense to you of taking depositions. Ask that your lawyer not schedule the deposition of anyone other than the defendant unless the lawyer discusses it with you first and gets your approval.

The same thing may be true for requests for records and reports, although the amounts of money involved are not as great as for depositions. Even though you may have already provided the lawyer with your medical and billing records, lawyers sometimes order them again out of habit. But the doctor's office will charge for these records, and may charge a larger fee to a lawyer than to the patient—and the lawyer, in turn, will pass this cost on to you. Also, lawyers sometimes want to get a doctor to write a report concerning your injuries. Such reports are sometimes important for your case, but they cost hundreds of dollars. Ask your lawyer—tactfully—not to order any duplicate medical records, or request a medical report, without at least discussing it with you first.

## Setting the Case for Trial

Setting a lawsuit for trial means asking the court to assign a date for the actual trial to begin. Often lawyers are forced to set cases for trial in order to put enough pressure on an insurance company to get a reasonable settlement offer. Getting a trial date from the court is a simple matter—your lawyer just sends the court a written request. It's what happens next that you have to be concerned about.

In the first place, many contingency fee agreements provide that the lawyer's fee goes up—often from 33.3% to 40%—as soon as the case is set for trial, regardless of whether the trial ever actually takes place. If your fee agreement has such a provision, you do not want your lawyer to set the case for trial unless it is truly necessary. This means that the insurance company has not come up with a reasonable settlement offer and there are no more legal maneuvers, short of setting for trial, available to pressure the insurance company.

Also, once the case is set for trial, the pace of legal maneuvering and preparations may speed up dramatically. The lawyers may schedule depositions and other expensive proceedings they had been putting off. And your lawyer may have to spend more of your money hiring outside experts to begin preparing for trial.

## Trial

If you decide that what the insurance company is offering is just not enough, even after you have tried negotiating and your lawyer has done everything possible to persuade the insurance company of your damages and the other party's liability, you may end up in a trial. Then you will have to rely on your lawyer almost completely.

■

# Accident Claim Worksheet

# Accident Claim Worksheet

## What Happened

Names of parties involved: _____

Names of witnesses: _____

_____

Location of accident:_____

Time of accident:_____

Weather condition (if outside):

_____

_____

_____

## People Responsible for the Accident

Name: _____

Address: _____

_____

Telephone (work): _____ (home): _____

Insurance company: _____

Policy number: _____ Auto license:_____

What person did:_____

_____

_____

_____

_____

· · · · · · · · · · · · · · · · · · · · · · · · · · · · · · · · · · · · · · · · · · · · · · · · · · · · · · · · · · · · · ·

Name: _____

Address: _____

_____

Telephone (work): _____ (home): _____

Insurance company: _____

Policy number: _____ Auto license:_____

What person did:_____

_____

_____

_____

_____

Name: _____

Address: _____

_____

Telephone (work): _____ (home): _____

Insurance company: _____

Policy number: _____ Auto license: _____

What person did: _____

_____

_____

_____

_____

**Witnesses**

Name: _____

Address: _____

_____

Telephone (work): _____ (home): _____

Date of first contact: _____

Written statement:  ☐ yes  ☐ no

What person saw: _____

_____

_____

_____

_____

_____

· · · · · · · · · · · · · · · · · · · · · · · · · · · · · · · · · · · · · · · · · · · · · · · · · · · · · · · · · · ·

Name: _____

Address: _____

_____

Telephone (work): _____ (home): _____

Date of first contact: _____

Written statement:  ☐ yes  ☐ no

What person saw: _____

_____

_____

_____

_____

_____

Name: _____

Address: _____

_____

Telephone (work): _____ (home): _____

Date of first contact: _____

Written statement:  ☐ yes  ☐ no

What person saw: _____

_____

_____

_____

_____

## Medical Treatment Providers

Name: _____

Address: _____

_____ Telephone: _____

Date of first visit: _____ Date of most recent or last visit: _____

Person to be contacted for medical records: _____

Date requested: _____ Date received: _____

Person to be contacted for medical billing: _____

Date requested: _____ Date received: _____

Reason for treatment and prognosis: _____

_____

_____

_____

· · · · · · · · · · · · · · · · · · · · · · · · · · · · · · · · · · · · · · · · · · · · · · · · · · · · · · · · · · · · · · · · · ·

Name: _____

Address: _____

_____ Telephone: _____

Date of first visit: _____ Date of most recent or last visit: _____

Person to be contacted for medical records: _____

Date requested: _____ Date received: _____

Person to be contacted for medical billing: _____

Date requested: _____ Date received: _____

Reason for treatment and prognosis: _____

_____

_____

_____

Name: _____

Address: _____

_____ Telephone: _____

Date of first visit: _____ Date of most recent or last visit: _____

Person to be contacted for medical records: _____

Date requested: _____ Date received: _____

Person to be contacted for medical billing: _____

Date requested: _____ Date received: _____

Reason for treatment and prognosis: _____

_____

_____

_____

## Other Party's Insurance Company (First Party)

Company name: _____

Address: _____

_____

Telephone: _____ Claim number: _____

Insured: _____

Adjuster: _____

Date demand letter was sent: _____

Settlement amount: _____ Date accepted: _____

## Other Party's Insurance Company (Second Party)

Company name: _____

Address: _____

_____

Telephone: _____ Claim number: _____

Insured: _____

Adjuster: _____

Date demand letter was sent: _____

Settlement amount: _____ Date accepted: _____

## Communications With Insurer

Date: _____

If oral, what was said: _____

_____

_____

_____

## Communications With Insurer

Date: _____

If oral, what was said: _____

_____

_____

## Communications With Insurer

Date: _____

If oral, what was said: _____

_____

_____

## Communications With Insurer

Date: _____

If oral, what was said: _____

_____

_____

## Communications With Insurer

Date: _____

If oral, what was said: _____

_____

_____

## Losses

Describe damage to your property: _____

_____

Do you have photos showing damage?  ☐ yes  ☐ no

## If Repairable

Estimates for repairs (name of repair shop and amounts of estimates): _____

_____

## Actual

Repair bills (name of repair shop and amounts of bills): _____

_____

If totaled:

Value at the time destroyed: _____

Documentation of value: _____

# Index

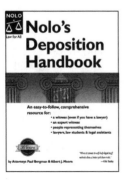

# Remember:
Little publishers have big ears.
We really listen to you.

**Take 2 Minutes & Give Us Your 2 cents**

Your comments make a big difference in the development and revision of Nolo books and software. Please take a few minutes and register your Nolo product—and your comments—with us. Not only will your input make a difference, you'll receive special offers available only to registered owners of Nolo products on our newest books and software. Register now by:

**PHONE**
1-800-728-3555

**FAX**
1-800-645-0895

**EMAIL**
cs@nolo.com

or **MAIL** us
this registration card

- - - - - - - - - - - - - - - - - - - - fold here - - - - - - - - - - - - - - - - - - - -

## Registration Card

NAME _____ DATE _____

ADDRESS _____

_____

CITY _____ STATE _____ ZIP _____

PHONE _____ E-MAIL _____

WHERE DID YOU HEAR ABOUT THIS PRODUCT? _____

WHERE DID YOU PURCHASE THIS PRODUCT? _____

DID YOU CONSULT A LAWYER? (PLEASE CIRCLE ONE)    YES    NO    NOT APPLICABLE

DID YOU FIND THIS BOOK HELPFUL?    (VERY)    5    4    3    2    1    (NOT AT ALL)

COMMENTS _____

_____

WAS IT EASY TO USE?    (VERY EASY)    5    4    3    2    1    (VERY DIFFICULT)

We occasionally make our mailing list available to carefully selected companies whose products may be of interest to you.

❏  If you do not wish to receive mailings from these companies, please check this box.

❏  You can quote me in future Nolo promotional materials.
    Daytime phone number _____.

**PICL 6.0**

**Nolo in the NEWS**

"Nolo helps lay people perform legal tasks without the aid—or fees—of lawyers."

**—USA TODAY**

Nolo books are ..."written in plain language, free of legal mumbo jumbo, and spiced with witty personal observations."

**—ASSOCIATED PRESS**

"...Nolo publications...guide people simply through the how, when, where and why of law."

**—WASHINGTON POST**

"Increasingly, people who are not lawyers are performing tasks usually regarded as legal work... And consumers, using books like Nolo's, do routine legal work themselves."

**—NEW YORK TIMES**

"...All of [Nolo's] books are easy-to-understand, are updated regularly, provide pull-out forms...and are often quite moving in their sense of compassion for the struggles of the lay reader."

**—SAN FRANCISCO CHRONICLE**

- - - - - - - - - - - - - - - - - fold here - - - - - - - - - - - - - - - - -

Place
stamp here

**NOLO**
**950 Parker Street**
**Berkeley, CA 94710-9867**

**Attn:** | **PICL 6.0**